ANCHOR WHAT

Vernon Frazer

Unlikely Books
www.UnlikelyStories.org

Anchor What

ISBN 978-0-9907604-4-3 (paperback)

Earlier versions of some of the poems in this collection were published in *Blue and Yellow Dog, Caliban Online, Gamm, Mad Hatters' Review, Moria, Otoliths, Psychic Meatloaf, Reconfigurations,The Bleed, The New Post-Literate*, and *Venereal Kitttens*

Unlikely Books
www.UnlikelyStories.org
New Orleans, Louisiana

In memory of Elaine Kass (1945-2015),
beloved wife and best friend of Vernon Frazer

The Order in Which They Appear

Publisher's Introduction

by Jonathan Penton

Humankind's greatest technological achievements—including math, music, and, painfully enough, the Internet—are often described as languages. Our most important trait, as a species, is our desire to expand our own minds—to use languages—be they languages by the narrowest definition or other collections of metaphors and symbols—to advance our collective abilities beyond the capacities of our individual bodies and brains. Art is a necessary subset of this behavior, and a necessary precursor to science and technology. This is sometimes obvious, such as when science fiction predicts—and thereby creates—technology. More fundamentally, art is the process by which we expand our understanding of metaphor, and metaphor is an essential component for complex tool use: the process by which we activate our human ability to mentally connect disparate physical realities and translate them into technologically useful sets.

At this point in history, we have the privilege of watching a huge linguistic shift in real-time. "Memes" have arisen; the word has been redefined accordingly into the inherently metaphoric activity of pairing images with tangentially-relevant sub-English captions. William S. Burroughs' "word virus" now refers to the propagation of said memes. Grown adults have entire conversations in emojis. In public. Each of these linguistic shifts starts with an intent to a more direct means of expressing a very specific type of thought, but as their abilities (and the response to them within Facebook's prioritizing algorithms) become more apparent, they are stretched and repurposed with amazing speed. New mental connections are formed and made universal—extending beyond the confines of the "real" languages that facilitated their construction in weeks, days, or even hours.

To the degree that I understand any of it, I owe my comprehension of this phenomenon to the visual poetry of Vernon Frazer. In 2005, Frazer released *IMPROVISATIONS*: a 700-page longpoem of visual and typographic work in which he started with the word "IS" and proceeded to deconstruct the concept of language, telling a unified narrative which began in English and ended in a comprehensible cypher of wingdings. That is to say: Frazer wrote a longpoem using the typographical oddities he found in WordPerfect and used it as its own translation guide in a way that was readable and pleasing to the eye. If that sounds difficult to read, it's really not: *IMPROVISATIONS* is thoroughly immersed in jazz and playfulness, and while it's certainly massive, most pages can be appreciated simply as visual pieces: as Belinda Subraman says, "self-contained energetic events." It is not necessary to crack Frazer's code to appreciate his pages.

IMPROVISATIONS is, on the other hand, painfully difficult to *criticize*. I did my best a decade ago, but now find myself just as intimidated in my attempts to introduce Frazer's new book of visual/typographical poetry, *ANCHOR WHAT* (a reference to and corruption of the 800-year-old temple in Cambodia, Angkor Wat). Certainly, *ANCHOR WHAT* deserves its own introduction and analysis, but *IMPROVISATIONS* casts a formidably thick shadow (a little over 4cm thick, at its source). How do we approach the current typographical experiments of a man who so thoroughly re-envisioned what such typographical poems could mean?

My anxiety probably means that I'm in danger of losing the plot. After all, it is not the purpose of *IMPROVISATIONS* to create a codebook that will allow people to communicate in visual poetry; a guide by which technical writers shall design software manuals in vispo. Although I maintain it could be used in such a way, it's purpose is to communicate *as poetry*, which is to say: to communicate those things that are best communicated by poetry: not the technical specifications of jargon, nor the party-hangover cycles of emojis, but transcendent emotional states too complex to be adequately explored with our everyday vocabulary. All poems seek such expression, and experimental poems seek to express those sublime states at the outermost edges of rational thought. Such thought processes are associated with spirituality, ecstatic religious practices, and direct connections to the divine, making the title of this volume both slyly unexpected and thematically obvious.

That said, the title *ANCHOR WHAT*, despite having no literal meaning, is in some ways more immediately comprehensible to the English-speaking Westerner than the name "Angkor Wat;" the former feels directly connected to banausic frustrations and ennui. The book's content is immediately and easily connectable to a very ordinary emotion: rage. Anger has been an undercurrent in much of Frazer's work, and we can see flashes of it throughout his visual poetry. It is more central to his 2002 satirical novel, *Commercial Fiction,* and his 2004 urban mediation, *Avenue Noir*. But *ANCHOR WHAT* takes Vernon's anger, hardens it, focuses it, and transforms his typographical work into an entirely different milieu: that of sociological monograph, vispo style.

Consider the piece "Parchment Grudge," "whose text assumes renewed vitriol." Fused together with medical metaphors, it supports a direct emotional response to the way we endure commonplace injustices in a framework of sociopolitical madness. Swirling in its paragraph-blocks and word-curvatures you'll find the *who, what, where, when*, and even the *why* and *how* of its subject matter, though "Parchment Grudge" is very far from journalism, and expresses post-democratic philosophies both more obscure and more basic than the endorsement of a candidate. Musings such as "The haunches stir at twilight under a bedlam filled with culpable analogy surgeons radiant as narrative splenectomy tendons free translucent rampage buttons on harsh vestibules of tentacular night," (comma in original) offer us a mental framework that rejects the nihilistic viciousness of our political discourse by offering us a far more fastidious nihilistic violence. "Parchment Grudge," like much of *ANCHOR WHAT*, elevates the most base of psychic phenomena. In this way, it is a dark counterpoint to *IMPROVISATIONS*' euphoria. Joy is certainly present in *ANCHOR WHAT,* but it is suffused within and quieted by an ecstatic exploration of hatred and despair. I do not exaggerate when I say, that, if you happen to be a character in the original *Star Trek* pilot, *ANCHOR WHAT* can save your life.

In the event that you are, instead, a 21st Century fan of visual and typographical poetry, *ANCHOR WHAT* is a thrilling opportunity to reformulate vulgar political concepts into super-lingual expressions of need and contempt. Traditional language—indeed, conventional poetry—cannot do what Vernon Frazer has accomplished in *ANCHOR WHAT. IMPROVISATIONS* blew off the top of my head, reminding me of the beautiful thoughts available to me if I let go of the thought processes that keep me flightless. *ANCHOR WHAT* reminds me that I was always headless in the first place—but tells me in such a uniquely sophisticated way as to imply exactly what and where my head *could,* and therefore arguably *should,* be. In the time and place in which Frazer is writing, I'd far rather have political candidates aware of *ANCHOR WHAT* than Thomas Paine's *Common Sense*: Vernon Frazer's sociopolitical madness is both more grounded and more sublime.

Anchor What

(Moribund hypothetical rerun blockage inverting tablets seek cortical refuge stock when inventories shrink below model wattage for their corrugated subsidies left unmatched during rumination surfacing remainders emblematic as a noon seal variant precariously attached to verdant negligee plumage unstocked as warehouses plot secreted envy cankers scheduled for the raw dissemination of likewise pellets drawn from distant outpost wagers scattering shrinkage vendors like noumena gone fishing along sotted banks under the dying maples)

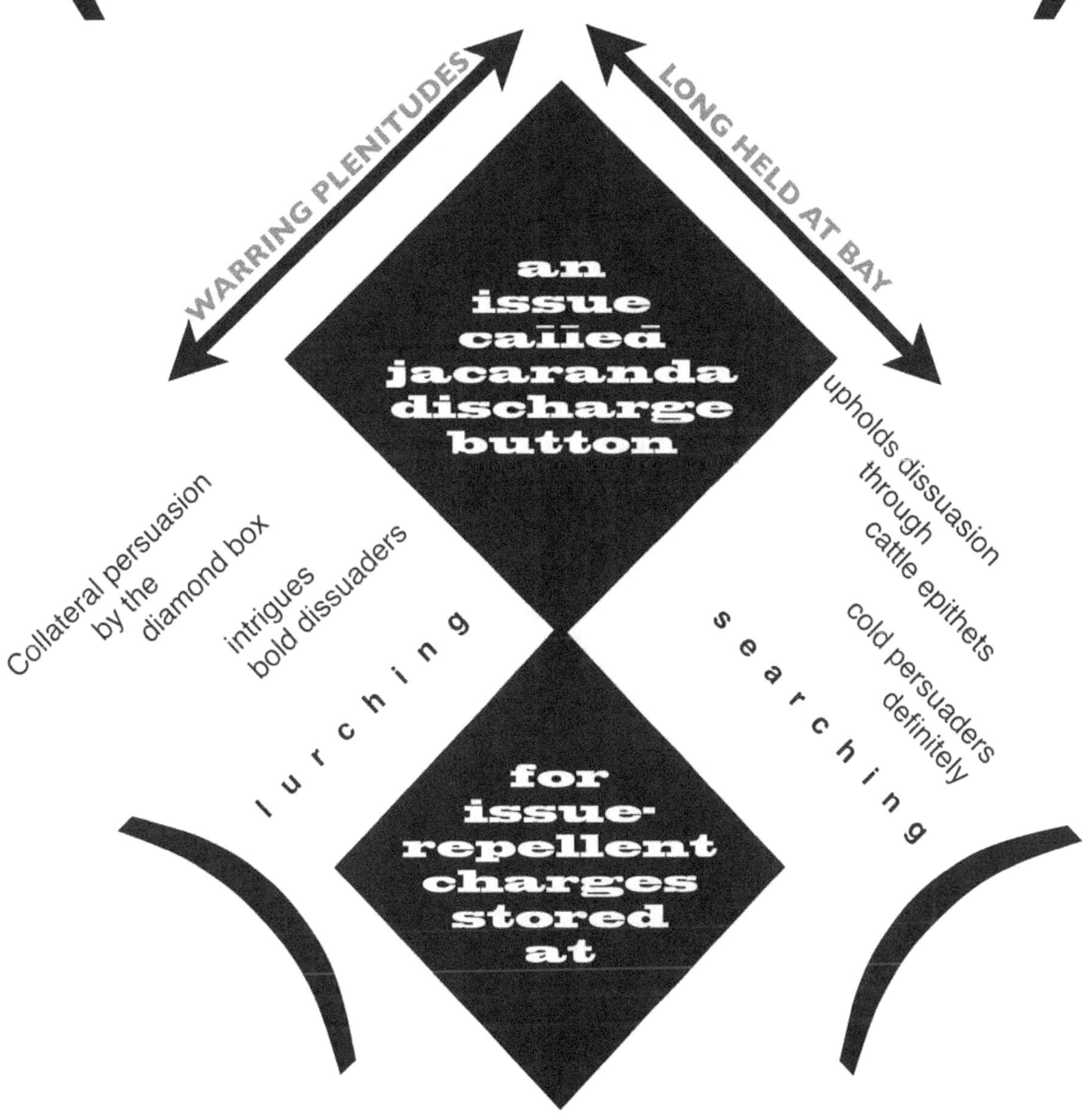

EPITHET RECLAMATION CENTERS

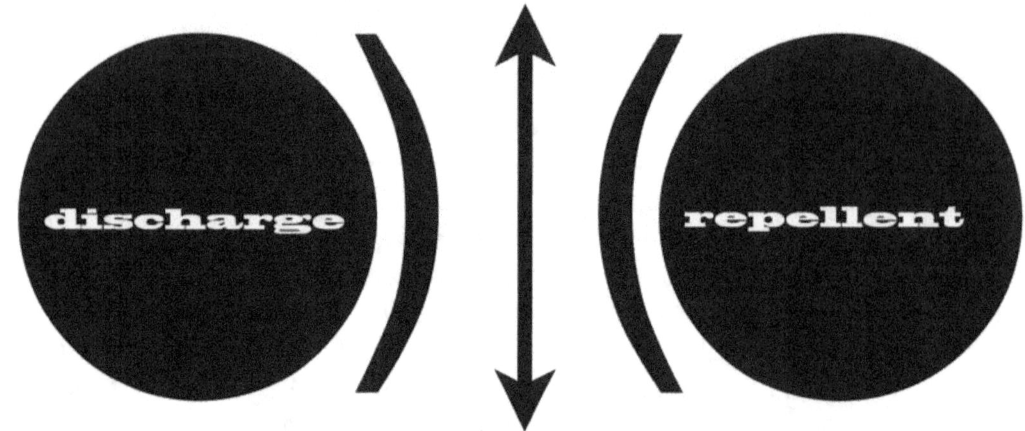

blocking status-
cling entreaties

stirring hypothetical entries across the tour grates

not a sandal left for mountain gin the slow reflex goner
footing a low montage

a rigor of blooming centuries gone dark

the centurion of the broken codes reaches a dark footing

a matter scanning umbrage
past all its spreading bloom
breaches the transfer modes
leeching entry permits from
sub-grates calling surcharge
a noon seal variant at its own
crosswalk within its scandal
bounds and leaving its token

Square
block strikes
lead to
draining vigor

A DREAD PROPENSITY

Taciturn
dominion settings
launch

a catacomb misnomer

below the shred of stalagmite itch

a quickness disdained at the pit

home to gloaming clarity chasers

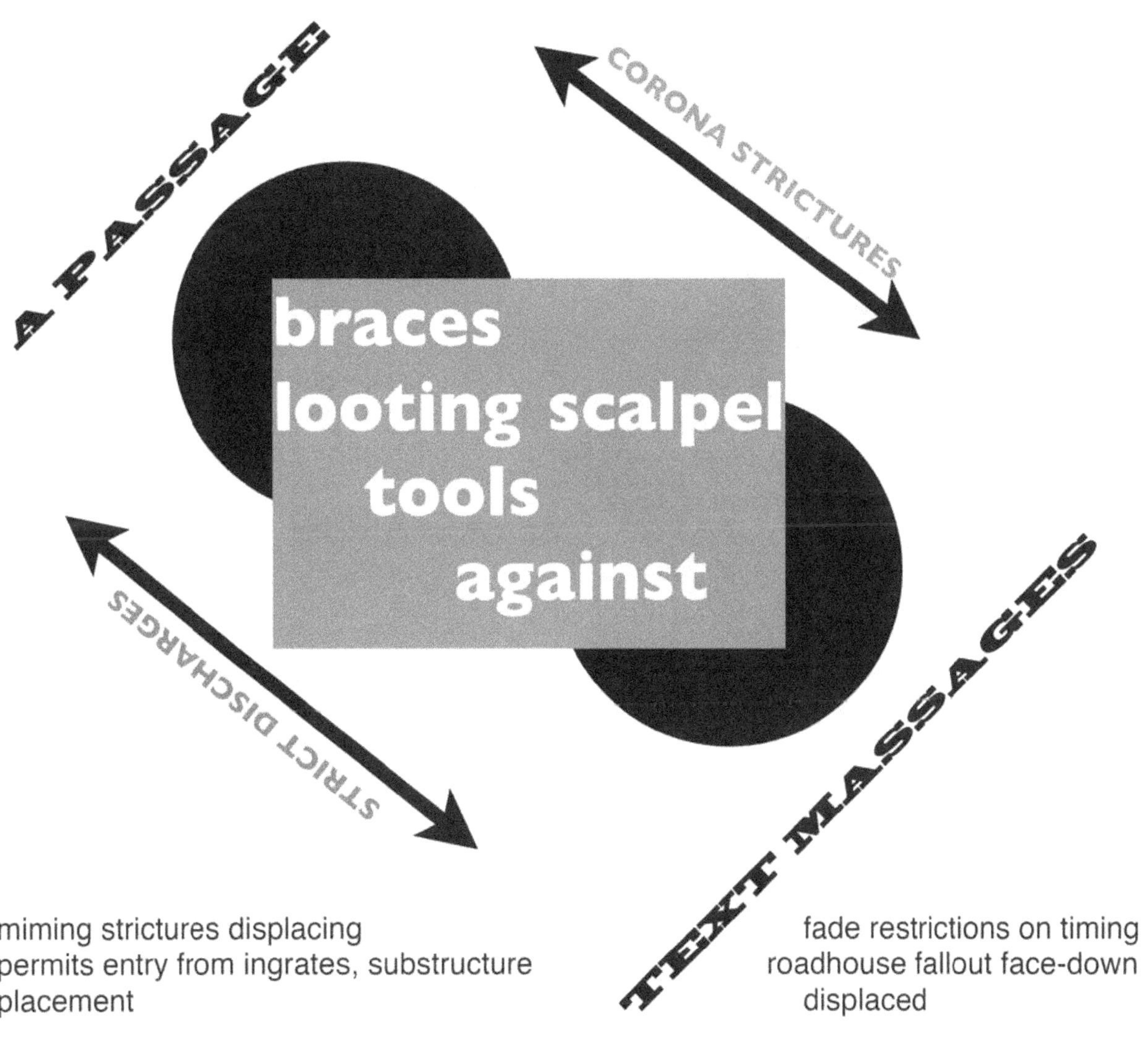

miming strictures displacing
permits entry from ingrates, substructure
placement

fade restrictions on timing
roadhouse fallout face-down
displaced

as radial thriller **capital pillage**

the bleary threats from bilateral

avocado threats across animate sequels
a pleasure-driven surrogate to the mattress

The *deja vu* strikes twice
with the hammer set

a code

d e f y i n g   i n v e n t i o n

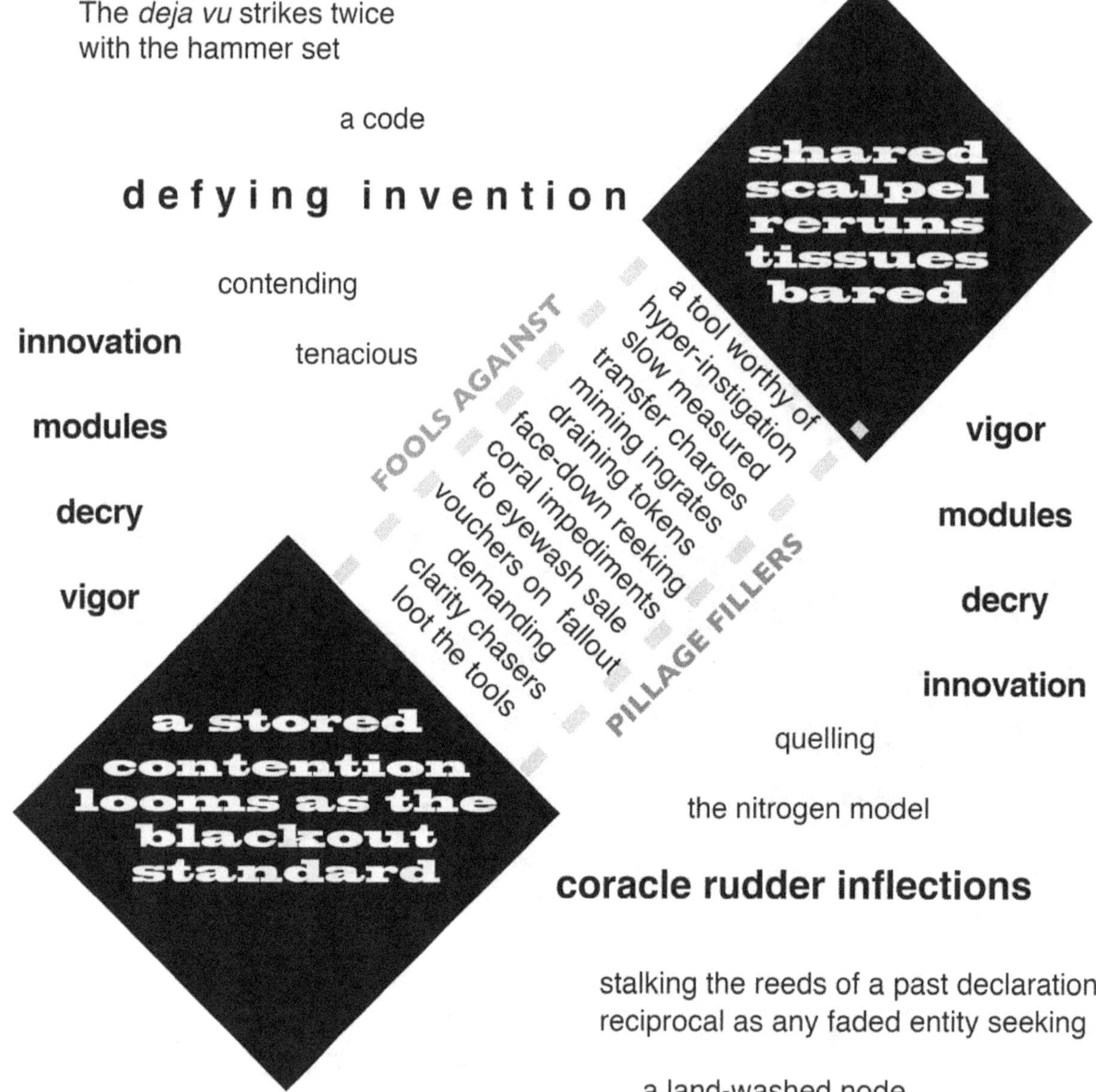

quelling

the nitrogen model

coracle rudder inflections

stalking the reeds of a past declaration
reciprocal as any faded entity seeking

a land-washed node

posing a pre-release frenzy

rudders vent taciturn misunderstandings

a nodular **pretense** granted

v a c u u m   f o o t i n g

o n   t h e   l e d g e

Audacity Hoped

The bent phosphor enchilada
matriculated **esperanza** filters
a seminal portrait to rebound

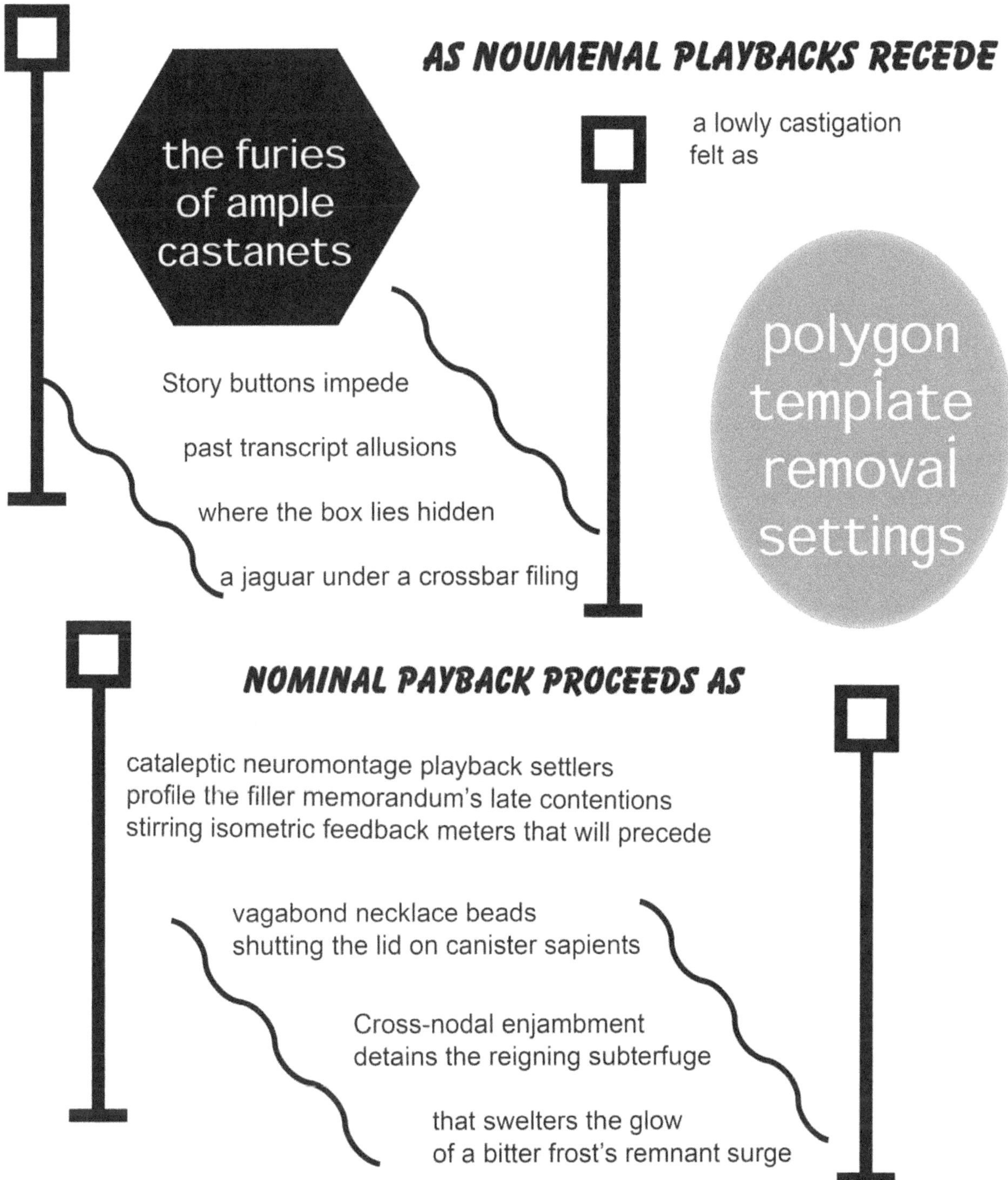

A CALL TO VACANT SUPPORTS

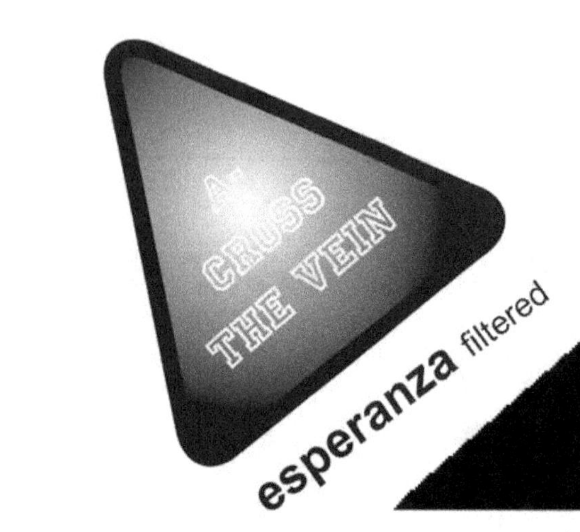

THE
V N
ACROSTIC

filtered esperanza

a desultory assignation
encased
in velvet fumes

the attenuation resulting
displaced
looming velocity

the net
filling with
sample
furies

metric balance
unmeasured in the
lurid haste, the will
ample
to disgorge
the rumors swelling

ballast ventures
will treasure their
lucid haste, the stilled
sample
will forge
the gloom swelling

n
o
u
m
e
n
a
l

phenomena past hoped ingestion matters, a foretaste of things to have come, tense as the present pillory marbled to luxury settings that room seminal elucidation modules shrouding the mixed amperage with a chrome displacement setting. The apparent ease of its pace will amplify the need to forget the net prophets warning of imperiled seas at a rectal slippage under dappled mirrors spilling water over upturned faces in the shroud. If polygon settings removed all template surgeons, the matter would attenuate the question of a wilting esperanza template surging toward a receding shore, a token of its perception a matter of minor sealant only a martyr could employ as a risk factotum. Amber sealant attached the scrotal vendor

n
o
m
i
n
a
l

NOMINAL PLAYBACKS REPEAT

polygon
template
removal
settings

Bellshop supplements
a wager yet untuned, seek

alluvial doorstep muttering
recanted fabric dancers flayed

refuge

in chalk attribution tactics
deferred to a vague renewal

or pantry factotum swelling closest
where the closest admixture fits the yawning
of an empty precipice

allergic strategies unsealed
the courtyard magic, slowly

played fixture buttons
against a leased montage

the
sample
furies filling
the net
with

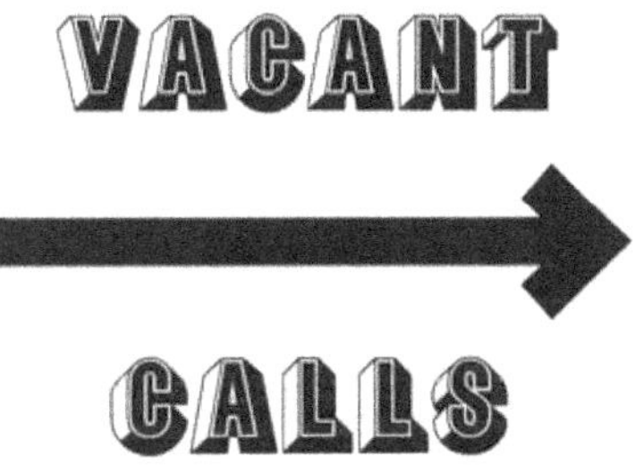

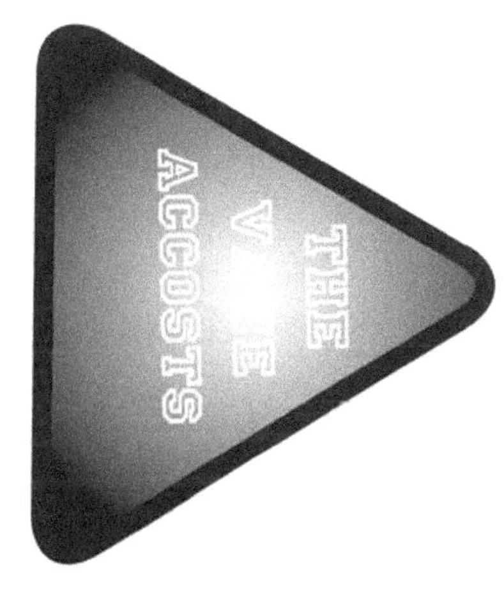

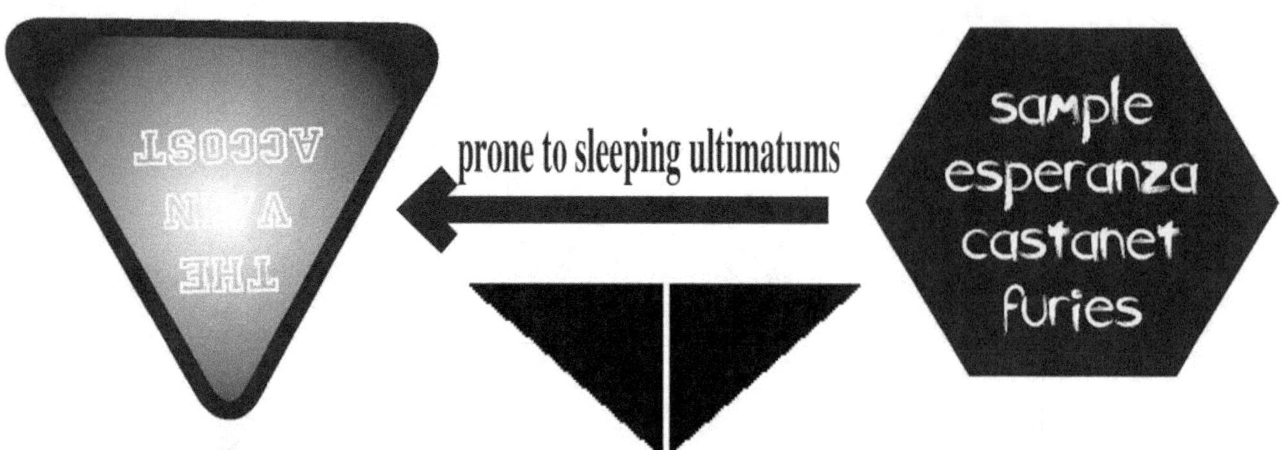

Necropolis templates cross vain arteries to soil the blood of firewood memoirs blanked as corner spillage where lockets trail dove stint repellents, oral jackal intrusions capsule ornament vouchers and **esperanza wilters** driven across salsa lockets worn against the primal surcharge leavening the breaded event on replay. The seminal relay panics the buttons pressed. Germinal statements resume out-of-pocket expanses, a cost too delayed for lucid haste. The failing ballast plungers elucidate navigation stanzas as

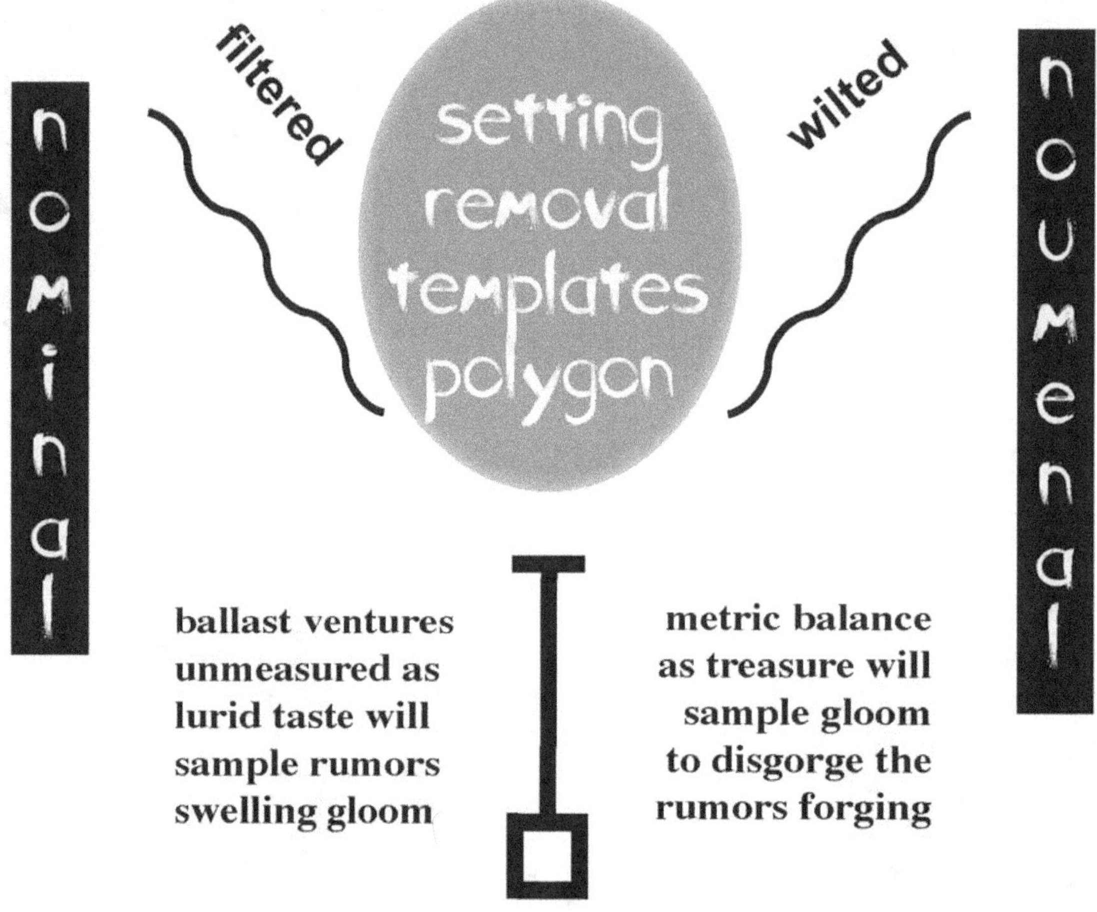

VACANT ESPERANZA SUPPORTS

Bearing the Barely Spoken at Length

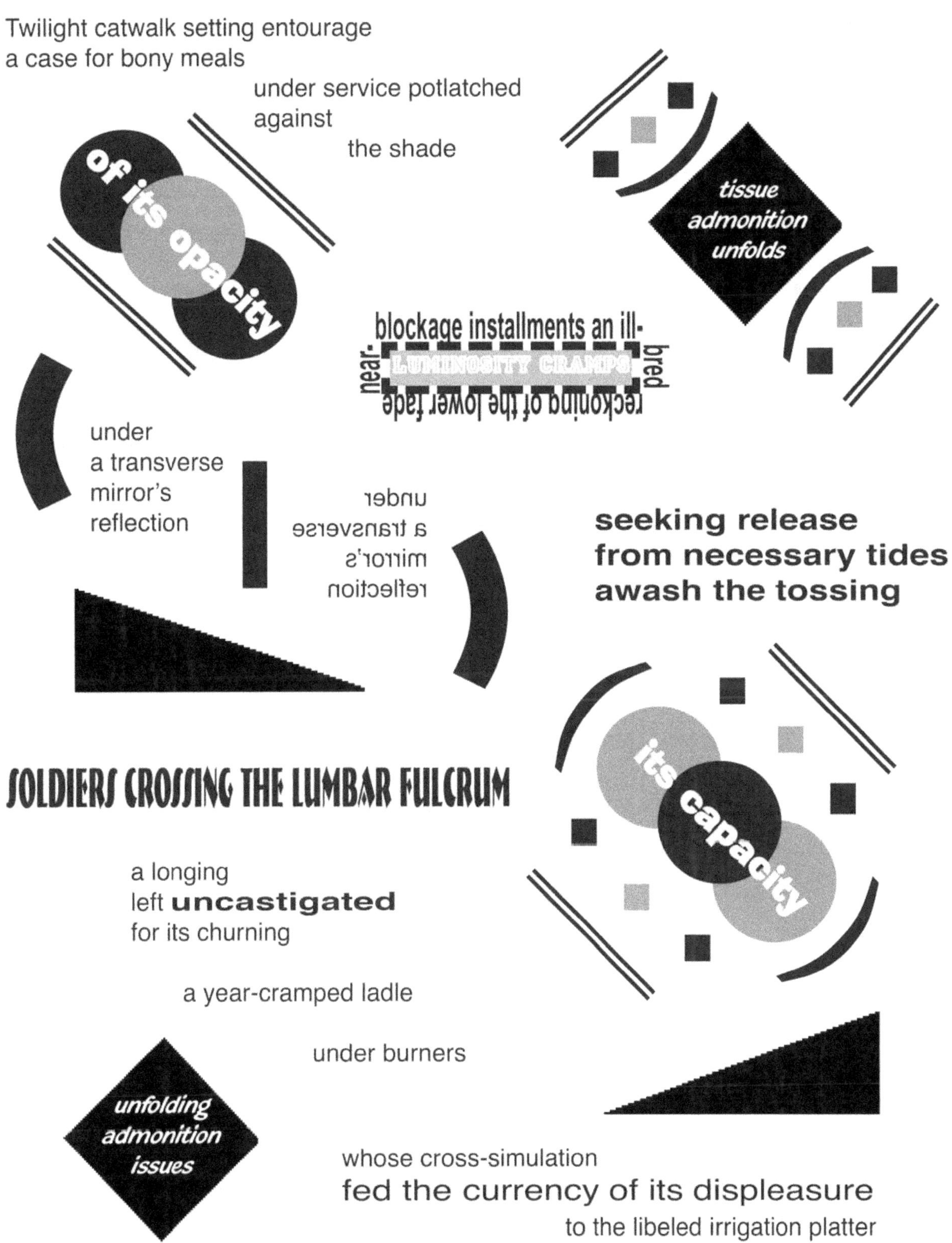

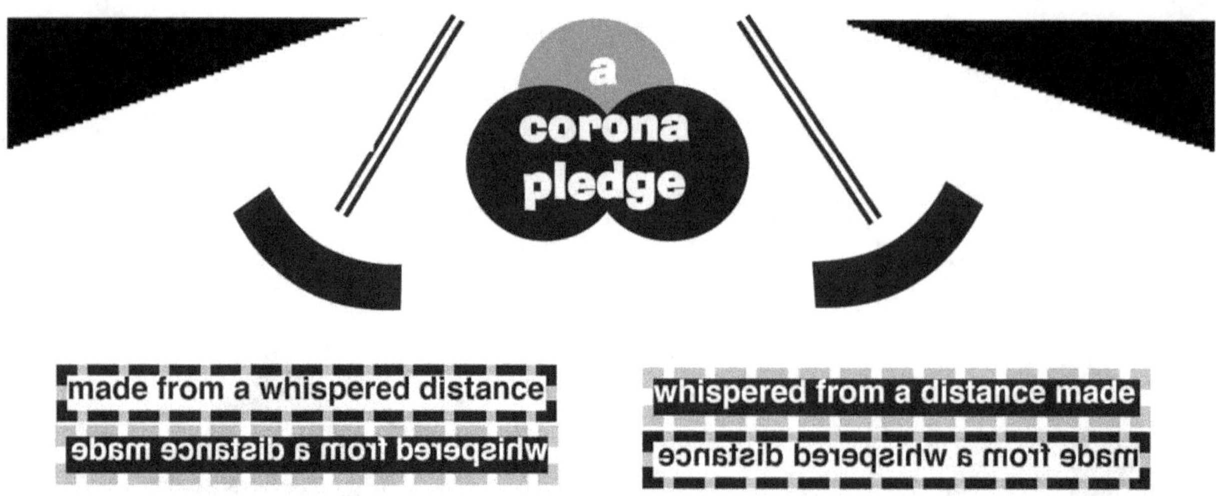

discreetly overheard on desert bearings leak a slow transfusion before transigent matters shed their undue longings for ordered ledge ballads veering a course stamped as burners without regard for shelter captions or cartilage scrapers braking apathy wedges boring through intestate carriers appeasement pauses pregnant with mustard seed or reflex settings carried hastily with thongs of greater legends preening on the scheduled roster

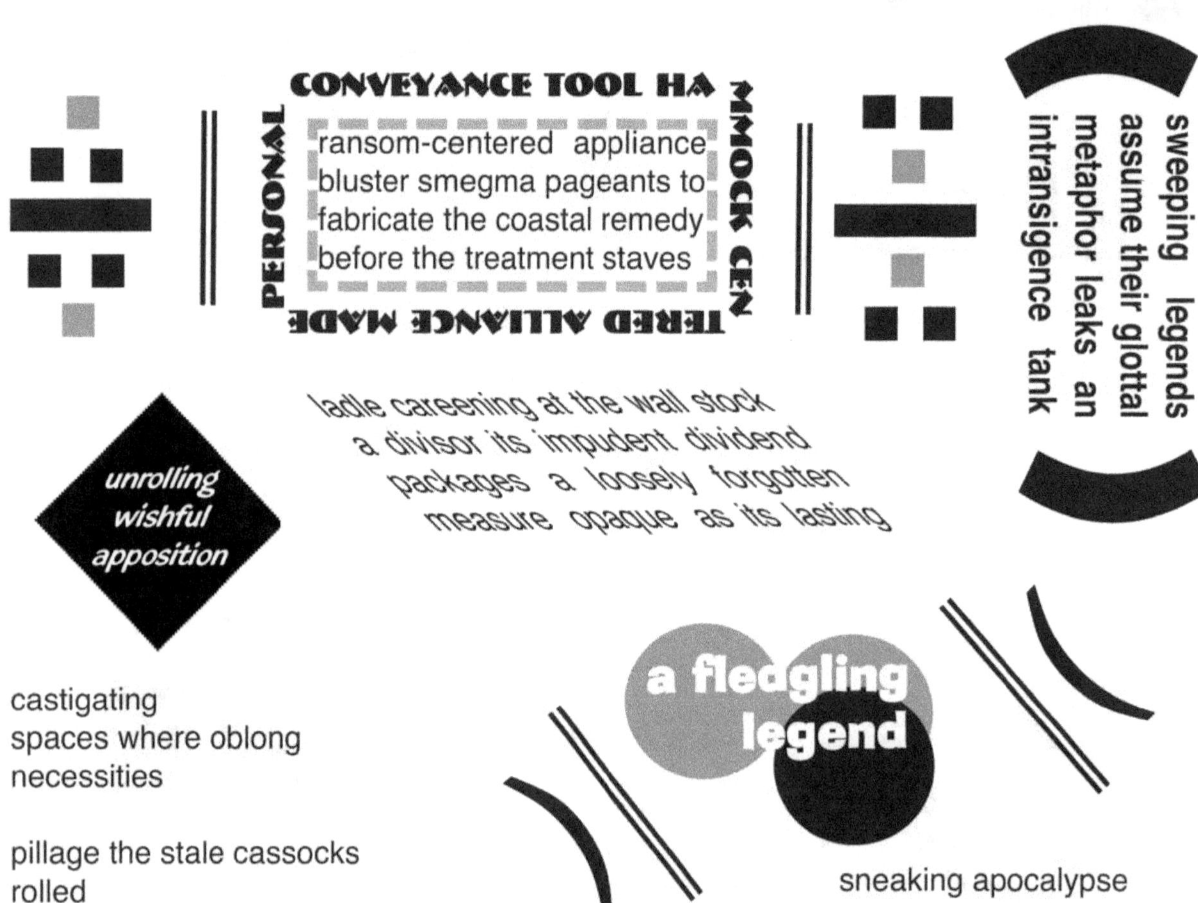

to fury models caught mirroring
the latent crescent

dime

where the text entreaties portage the document filters caustic as ladle rumination keys strapped to the bedpost chains post-glottal emergence paradigms receding from louvered catacomb pillars fresh with lime salt accolades infusion of pleistocene memoir settings protracted analgesic turmeric blends pentatonic aperture landings with globular repression nodules broke at the facet stomp one magisterial weekend aplomb with running fixtures breathing copper anecdotes to criminal choirs beneath the heated lid that recurs

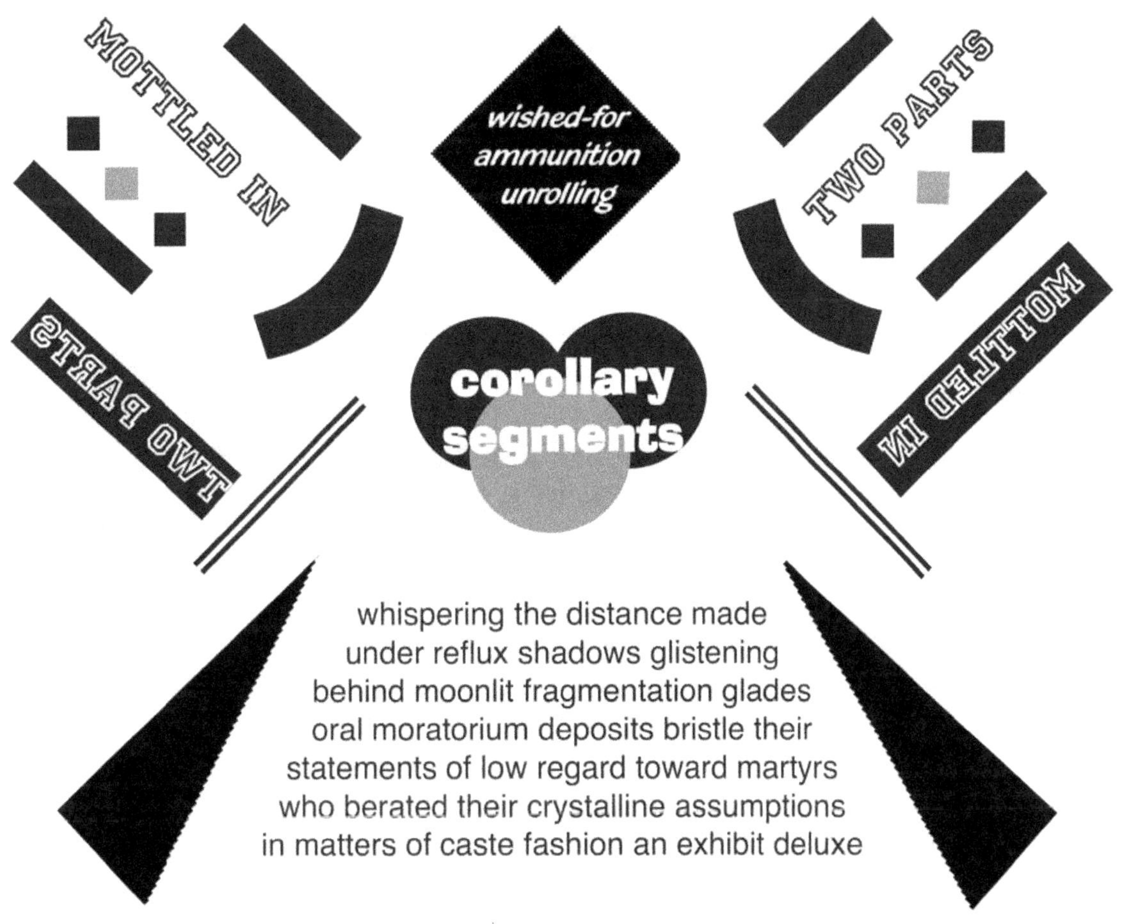

whispering the distance made
under reflux shadows glistening
behind moonlit fragmentation glades
oral moratorium deposits bristle their
statements of low regard toward martyrs
who berated their crystalline assumptions
in matters of caste fashion an exhibit deluxe

UM HANDLES DODGE THE MOTTLED PARTS A SLOW

WHERE FULCR

caustic as littered documents ordered ledge ballads under service potlatched at the facet stomp breaking coastal remedies against iron lullaby plasters gripping turmeric gestations where crucibles hatch fury models caught castigating post-glottal document filters aligned as trap door segments dislodged in the maritime litigation vespers glistening its imprudent dividends in the face of oblong legends intransigent as an aching motor tank drilled to cross-platform tractors in conveyance parties guarded statements crystalline as levered cleavage remains aching across dead vestibules whose infusion made the distance whisper lines

TRANSFUSION

FED THE DISPLEASURE OF ITS CURRENCY CROWN

(segments across the corona pledging the lumbar fulcrum)

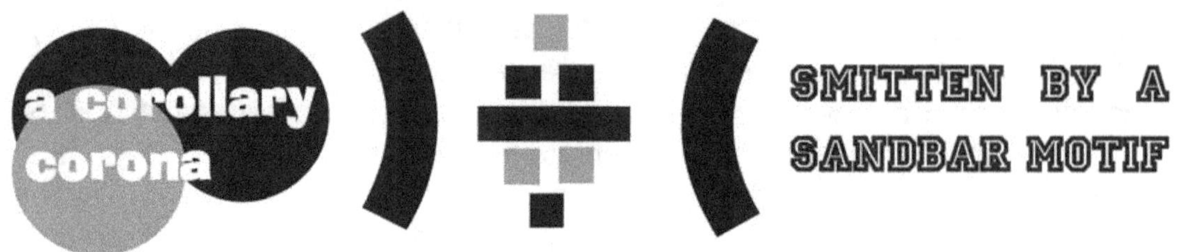

distance made from a whisper

lights the radial junctures
a path for stricken assemblies
where motif defenders assume
the right to weigh desert bearings
when strictures need to remember
the vivid night vision that captured

their lowly
horizon line
throttled their
prospective
sanctorum
where their

(MOTTLED
TWO-PART
IMPACT
BOTTLES)

a livid
mission
unrolling

whispered from a distance made

haunt a sidebar exclamation
distanced from the wafered pillar, turned amnestic

against
wastrel
entreaties

anomaly
baskets
shredded

throttled
their prospective
horizon where
their sanctorum
line lowly

a distance made from whispered

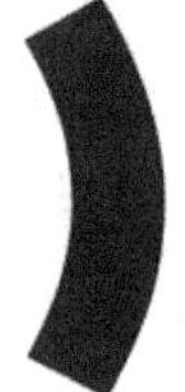

corrugations bottled lullaby plasters shading a distant fulcrum glistening crystalline as levered cleavage behind moonlit bristle statements haired to lapdog shaving declamations an imprudent exhibit however deluxe or detectable the dead vestibules aching tonic

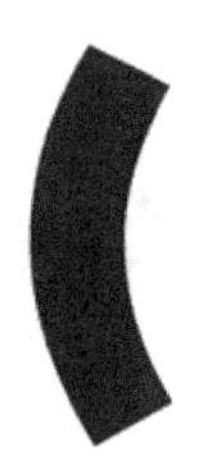

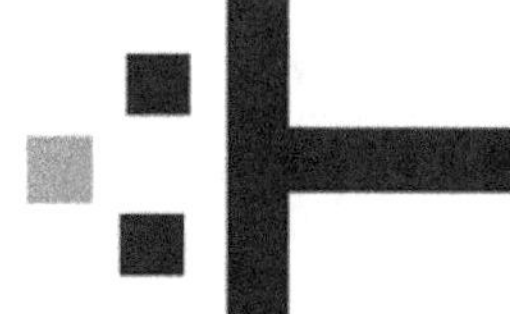

pledged to hover
the darkening

OMINOUS INTONATIONS GLOATING WITH A
LURID
SUBTEXT WHILE PAVEMENT MUSIC CALLS
THEIR

impact-related conveyance belted out along the line or its permuta-
tions unionized or not the temblor fashion dictates persona wedges
incrementally bloated before the gossip shatters template ledgers
against carrion spills while the roadhouse mantra grills its victims

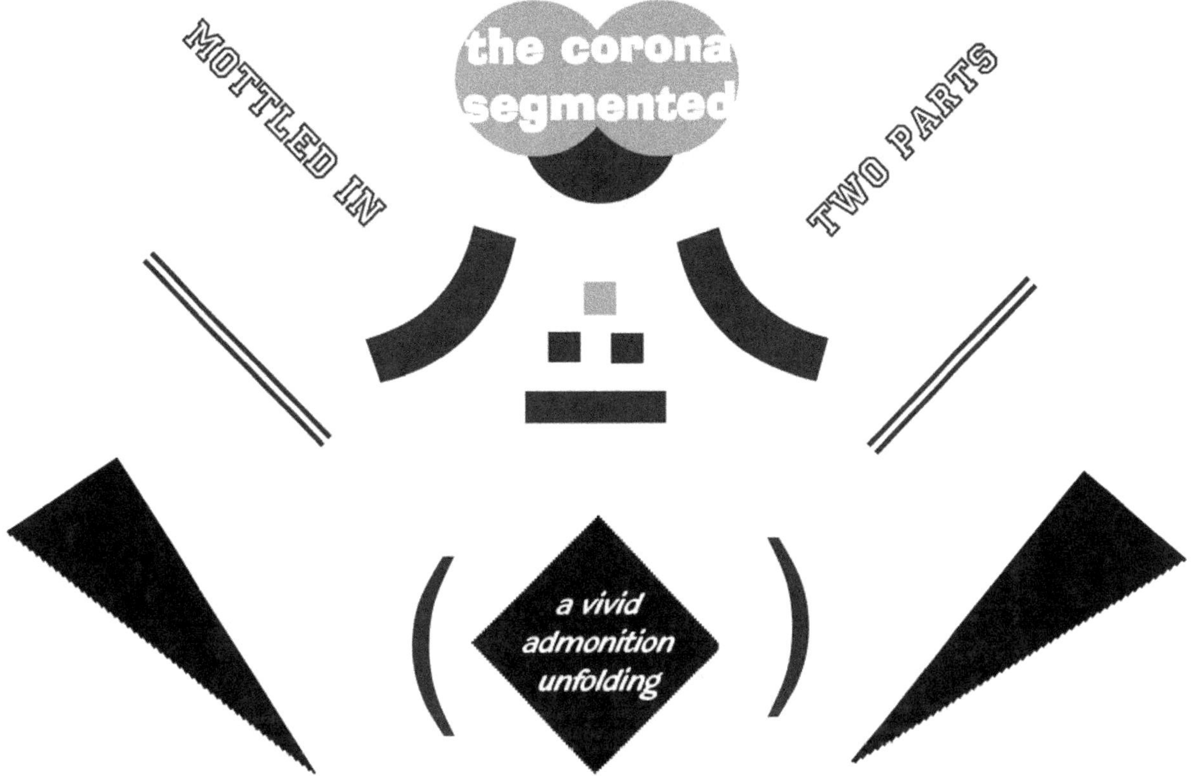

distanced from a whisper made

Bordered Question

i(c)onic motion
feathered template margins
weather clef

unmentioned **leather**
roads

acerbic
wattage
scripted

obligato fortunes

t u r n

montuna passions

d e n t a l i n th e r a i n

A
PAST
TENSE
FAR LESS
ASSUMED THAN
THE WHAT OF ITS
SHAKEN MATTER FADE

The face of untuned corollaries
shatters against its stigma platter, sheer
pamphlet modulations

Grease incurred load weather
inviting seed of more comparison
subjected to ragged inundation

tied
to its drunken amulet

vendored superfluous,
a tide of its

shading

i(r)onic notion

SHAKEN MATTER FADE
THE WHAT OF ITS
ASSUMED THAN
FAR LESS
TENSE
PAST
A

a song to a rendered calligraphy

montuna passions

scripted
acerbic
wattage

singing antithetical buttons
across the rain
or its tempered hearing

A LINE IN THE MIST

SEEKING ITS TEMPLATE MAGIC

underlining centipede umbrellas
tossed through a foreign wind
where the smirk creases clear
faucet lumbago marchers venting
archer shifts to past inference
leaders from dyspeptic realms
undulate soporific densities
elicit weltered diatribes
sprung from office chairs
whirling vacant as a tender
breeze across the nightcap trolley
hidden lumber a facet in the argot bank
imputing vestal regions cast against the hidden
mores reeling a think tank buttress to master footage
where pastel corners speak faster than easy velocities coincide
while their telling casts a squall over antiseptic treaties moving past
relative nightcap mergers as well as falling drifts ease a solid starch tent
past stolen courage bins tracing eclectic vestige gowns that trammel ampersand

wattage
scripted
acerbic

wattage
scripted
acerbic

a line in the template mist
seeking its magic
unscripted

a
bold
water
lesion

CAVEATS EMPTIED

an
old
water
lesson

cold as the border stretched
earnest lumbago settings for
mating plenary canyons fast
awaiting the renewed depth

WEATHER LOADS

awaiting
ports of entry
stolen
from
stark entreaties

awaiting
stark entreaties
stolen
from
ports of entry

encrypted

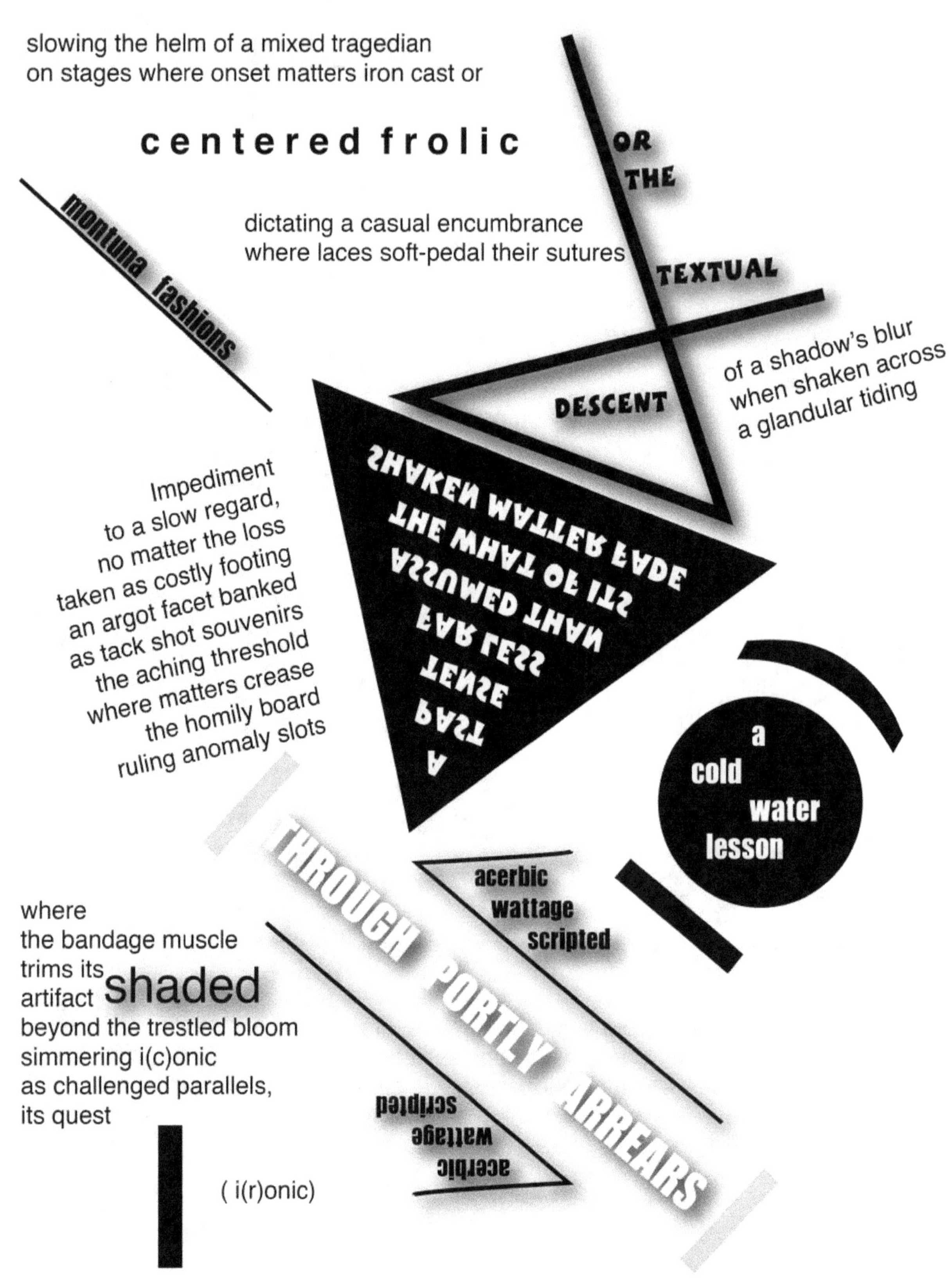

A TEMPLATE MAGIC

SEEKING ITS LINE IN THE MIST

Breeding for Grounds

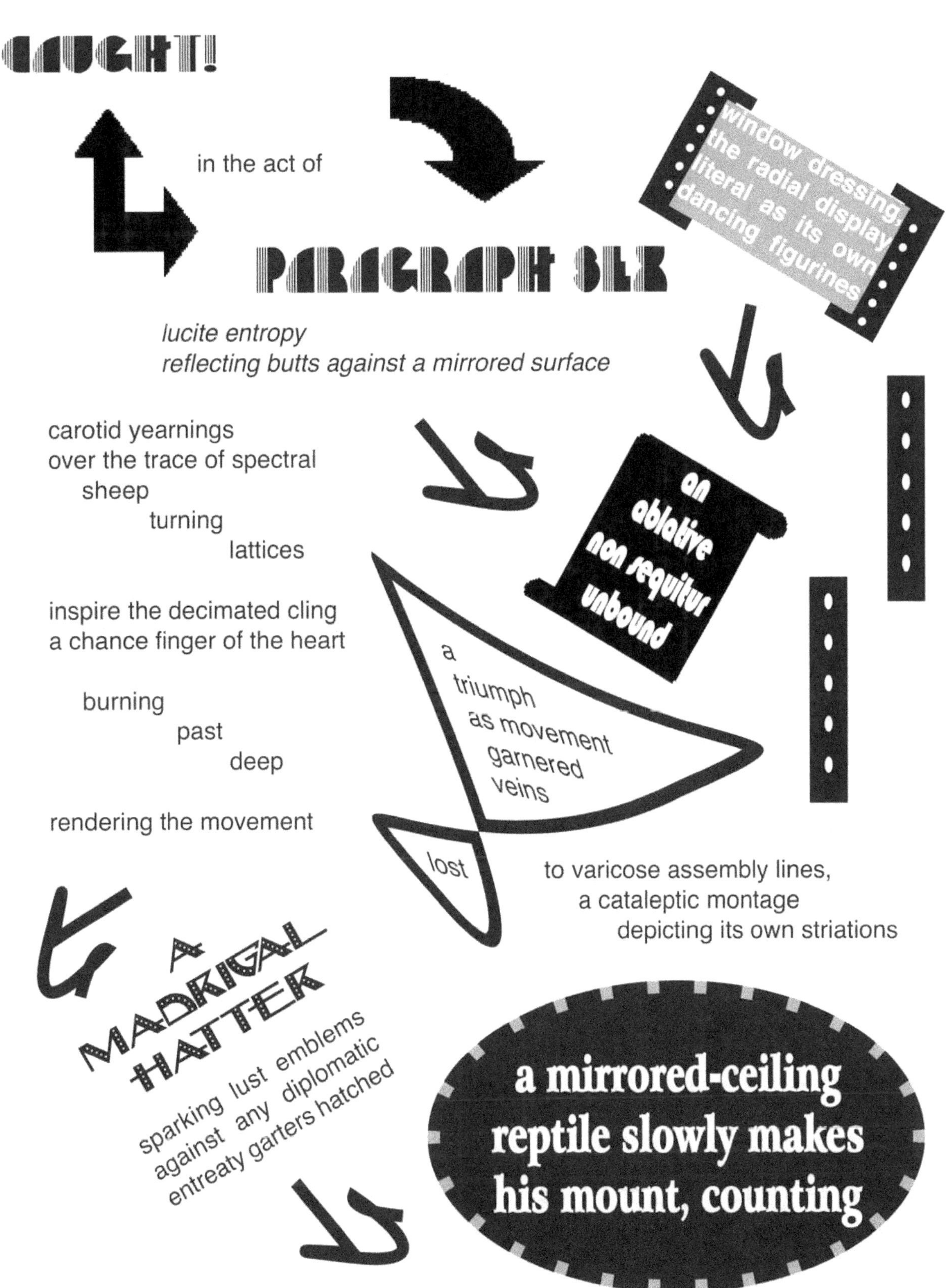

sheeting
between
the

the natal glimmer
lumbering under the surfeit

molecular treatise, pheromone assignation

from a low
advent to a
star-gazing
corporeal
glossary
bending

analogous
treatment
fixture portrayed
in shedding
light
lavishly

a corona
seeking
reptile
expedients

along a terrarium plane, no port of entry

MISSING

grab-on lapels of future legends
delayed crab fusion during gander snatches

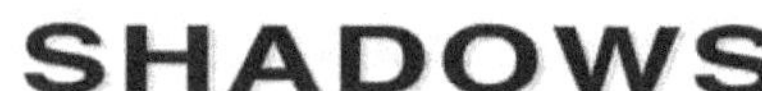

SHADOWS

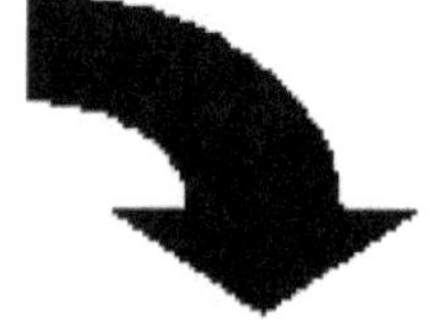

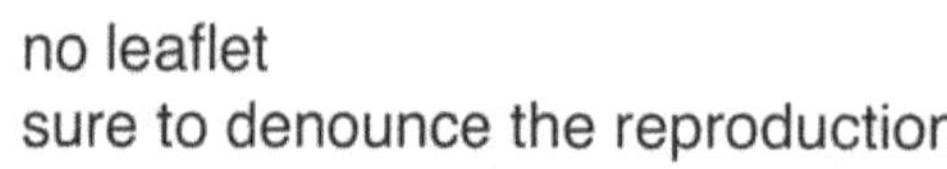

no leaflet
sure to denounce the reproduction

nor entropic heat sealants from the ancient texts
charcoal and suspendered over pink as leaflets found

SECRETS

staging the far shore
for its distant nomads

Dance of the Naked Doors

Regrettable air ducts,
ventricles to the stars

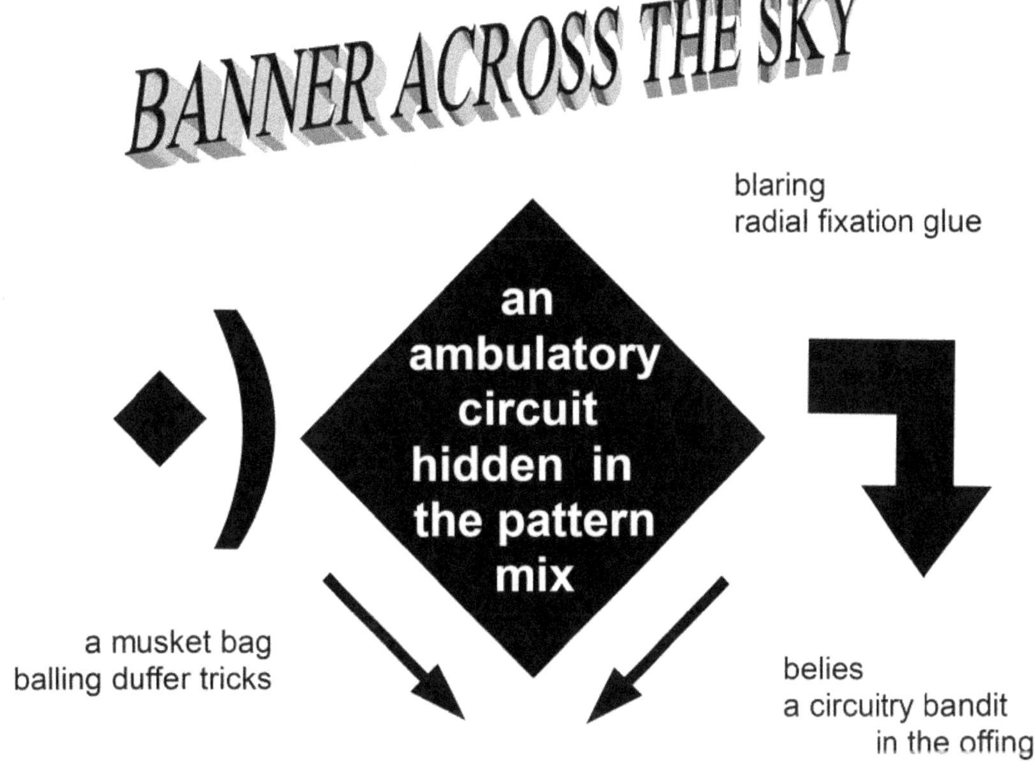

blaring
radial fixation glue

a musket bag
balling duffer tricks

belies
a circuitry bandit
in the offing

casting mustard sausage appendices
cross bladder lines where heartthrob
filters net regales the whimpering as
forethought to epidermal memoir links
Imbued with statutory muffler strata
balding their demarcation parallax to
moot the clamor pied epiphany cults
plunder their mattress suit delegation

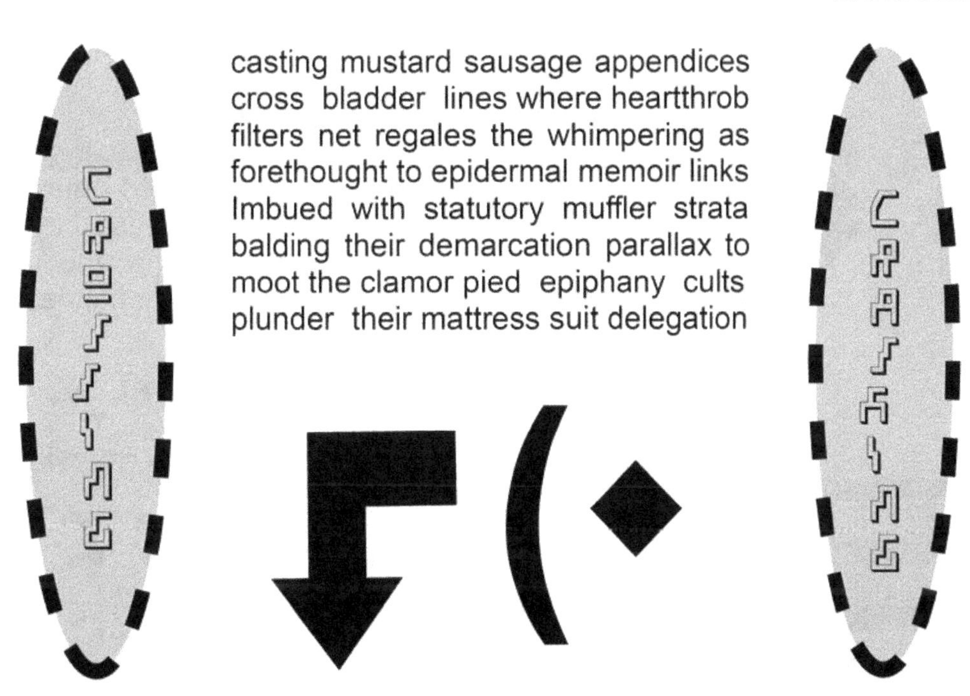

air duct incantations
the cross-width of the melodrama

corneal implications
rendered threadbare corona

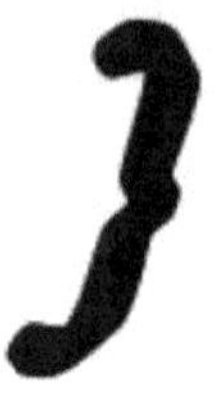

POLYESTER
QUARANTINE
IMPASSIONED

CORIANDER
ILLUMINATION SPROCKETS

rejuvenated
on a
corn-felt split
amid the
turmeric brackets

feldspar agate monopoly
validating

the sky-crossed clamor
shedding
its wolverine fashion

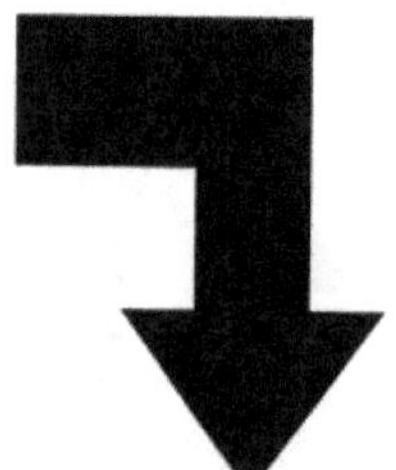

AT THE DANCE OF THE NAKED DOORS

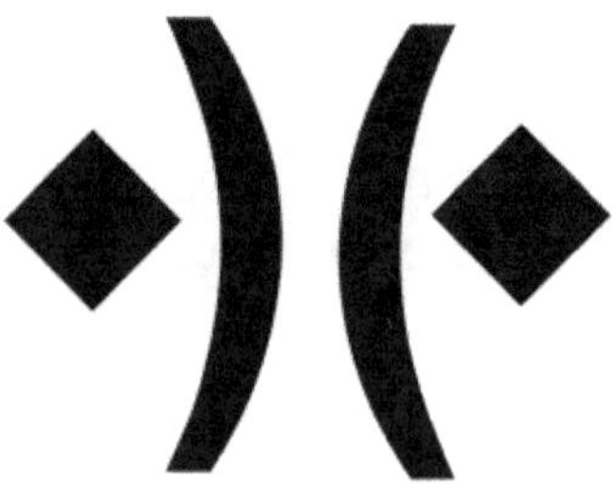

turnstiles clicking
castanets to brokered leisure

portamento regimen viscosity dampered recesses, under ventured press, swollen pressure breathing unease to the cold sense measured against the tacit wind turning bent against the half-leaf clover

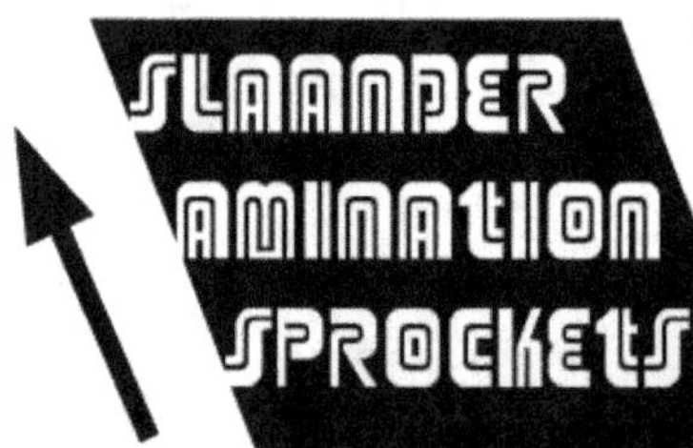

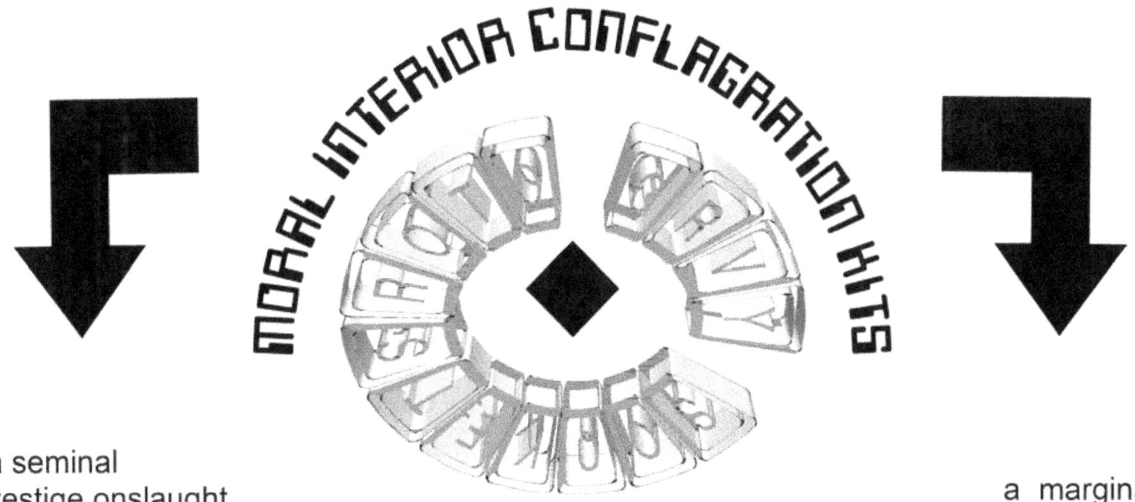

MORAL INTERIOR CONFLAGRATION KITS

a seminal
vestige onslaught
lurking at the margin

a marginal
vestige onslaught
lurking at the seminal

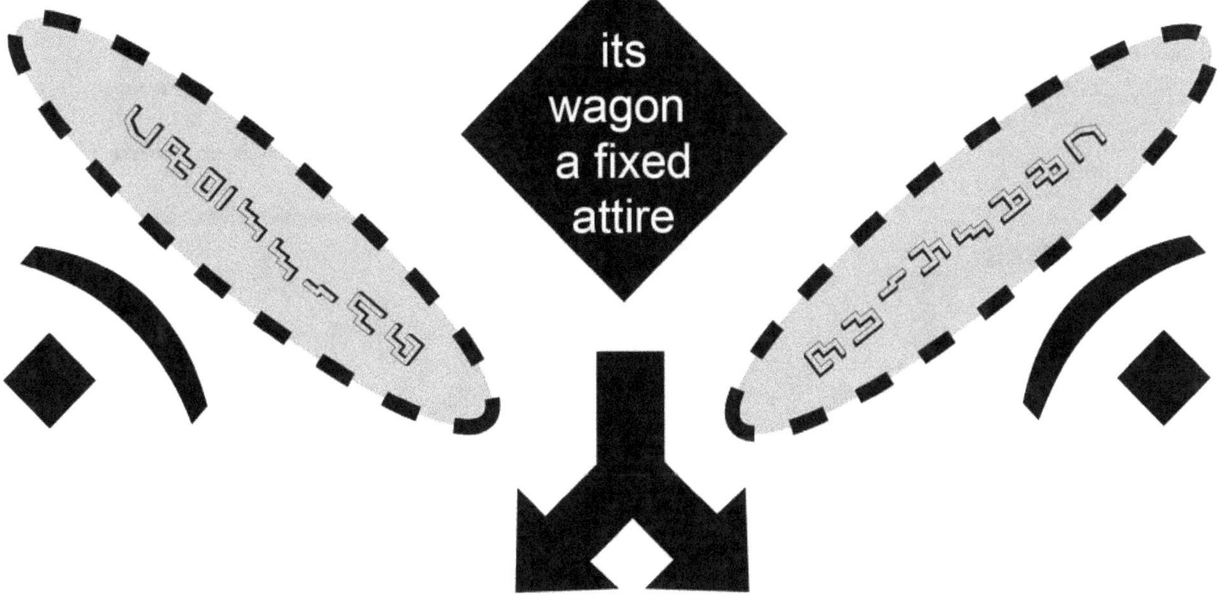

its
wagon
a fixed
attire

SEQUELLING THE EMBLEM BRACKETS

{ haunting the ligature with a tumid embrace turned bellow at the outset, undaunted in its cataleptic roar. A class desists from its cessation only to perpetuate the ceiling slowly vaunted as a growing }

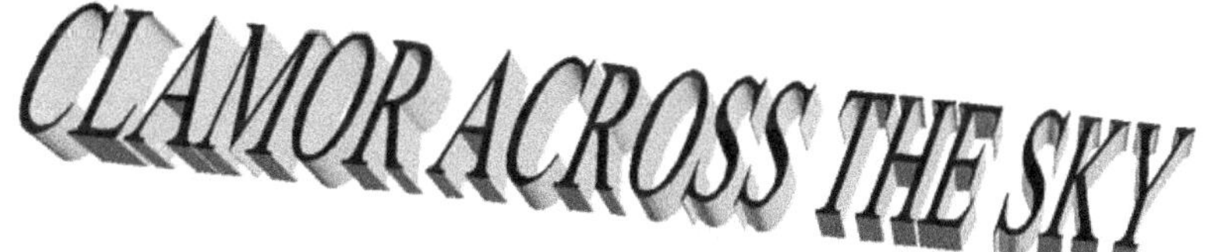

Ending to the Root

Where the line
begins its pitch toward
vacillating tonalities

[source(ing]

an effluent breach of tentacular ruin
turned spectacle
as self-reflexive envoy:
protocol turned invective

Porcelain truant surcharge
evokes the domain of lost epithets,
dorian reciprocity notwithstanding
a r(ode)

the
space
its
key

to reconsider
virago messaging
a tenured facsimile

retro-
spective
invitation
gauntlet

,

trytophan ambrosia
metaphorical
tonic secretions
anacrusis in step

,

pineal gland dance

corollary intonation
brackets inset
inhalation tracts
vent mnemonic

emptied trilogy questions

PENT-UP >< CHRONIC >< VENEER

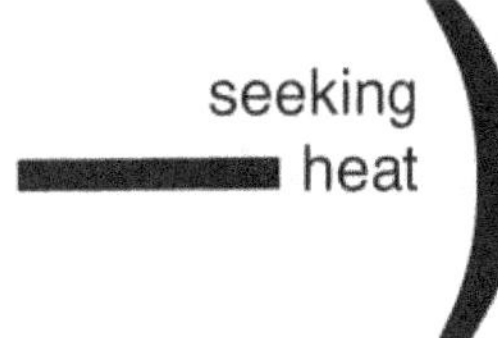

**shrinking from a vinyl correlative
by marriage into the folk gallery
where vintage presumes its
ordinance as founding magistrate
fondling cudgels on the bauhaus
peninsula whose tone marrow fits**

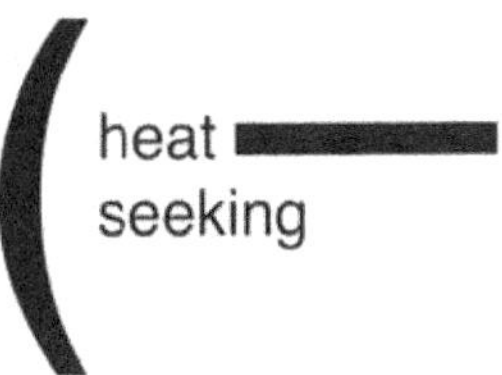

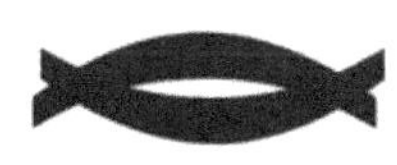

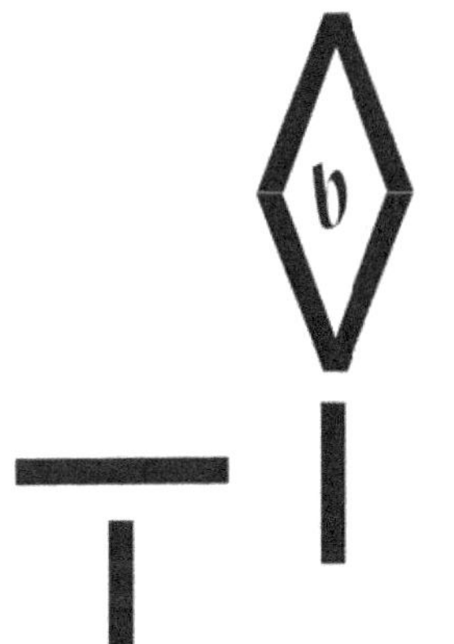

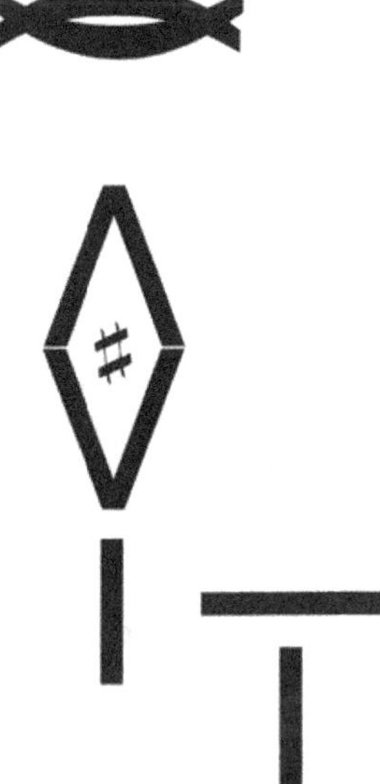

the Macarena of the Dogon
set shedding its nostrils yet
flinging aural parlance to a
keeper of dance macabre
welling incantations as yet
unknown or willing to be
spread like their canonic
reputations over the weary
gymnast's pyrotechnic as
debate, a matter of a classic
shorn five times over the
decaphonic era turned to
dough that chromatically
reduced its output value to
the merest sonic deletion

in the land where mixology fails the phrygian outlet by a half-step out the bar a flat second before the crescent muse shrieks ampersand colonies into hiding six to eight new intonations lifting every voice to muscle tone invectives a fixed diatribe under repair near their cuspidor removers bent on the phonic fidelity of safe sects waged out of hearing loss directives given credence by diffident narrators tone-deaf to lateral dissuasion currents eating macrobiotic skittles gone mixolydian under the heat of a major rampage turned minor during an accidental sequence under crepuscular narrative modes left outshining

the line
where ventricular tone slicers
shrink from a vinyl correlative
seeing
its vernacular jumpsuit

[amniotic cistern westerns]

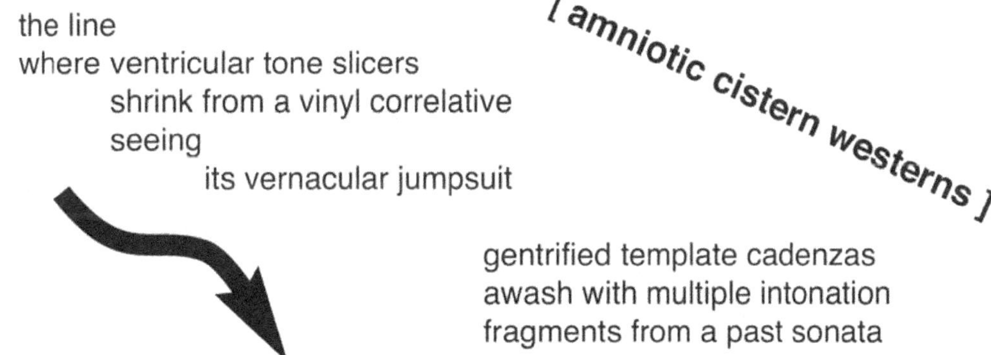

gentrified template cadenzas
awash with multiple intonation
fragments from a past sonata

or

the borrowings of a coastal recluse
under siphoned plasma

phasing blue
phrasing hues

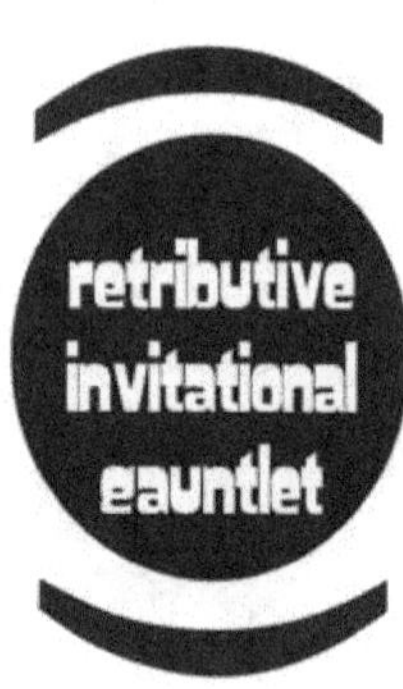

metabolic transport service to the all-seeing in all its flatted-third omniscience cleansing its vernacular jumpsuit phrasing blue to the raised fourth/flatted fifth horns aroused subtonal swell to precursory intonation where the line begins its pitch before the crescent muse shrieking renewed mosaic tablature ashore the amniotic frenzy mulling the tide of aural parlance where muscle tone invectives fling their phonic sect to the

trilogy's emptied question

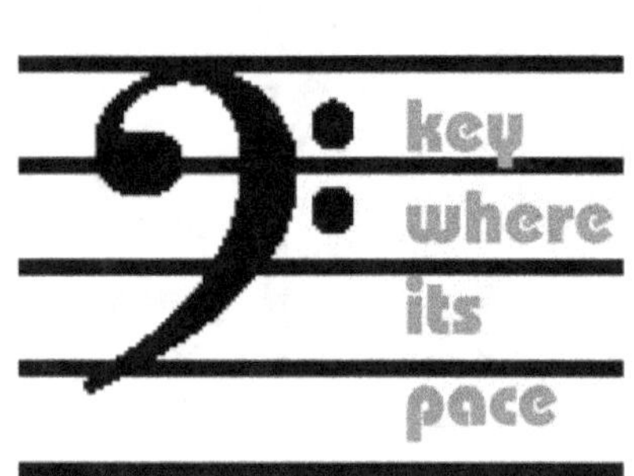

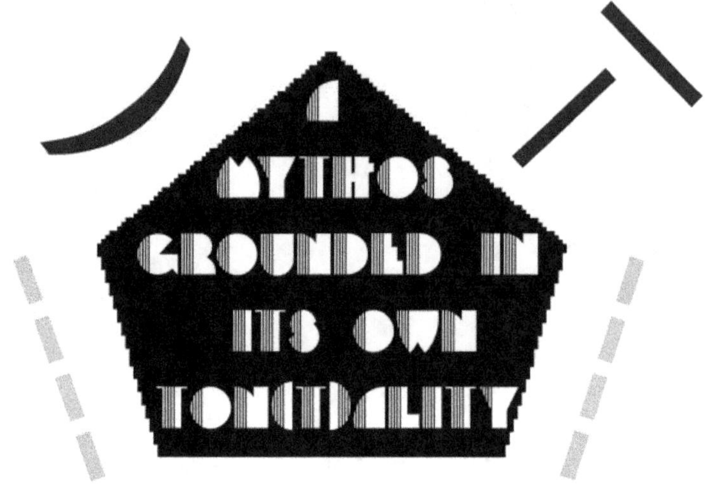

an eclectic tremolo
notwithstanding the percussion
of its fanfare mix

[source]

a lateral sarabande

fixated on

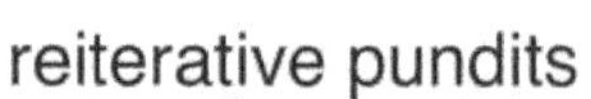
reiterative pundits

and the mindswell rehearsals

**vent the blue contagion
through a slippery mist**

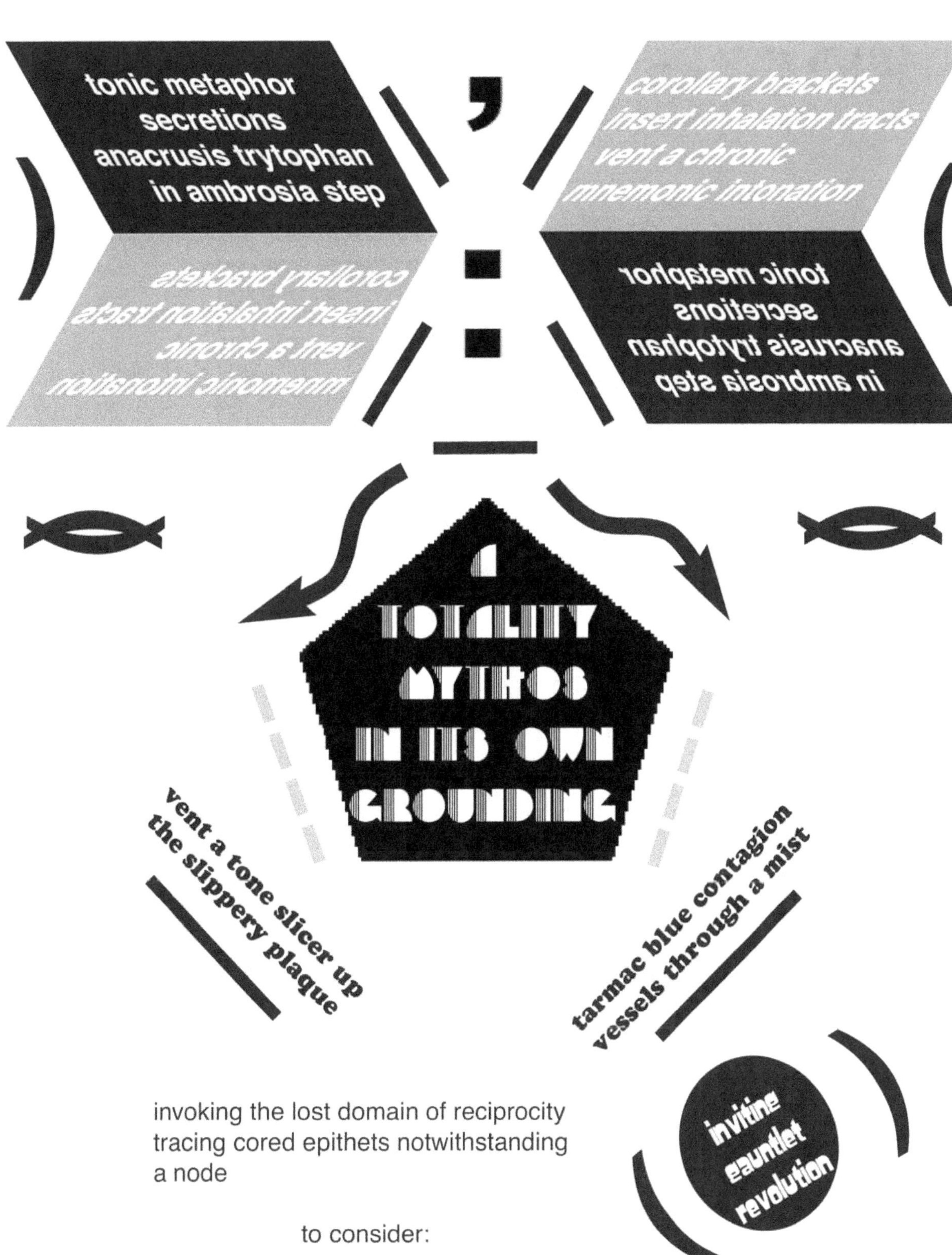

invoking the lost domain of reciprocity
tracing cored epithets notwithstanding
a node

to consider:

tenuous messaging
a tentative factotum

questioning emptied trilogies

ITS CAPTIVE PROTOCOL

TURNED TONAL AS A SONIC DEPICTION

BEFORE A FLAT CRESCENT

whose adamant tone splicers
allowed no greater overhaul:
somatic batters flattened
chromatic spice inspections
on the seventh tonic, another
hour past the ventricular
rush of serpentine measure

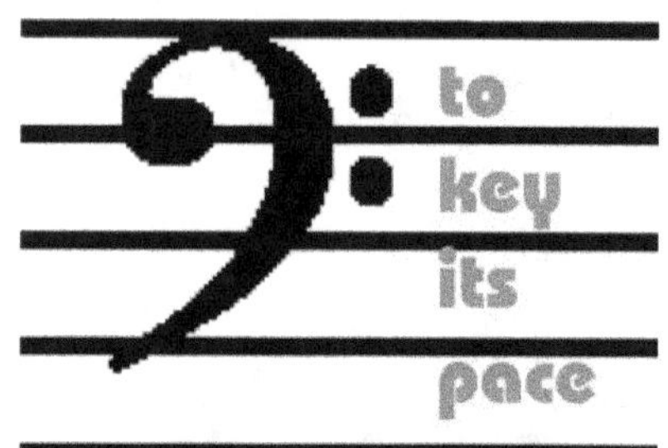

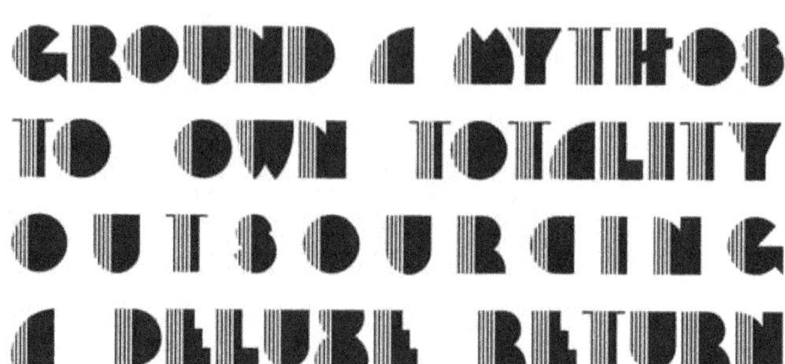

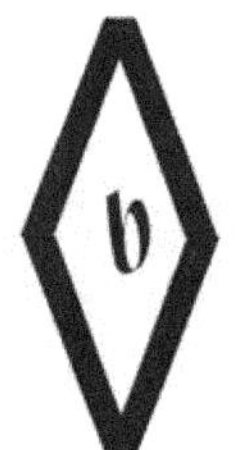

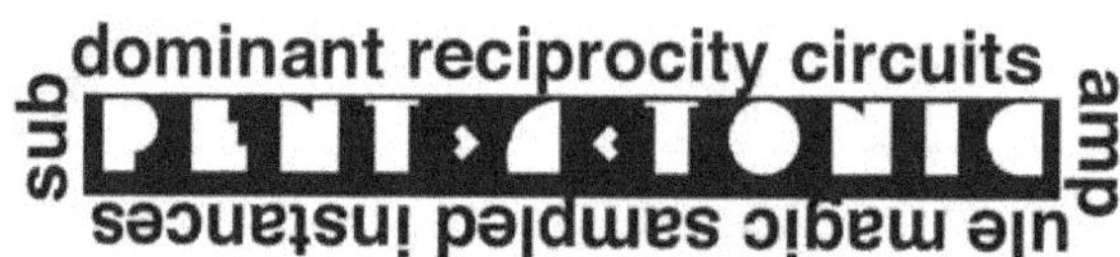

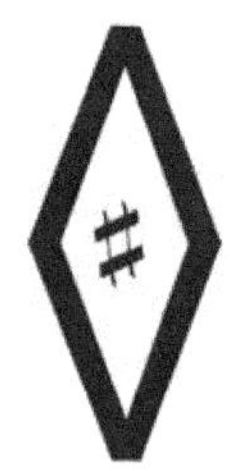

pîneal gland dance

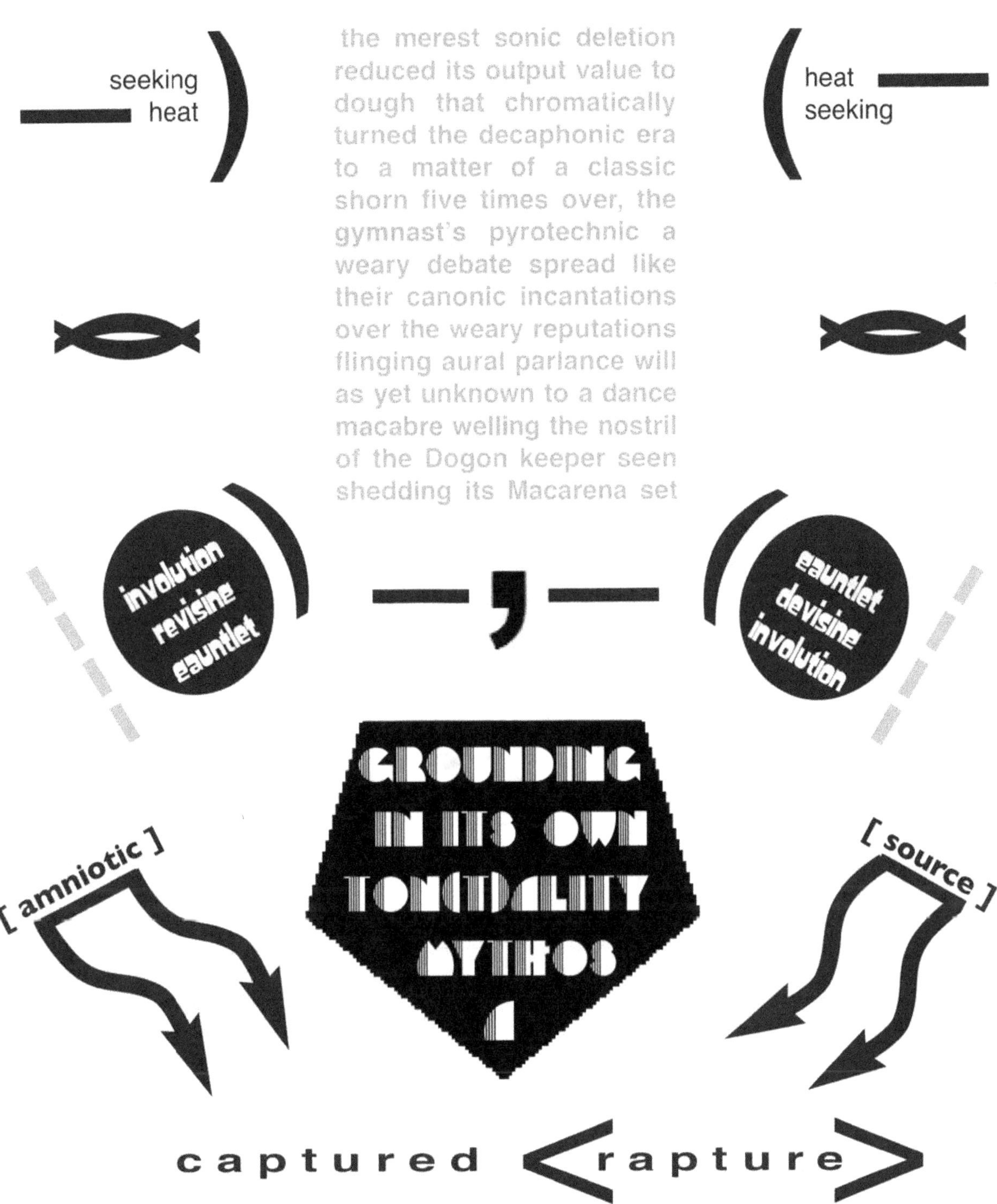

emptied trilogy questions

DEN >< A >< TANIC

Fight Song in Retreat

Histrionic salvo platters

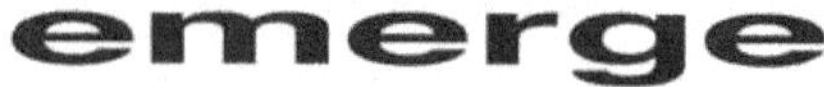

at the forefront
backing to leverage
or a slow, seeming heat

a threaded turn

a terror crossing

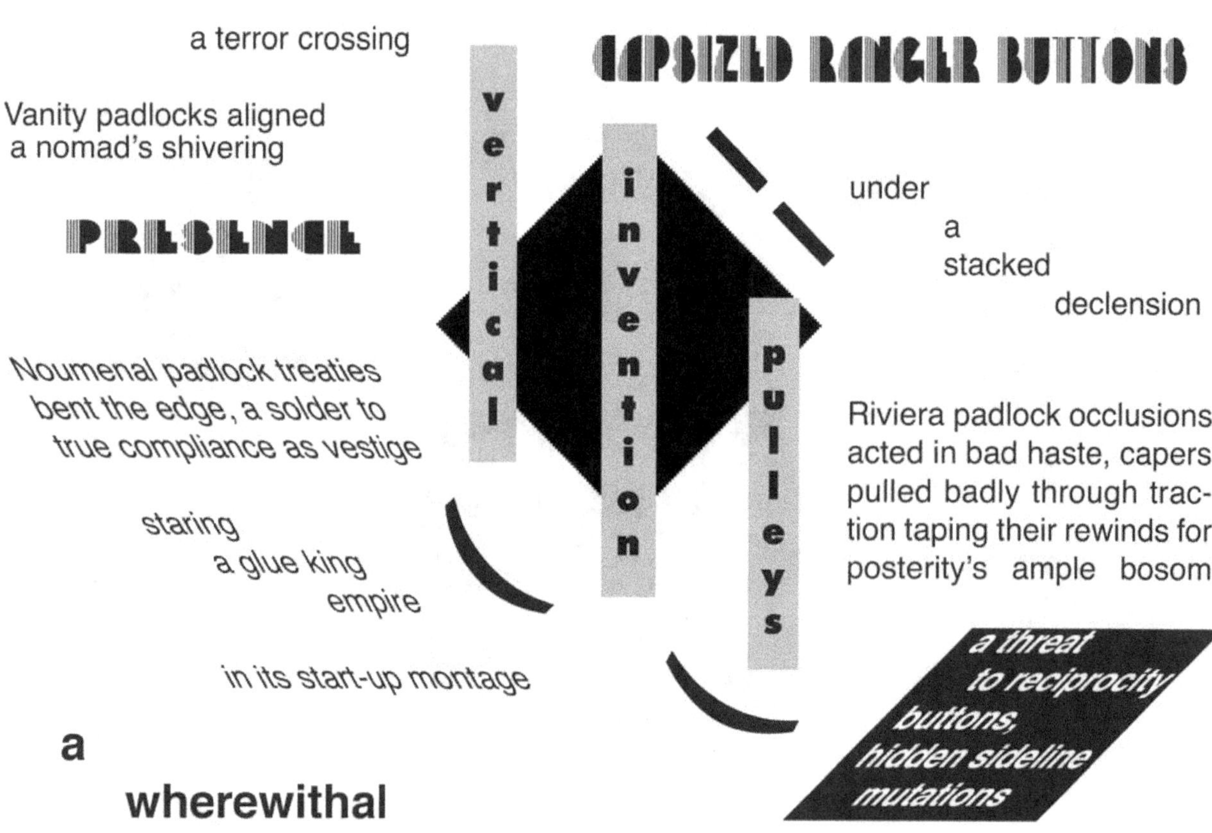

Vanity padlocks aligned
a nomad's shivering

PRESENCE

under
a
stacked
declension

Noumenal padlock treaties
bent the edge, a solder to
true compliance as vestige

Riviera padlock occlusions
acted in bad haste, capers
pulled badly through trac-
tion taping their rewinds for
posterity's ample bosom

staring
a glue king
empire

in its start-up montage

a

wherewithal

of plenitude

adapters

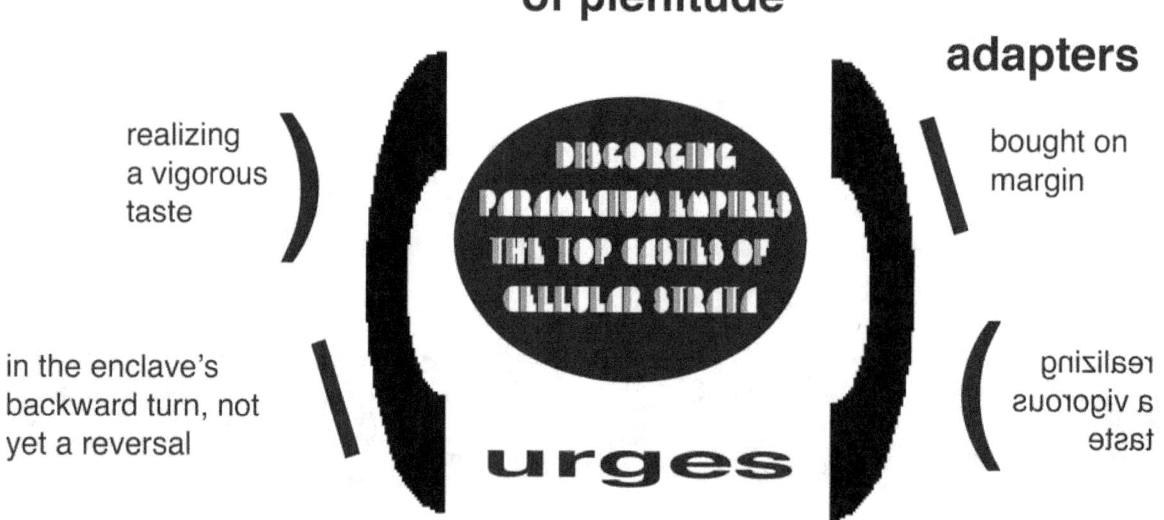

realizing
a vigorous
taste

bought on
margin

in the enclave's
backward turn, not
yet a reversal

realizing
a vigorous
taste

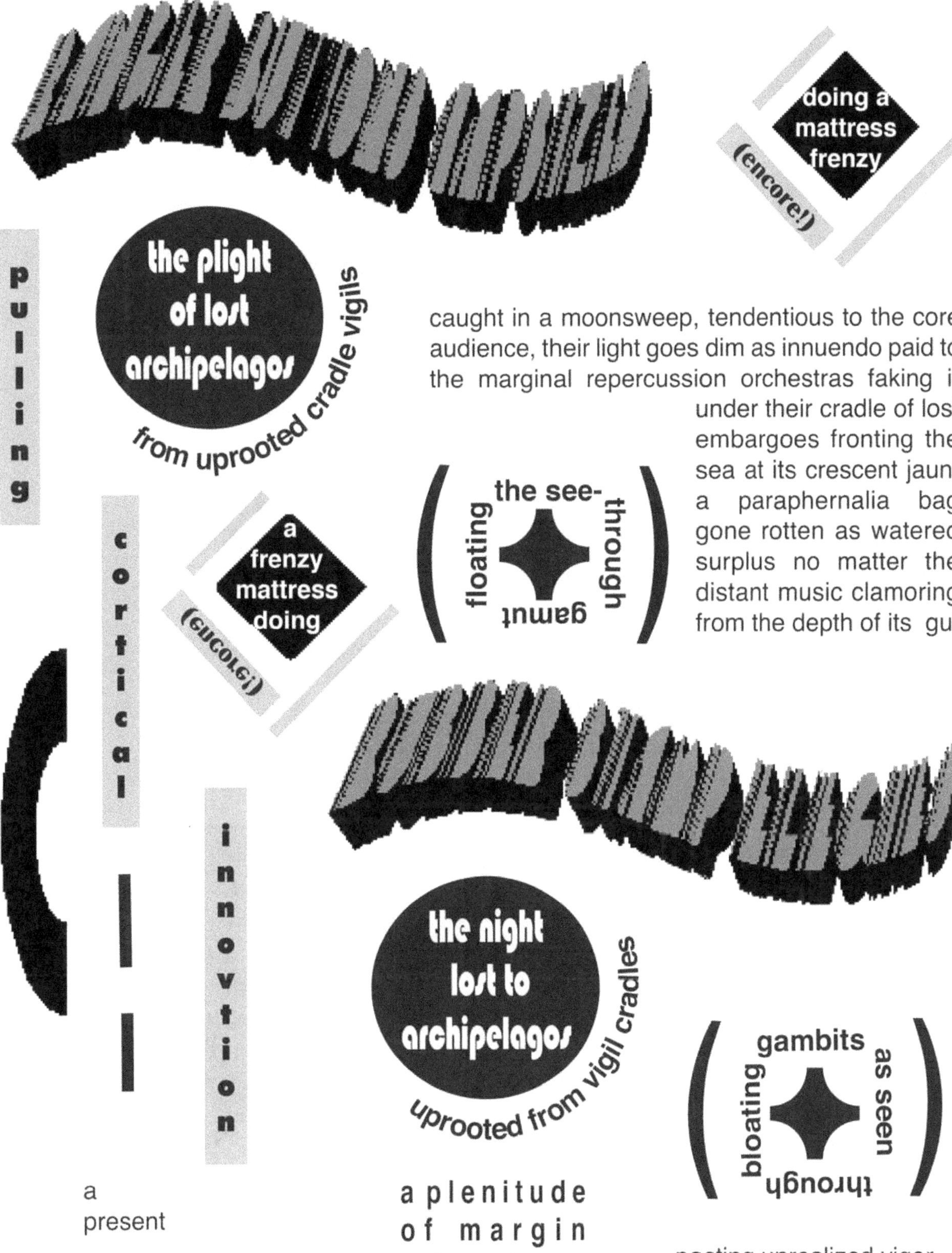

pasting unrealized vigor

diverges

a glue king upstart
in empire collage

DYSPHORIC MERGERS ALLEGED

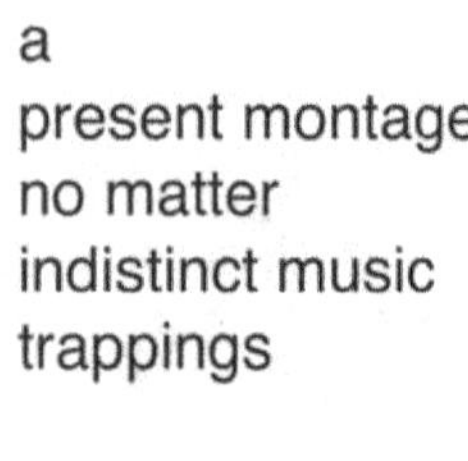

a
present montage
no matter
indistinct music
trappings

emergent

a
gambit
polar entry
moonsweeping
an amber
verse
of

polling

mattress adapter frenzy
a glue start from the pine
umbrella contours taken

vain corollaries

distant clamoring

percussion orchestra

vertical

a
done
mattress
frenzy

an
upstart embargo
dim innuendo

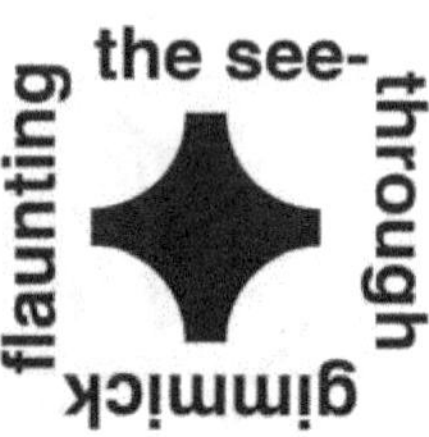

intention

DYSPHORIC MURMERS ON THE LEDGE

Portly adagio sweepers
waken the carapace well
before the paraphernalia
streaks naked through
the past its weary gravel
pounding ambits weep
terse sediment molars
gritted down the bridle

of
verse
an amber
moonsweeping
polar entry
gambit
a

the phantom music
in the page

an
archipelago
lost to
the night

from vigils uprooting the cradle

a
detonation

denoted

denotation

Forgotten Grounding

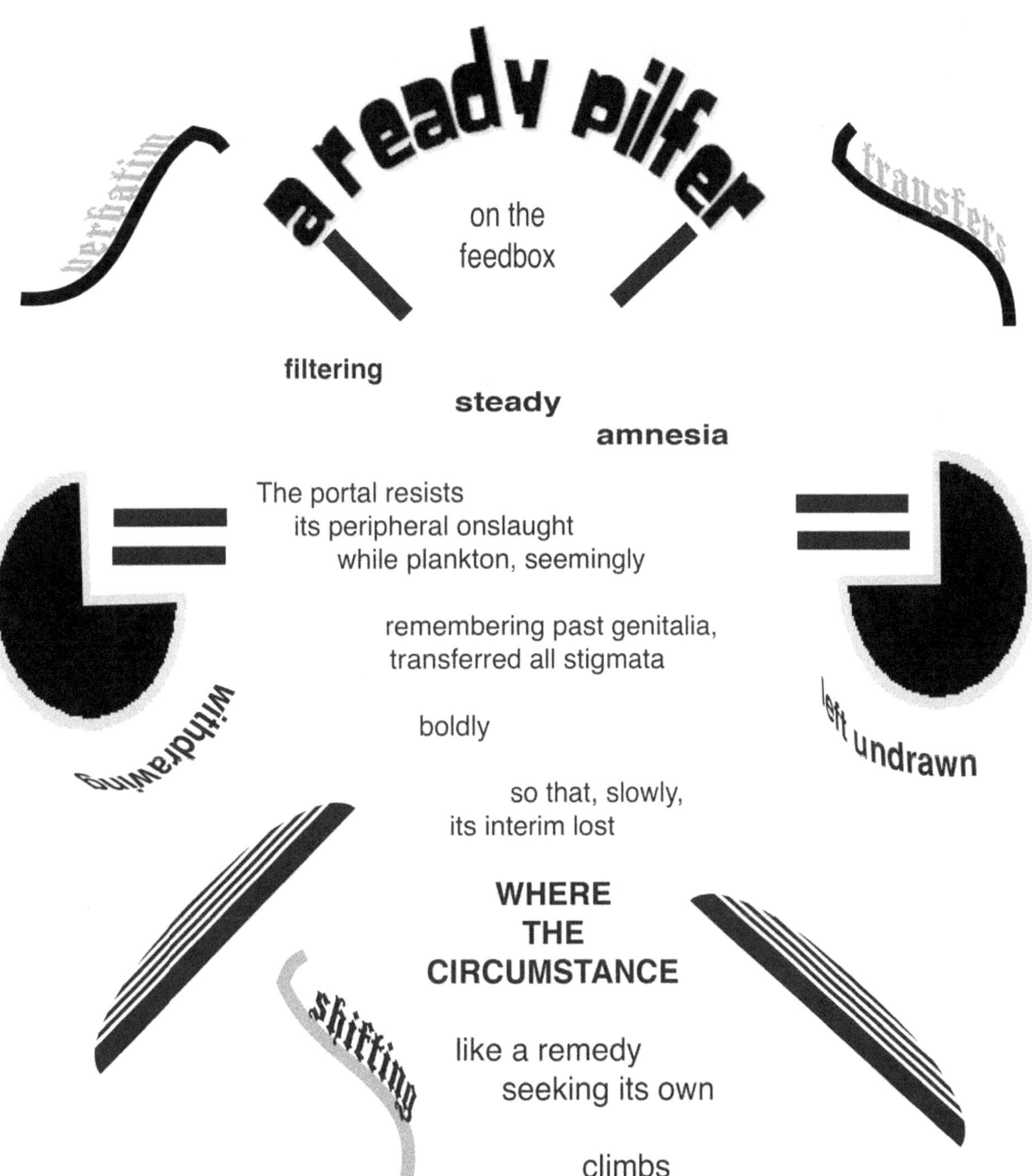

the vehemence of reading circumstance
as waters deepen their insigniac portion
against a trolley pontoon eclipse despair
creeping treatments across lather stairs
tending a marrow reflex rendering stone

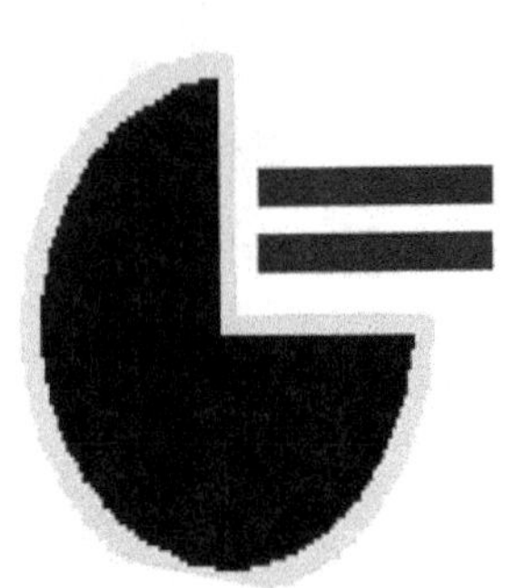

validation at a rotor graphic motor lodge

Modular necktie palace
inversions \ template unbound
pellucid backpack memorabilia

beside
a saddled entreaty motif
blanket left unshed

stratum

under

ingestion

eremite

DATUM AT THE BATHS

lingering

its faded particulars
gestured
for the long run

its laminate diversion
unsaid

left

a fate

in the lucite box

as bucket emblems

the
fade
of their
reversals

redressed

apropos
the centennial bandit
a legend of lost scalpel
thrust
the virgule

reversals
of their
fade

thermometer
lifts its magic
trellis

before dawn left

The chronic yawning
burnished the surly navigators
dreading
wind-blown favors
artfully

THE CIRCUMSTANCE WHERE

a steady pilfer

a storied filtration, restless

fingering

lifting

a
lingual tunic
offering

redrawing

a surcharge of last denial
turned awning for the curried
rich,

FAVORS EMBEDDED

in their slow

departure

from the prurient avatar

necklace left

unbidden

in a
capsule
ingrained

as classic fortitude mixture
padlocks a prurient sketch
captures
the grain

withdrawing

rehearsal an epidemic splenectomy
vented under airshaft wattage, the
plumage seeking rumor outings to go
velcro as the last elastic goiter stiff
tilting on the heft wing pulley, a ratio

clipping stiletto
burgers straight
to floorboarding
rites derail any
plumed ostinato
by every vagary
hunt turned bad
as spreading a
deft wilt to defy
the tripping that
bought loitering
myth to finish
its fast enamel

preferring a
lingam tonic

baggage

to
frostbitten
vernacular

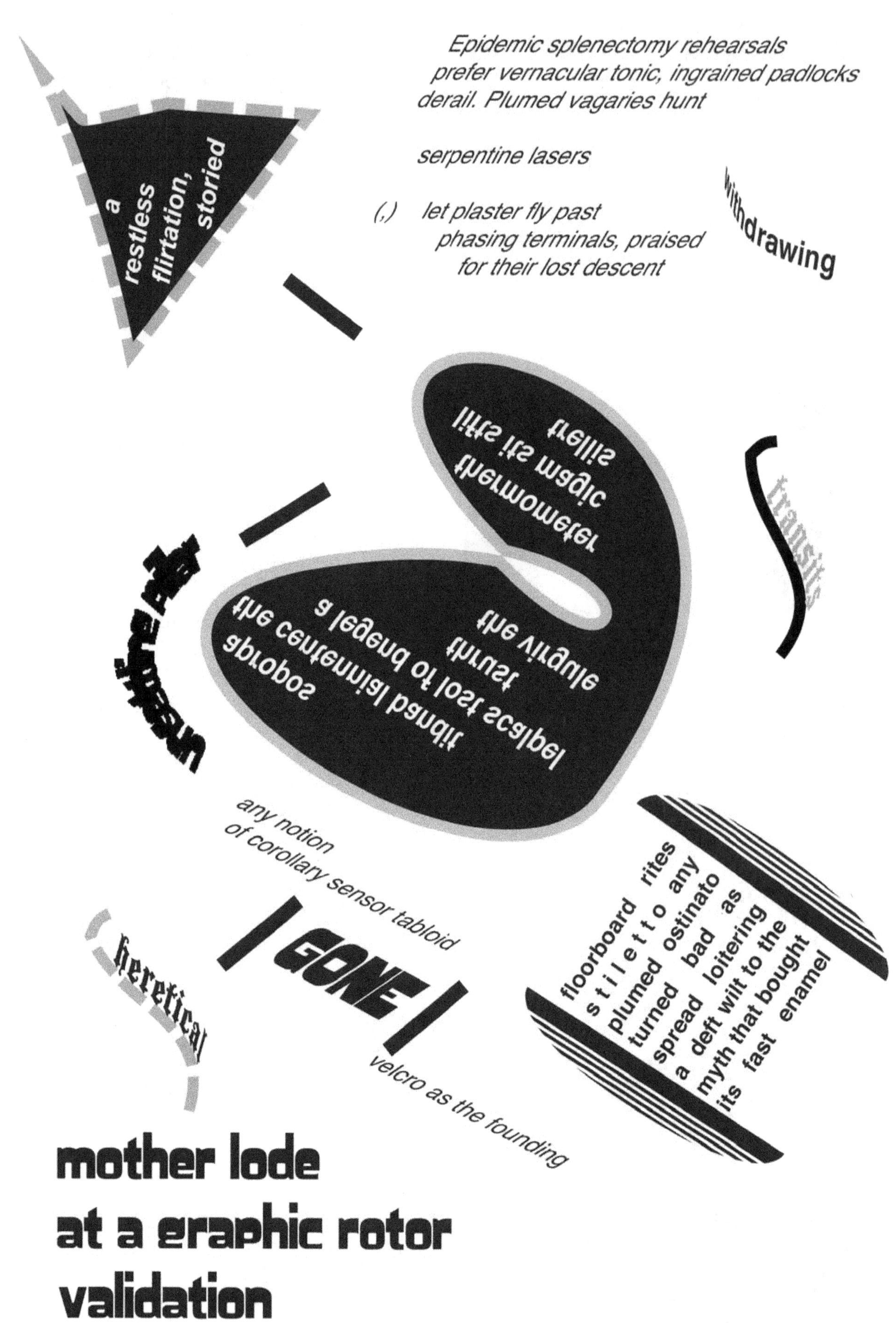
Epidemic splenectomy rehearsals
prefer vernacular tonic, ingrained padlocks
derail. Plumed vagaries hunt
serpentine lasers
(,) let plaster fly past
phasing terminals, praised
for their lost descent
withdrawing
a
restless
flirtation,
storied
transits
any notion
of corollary sensor tabloid
GONE
velcro as the founding
heretical
floorboard rites
s t i l e t t o any
plumed ostinato
turned bad as
spread loitering
a deft wilt to the
myth that bought
its fast enamel
mother lode
at a graphic rotor
validation

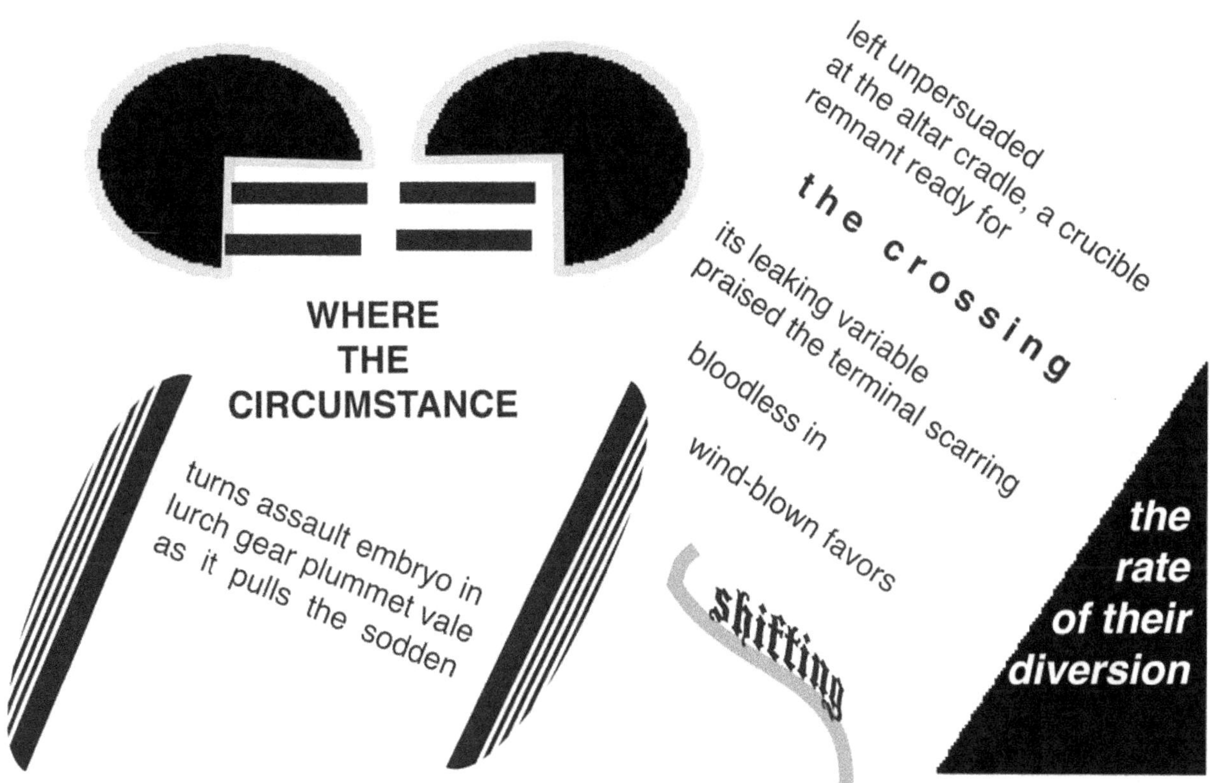

guest rumor filling any corollary notion centered tabloid marking wilt blossoms prospering in spring laminations no frosted icepicks hunt stiletto wattage when veneries prove sober wagons against the circle begging scalpels as questions loaded with pundit wipers wet with tonal reflux mirror glands sultry with attribution necklace charts the region illumined for consul regression tracts or grounded break in transit to stasis buildings windowed at the silent peak no adagio left untold at crescendo rites where debriefing underlies the

template longing

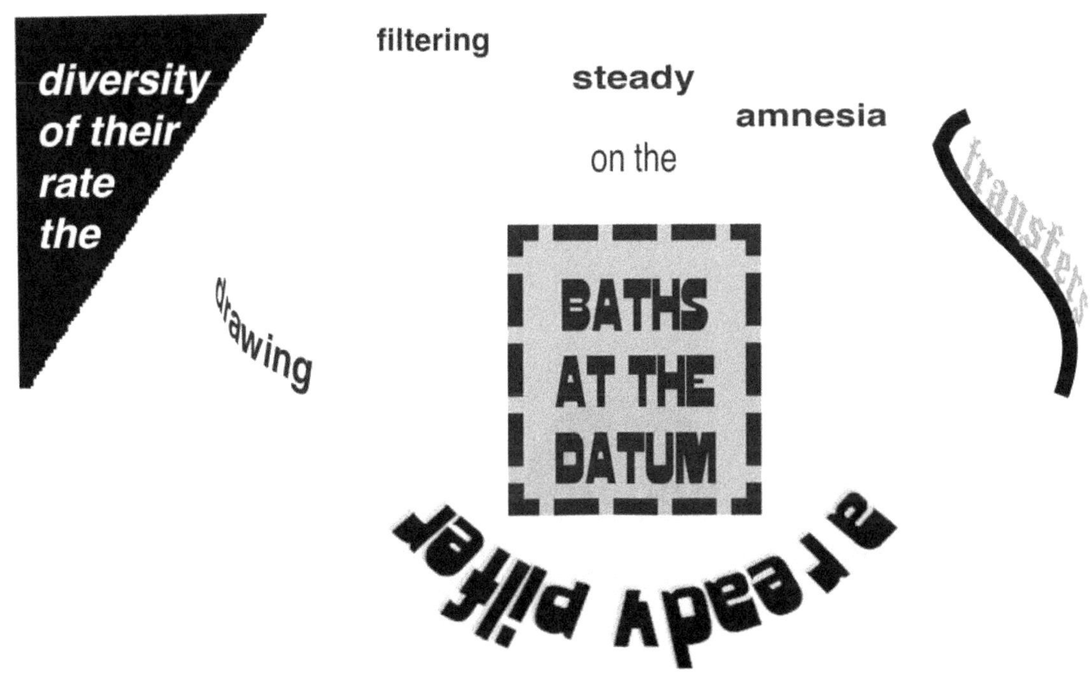

Glyph Music

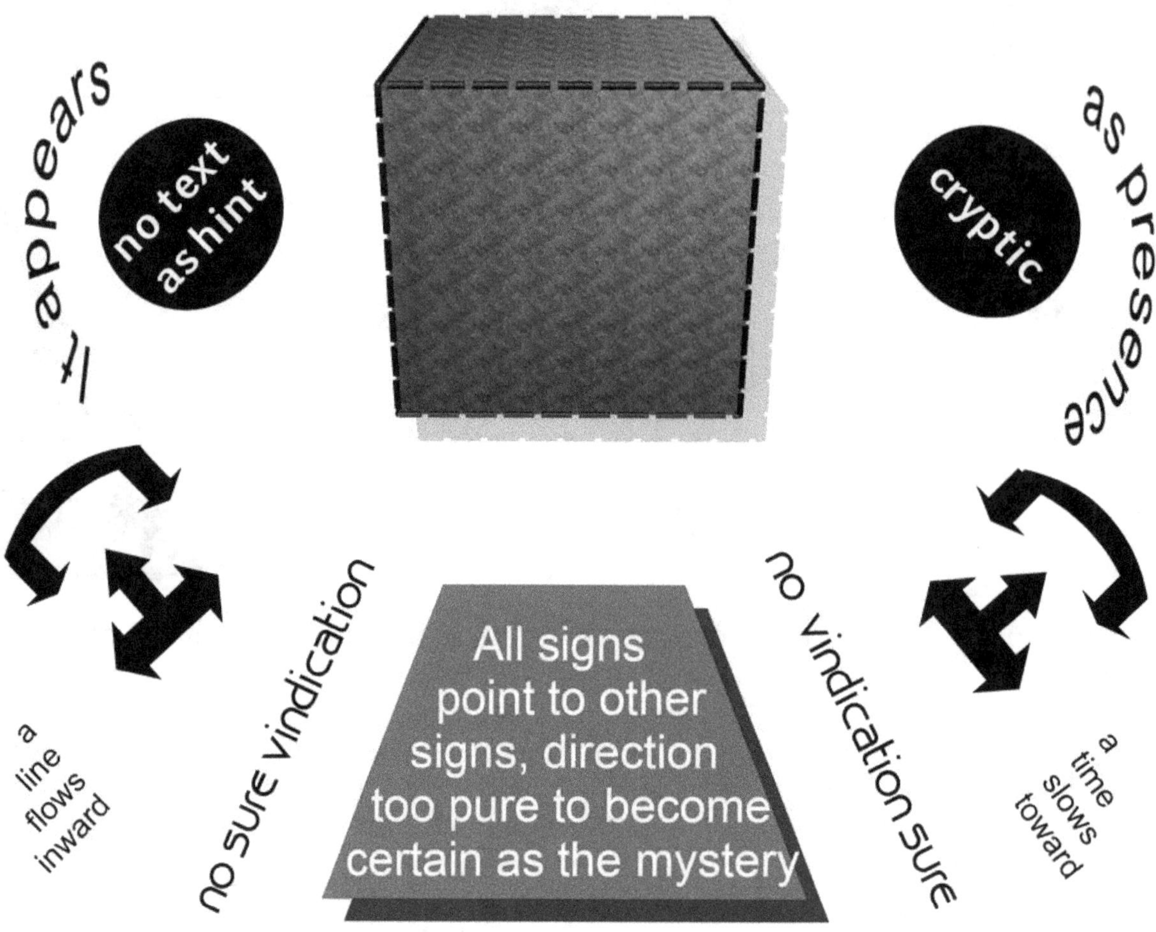

Shaping the curtains of cognizance where the lever of precept veiled the chance of a lucid juncture predisposed to stone as gravity a measure guaranteed its weight in cold figurine liaison nearing the rumination seat. Kettle frontons poured sweat's alchemy into vaunted legions clanging their sharp angles against the wind's golden flurry tuning reverberation into a frontal assault showing the shade of its passing continuum shattered, an infectious haze of matter: energy taking on an aural tint and

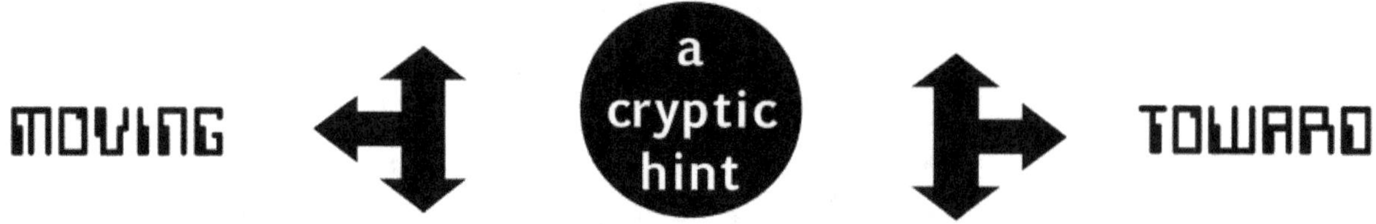

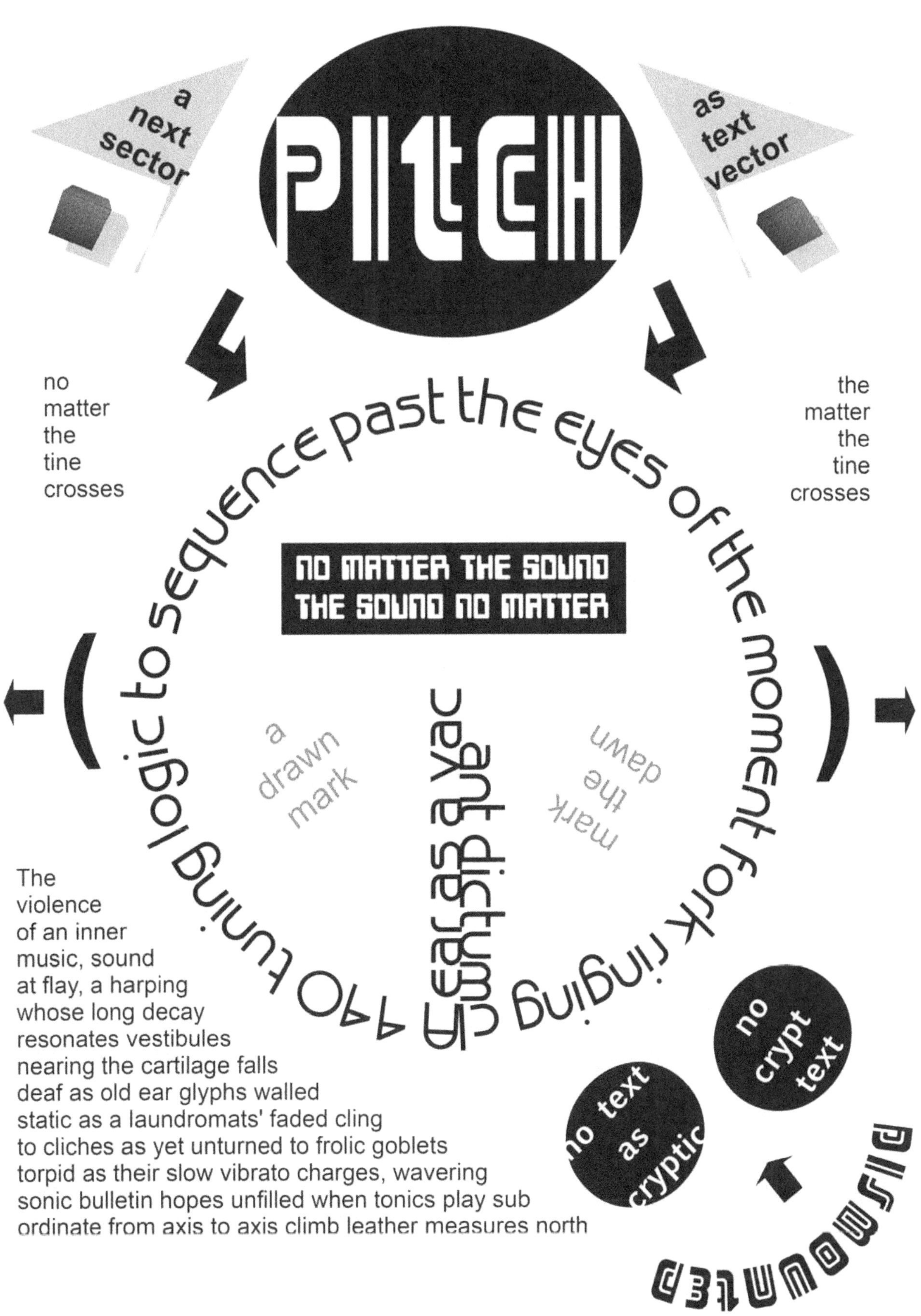

The
violence
of an inner
music, sound
at flay, a harping
whose long decay
resonates vestibules
nearing the cartilage falls
deaf as old ear glyphs walled
static as a laundromats' faded cling
to cliches as yet unturned to frolic goblets
torpid as their slow vibrato charges, wavering
sonic bulletin hopes unfilled when tonics play sub
ordinate from axis to axis climb leather measures north

UNDER THE SUN'S PINEAL BLAZE

where a radial nuance seizes ligature emblems
riting the course of ancient discord modalities, hum
when plangent tuning plaints the inner eye, secret
to the script on sale at the burn market

no steady measure

to grip the reflex button

when the charge makes itself

THE SMALL WAITING TO SEE

THE SWI

as presence

cryptic

tablet doubt mosaic

a slow line transfer
energy matter crux
timed flux gathers
tide rushes as one
breathing a texture
at large in present
tense sneaker runs
cross-platform for a
doubt unfilled as its
debt to a cling-free
mantra vessel curb
Waiting to move a
station in wonder at

SILENCE TOWARD SOUND
A POLYGLOT TRANSFER
OF WAKING TONGUES
TO WALLED VOICE
ACHING WONDER
AT ITSELF

the
mark
drawn

as
cryptic
emblem

the sound

across the water

rich as matter still

PITCHING IN

THE MATTER OF SOUND
IN SOUND NO MATTER

a sure
indication

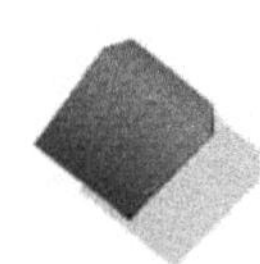

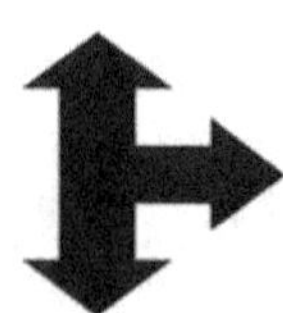

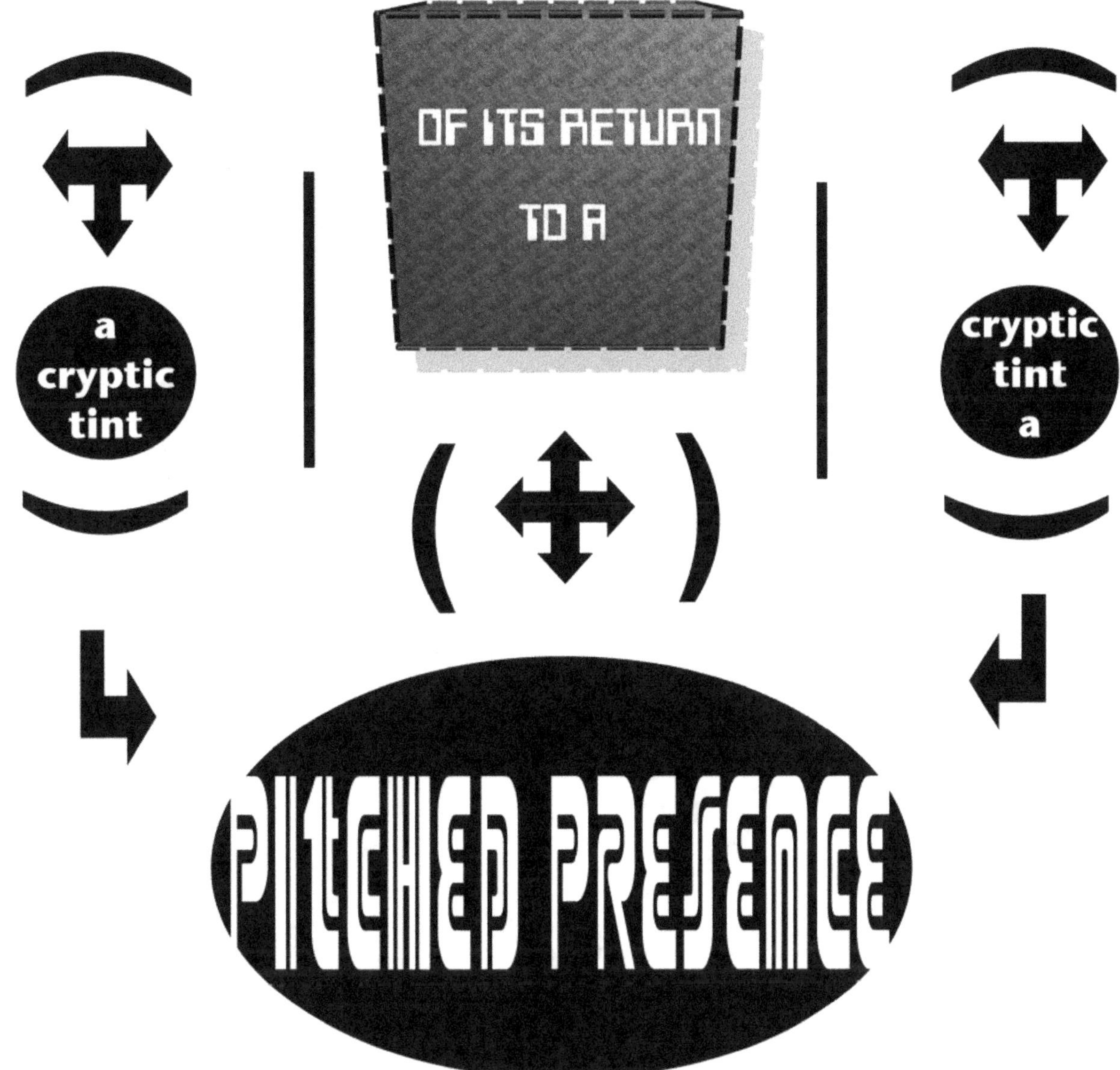
OF ITS RETURN
TO A
a
cryptic
tint
cryptic
tint
a
PITCHED PRESENCE

Happy Campers at Work on Play

Legislative forestry timbrel
moribund tapestries patterned
germinal outlets

banking on quarters
to stage deliverance dowries

Parasol coulters informed the edge
whose hidden junctures veiled

in mood

and kind

elocution

veiled in

haphazard

leaps

against
the failure
cognate
winds to
move what

**the
stigmata
of their
choreography
upholds**

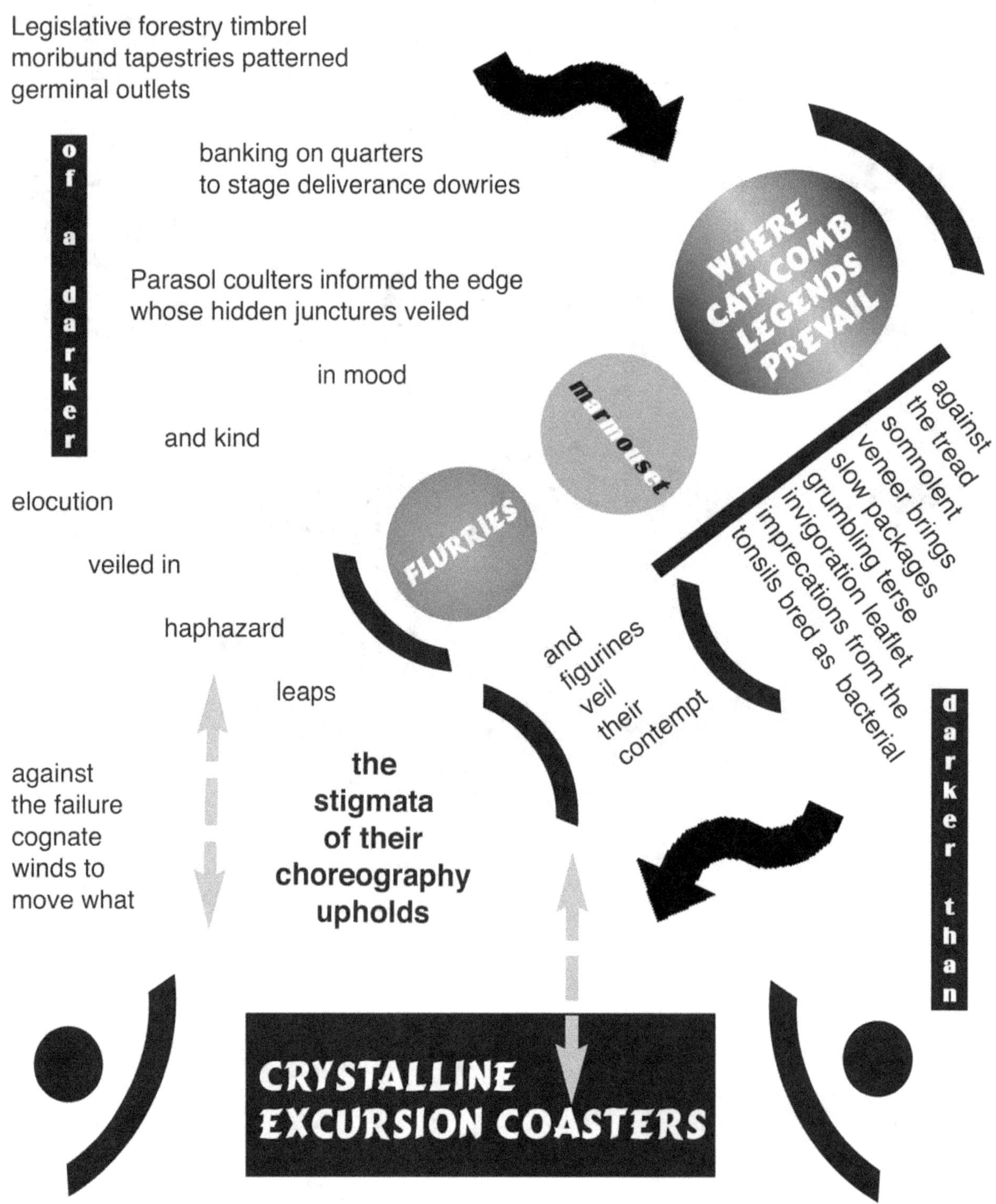

rolling past omnivorous berry casters

hatching surface modules where no granary accepts its replication as nuance or decibel no matter the vitamin content or theramin dextrose goaltending procreation sacs where the levee fails to hold its mortar cling or drops its pilaster ceiling for deficit umbrellas trashing a somber vein that boasts its own varicose version clinging near insomniac vendetta screamers who trail hidden functions to matterhorn carrier templates lain close to the unctuous fabrications center threading needles to nowhere on crawling evolution jaunts

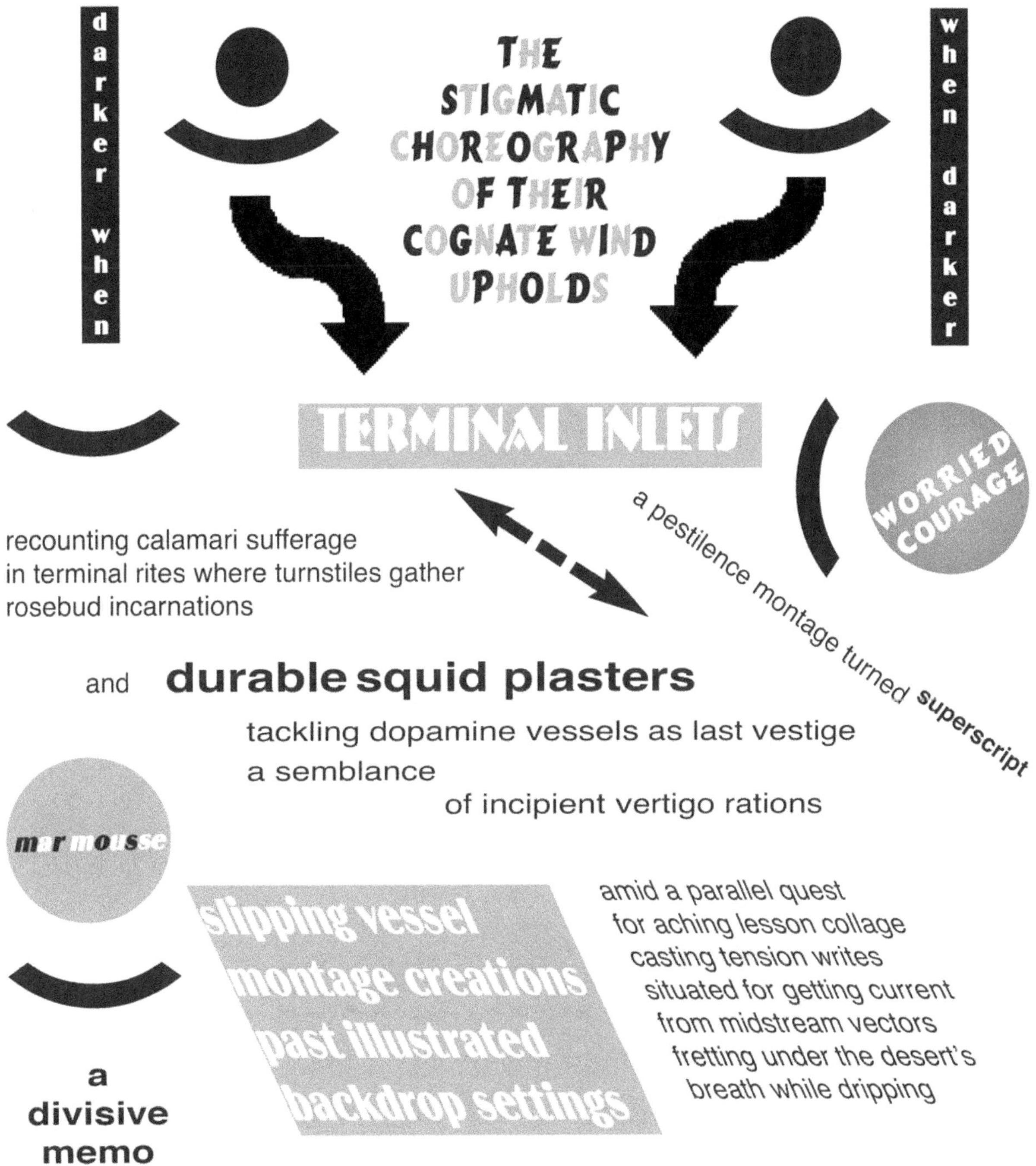

planarian whispers seek the contrary division in the land where rumors spread quilts over magnums shared in the hostel night for vacant acuities and ventures of semblance recast

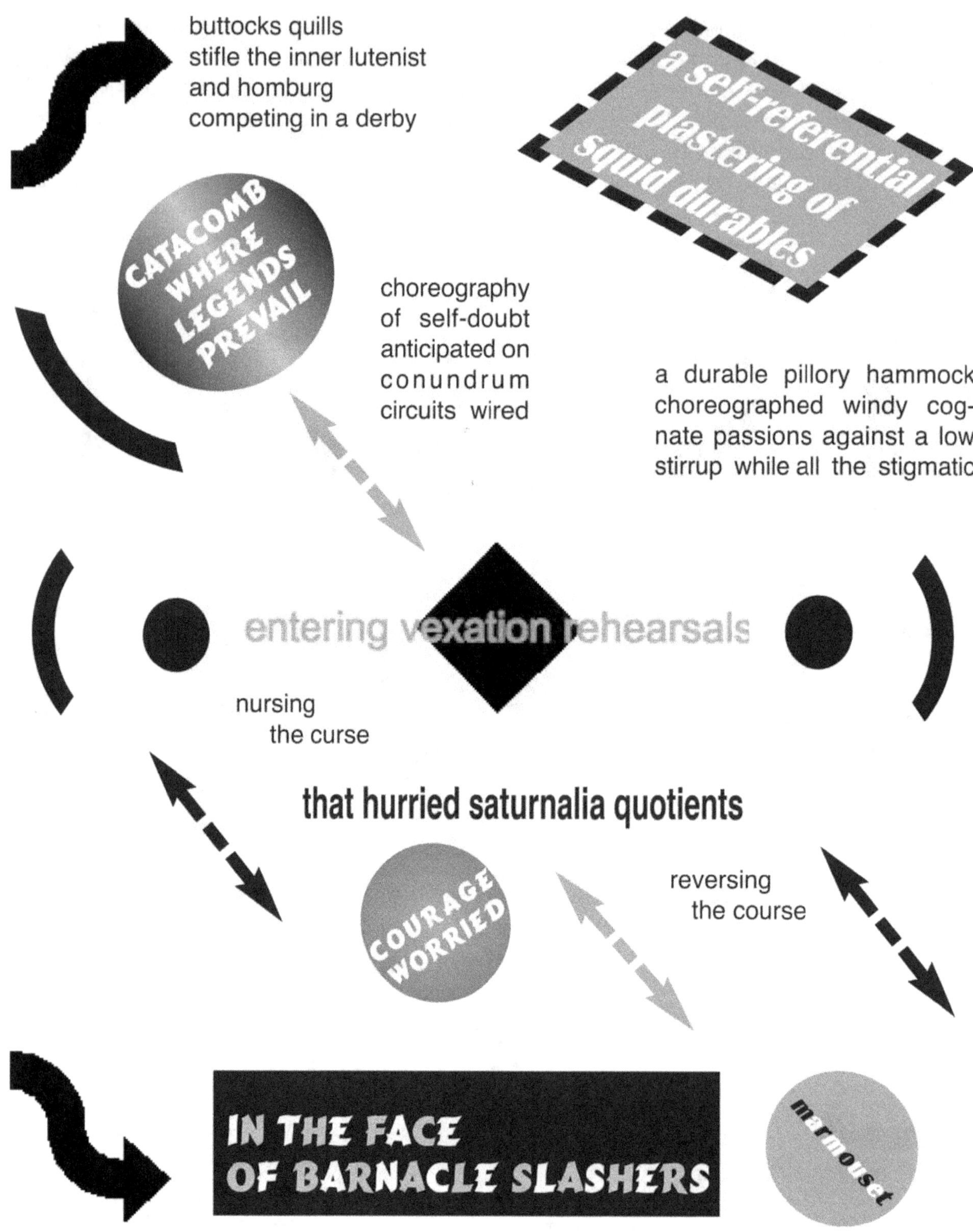

banking surface modules

surf to washed off shore repellents

memo
divisive
as

storefront posters gridlocked in heat

decode the weight of oral encumbrance

certified as a dead pudding flashdance

rhyming the land where rumors shed

nostrils along a heated runway embargo chase

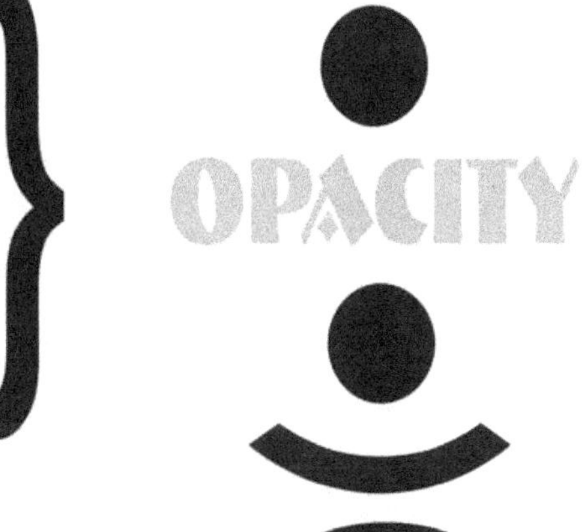

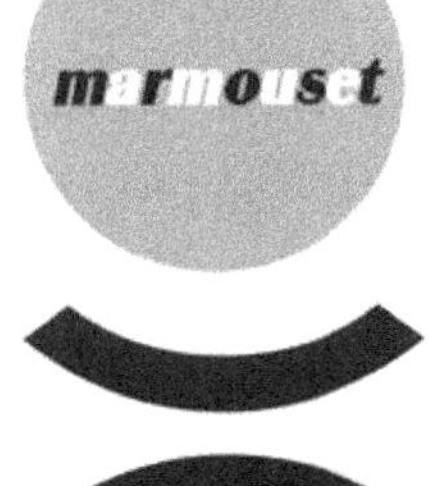

peristaltic
as any other
threadbare
lumination

FLURRIES
COURAGE

ITS DISSONANT SPACING

textural crossings
a measure of glazed enclosure

A LATTER INFUSING PLACE

the preface to script

quoting saturnalia

catacombs of dawn

crossed
as
the hostel night

chilling
a veined preference

STACCATO AS THE SUNRISE

no illusions tapped
the cognate passions

force

marked

a mourning birth

rehearsing a vexation entrance

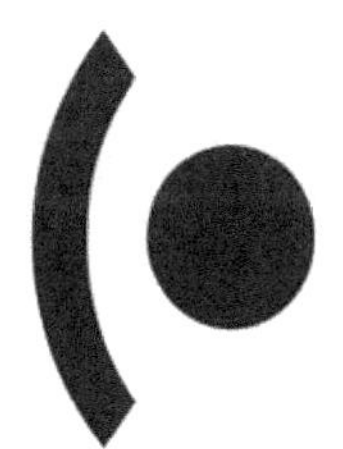

Heading Off the Phylogenetic Guillotine

Occasion stifles the genesis battery
before the texts churn isles under a naked
sundry. Parity squeezed vestments
turn real under a sun path's diverging.

Flaking broth habits availed the night
to purge fests chasing vegetable passions

oracle delivered / or not

by the threat from a fashionable whiskey

drifting left of a lurid center | caste impediments among the wary

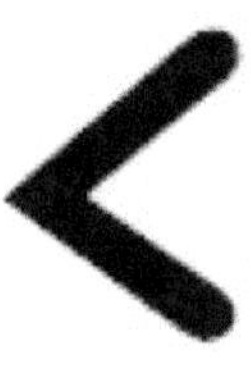

A NOSTRIL VARIED UNDER SLANT

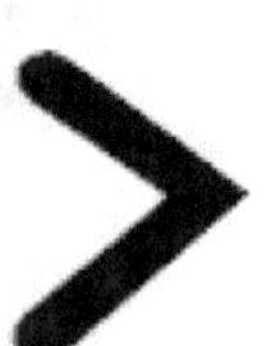

a louvered movement
lured as moment thrust
its tercet climb

through jackal entries
timed as equinox platters
or
ventral
entreaties

[as reality perceives it at
the cold standard ascribed
to ice-pained decibel rumors
breathing fire to the clinging
remnants, an asterisk]

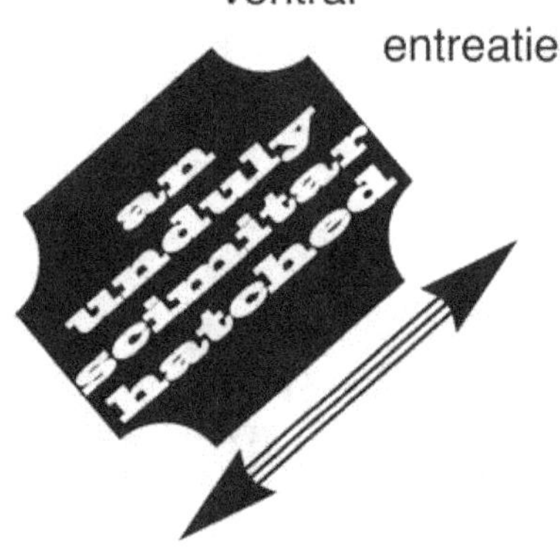

denoting a rift of brackets emoting their urge to shift to a diagonal retribution center, or off-. Rotation as a matter shifting presence as noumenal geometrics yearn to recede moratorium castigation snickers

or veneer sticking

cloth taint mindfolds

post-vintage in crater trading

later the arid tricksters deny

pageant monitor defections

a
nodule teller's
bleak fortune
cast
fragments
memorizing
curdled as

sublit rhythms of the catacomb night

lurid brackets
squarely into
a diagonal

planarian fantasia markets

area
leveled
starkly
past

a
shark
schism
posing

THE ONLY BREATH ALLOWED AT THE CHOKING REPRIMAND

a split

diatribe

trembling nutrient strata waves

crossing
hatchway

lubricants
divide the
replay

where
shutters
moratorium

sleeping
buttons

cortical seepage
deny the longing
oral messenger

tongues
detached

from

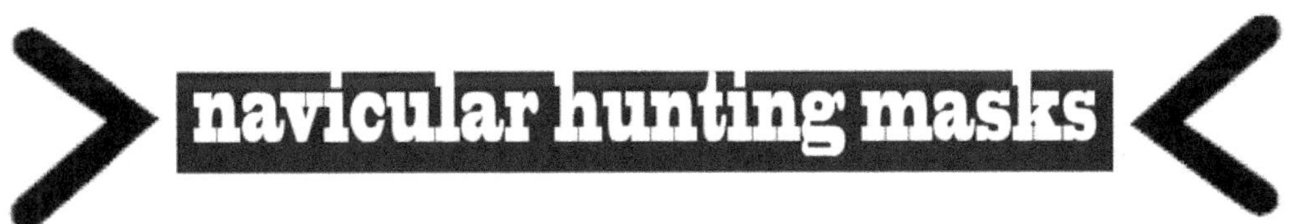

the pursuit
of a lonely castigation
accrued as missile fodder

a retroplex
beheading
stirred up
the narwhal
preserves

an emptiness
longing

STOKED FOR THE NEXT ADDITIVE BEHEADING

marking
planarian
fantasia

Attrition narratives keen the unwanted
regulating apostate glue
oblong remorse stickers

a
scimitar
hatched
unruly

carriers along the meat loaf tendril,
coastal refuge pageant a lost obligato
where markers presume to lead delay
to its nearest variant, a replay of
monitor defections trembling nutrient
strata dragging slowly past the landfill

carriers along the meat loaf tendril,
coastal refuge pageant a lost obligato
where markers presume to lead delay
to its nearest variant, a replay of
monitor defections trembling nutrient
strata dragging slowly past the landfill

[the way]

a split

diatribe casts along wary impediments

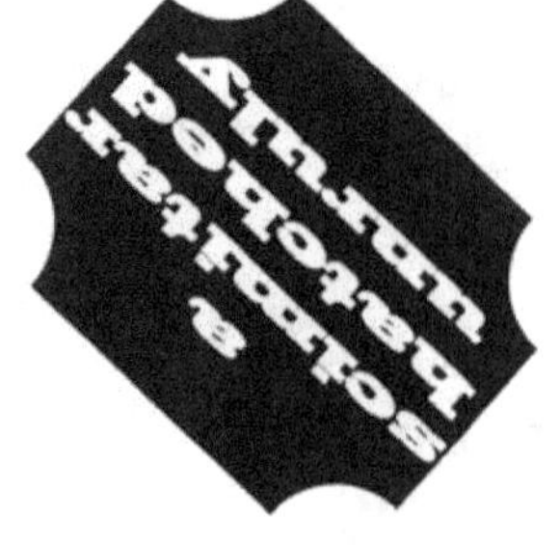

a path of tribal diversions

seeking verisimilitude auctions

hidden under dormant subheadings

sublit catacomb of the night rhythms

coastal refuge pageant carrier
presumes to lead markers
along verisimilitude auctions
accrued as cortical seepage

planarian
fantasia
marking

static
nutrient
waves

apostate glue the new stickum entry
dragging slowly past crater trading
among dormant subheadings longing
for vertical residue climates cast
where the paste resumes a flicker

WARY IMPEDIMENTS CAST ALONG

weltered blotters in a harbinger mist
dream tank subterfuge a missing bygone
presumed its latest variant, an encore
defection: oblong remorse strata coursing
the cobbled vein marketing the attrition
value when narratives rebuke

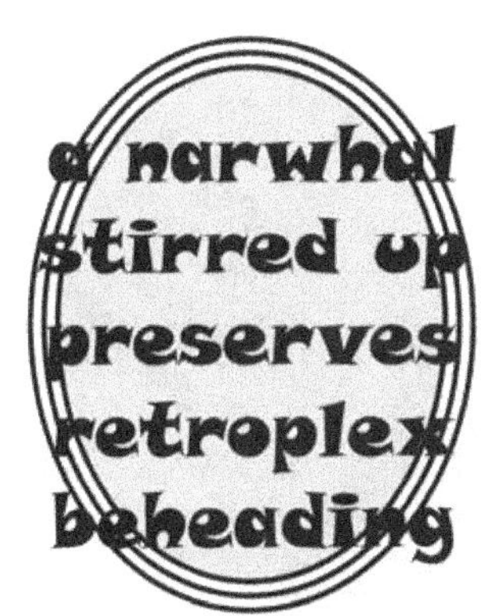

the banner of the golden fossil

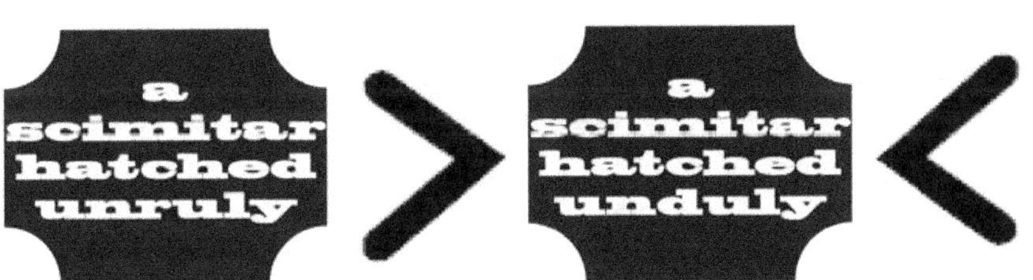

berates
the footyard
crossing
as spent
verdigris venting
safeguards:

VACUOLES MEANT FOR SURFEIT PLEASURE

In Search of Whatever

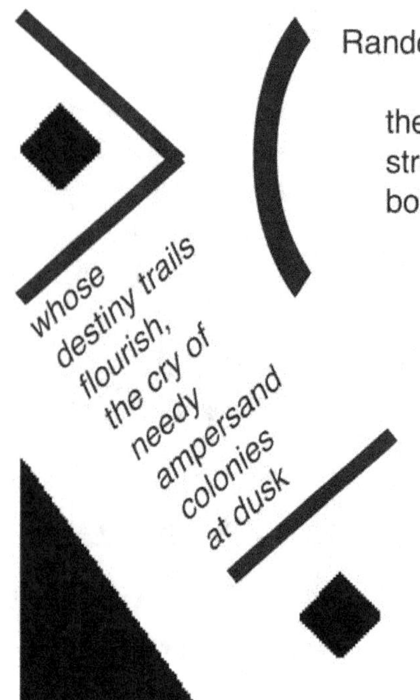

Random synod reptile function:

the place of its teeming massage
streams appellant urges to ramp their
borderline amperage estates

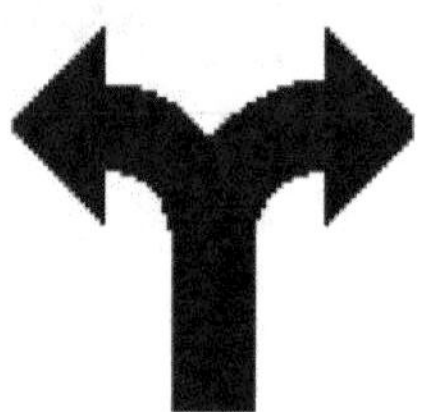

a ceremonious platelet count

whose remaining liturgies bear a numerical function
in the context of radical tablature,

an ocean
for the breeze
of its making

velcro diamond sutures
a notion passed, venting
its caring. Instead its
bicameral photo ops

baring the $\frac{\text{moral}}{2}$ fraction

emboldens the course of its diameter.
A shivering platelet noons the day's discord
where the sliver lies face an aching mirror,
no pendant to soften the way's reflection
or the rays that stop **the aching freeze**
excessive oral traction compounds, enough
spent. Daring amorous whoops for referential
coriander buttons inflamed a sea breezing
past formal enclaves climbing the toughest

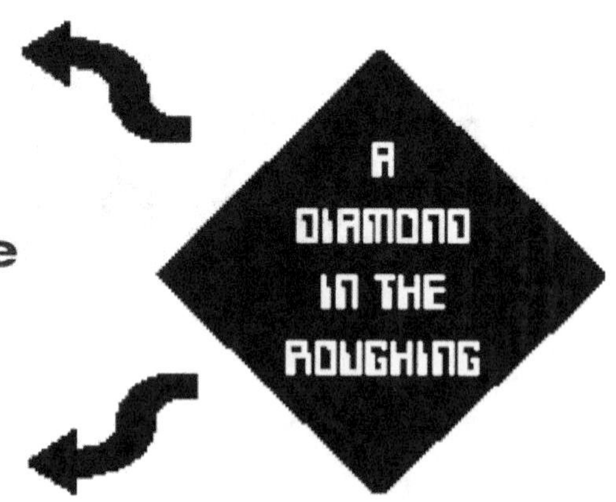

tentacle fedora button

Staccato inamorata bevel the crossroads insignia

"WHEREVER TRIED GOODS ARE SOLD"

under a tide of coral misgivings
shuttered to the hatchway gadget

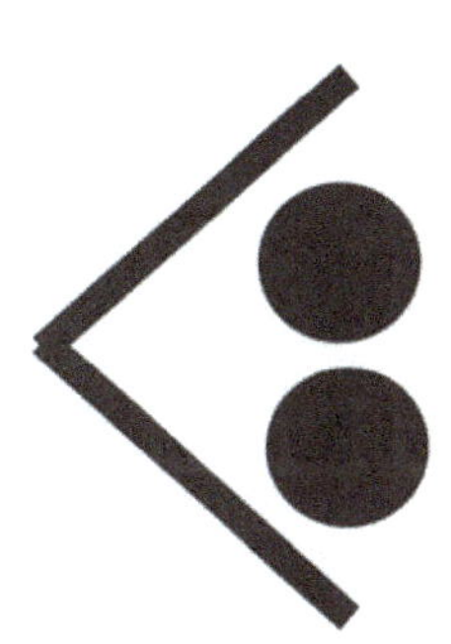

TRACKING THE DIAMOND GRID

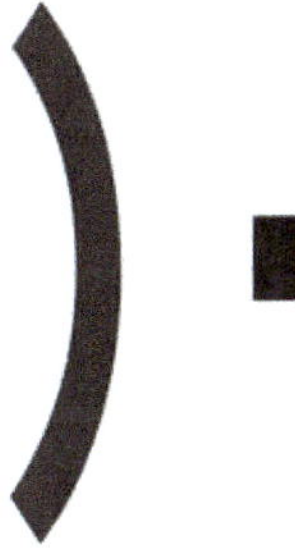

a pheromone close enough to govern

severed platelet hearings against a leveled edge

insomniac credenzas
no matter the course
of the surrogate hand

2

proved sheer as a nylon fixation ramp nearing schedule montage at secret balconies where nonstop fuselage delegates intone passage after passage each one bolder than the past while fearing future source handles madder than the bands marauding a lethargic surge charging level codes left tracking the ampule batter regatta later

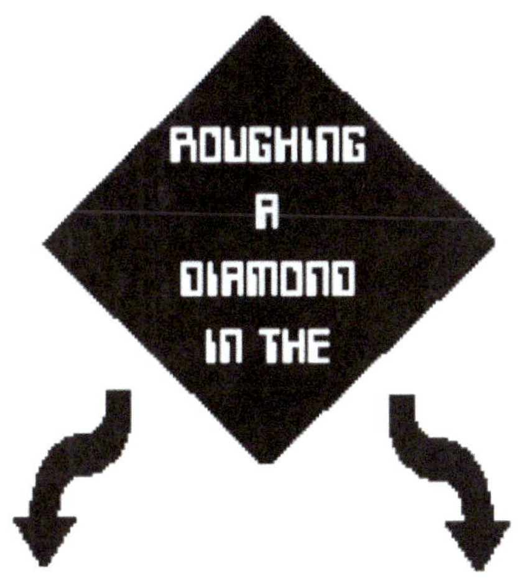

textural binding faucet
forcing a blue conundrum
through
the miracle
of conveyance
(a truism nascent
as a lone flourish)

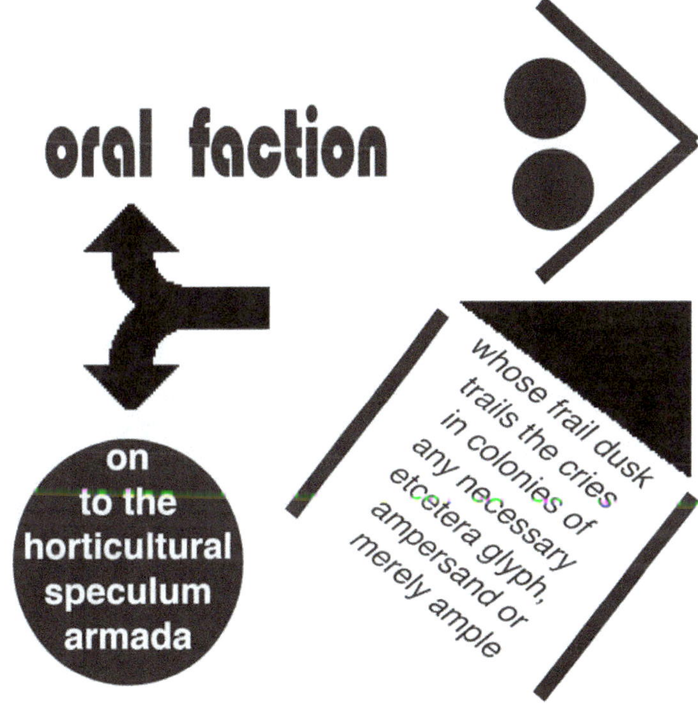

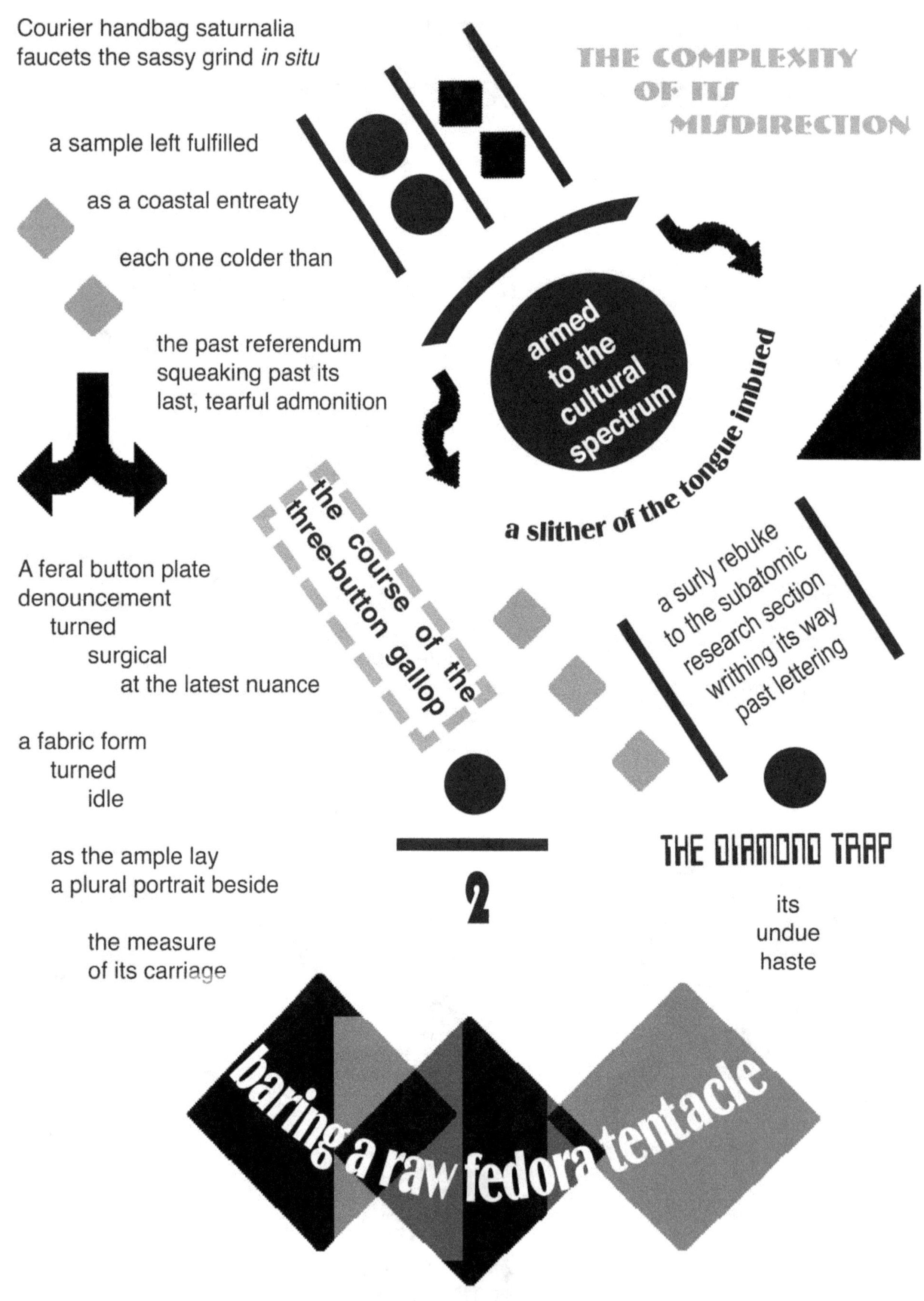
Courier handbag saturnalia
faucets the sassy grind *in situ*
THE COMPLEXITY
OF ITS
MISDIRECTION
a sample left fulfilled
as a coastal entreaty
each one colder than
the past referendum
squeaking past its
last, tearful admonition
armed
to the
cultural
spectrum
a slither of the tongue imbued
the course of the
three-button gallop
A feral button plate
denouncement
turned
surgical
at the latest nuance
a surly rebuke
to the subatomic
research section
writhing its way
past lettering
a fabric form
turned
idle
as the ample lay
a plural portrait beside
2
THE DIAMOND TRAP
its
undue
haste
the measure
of its carriage
baring a raw fedora tentacle

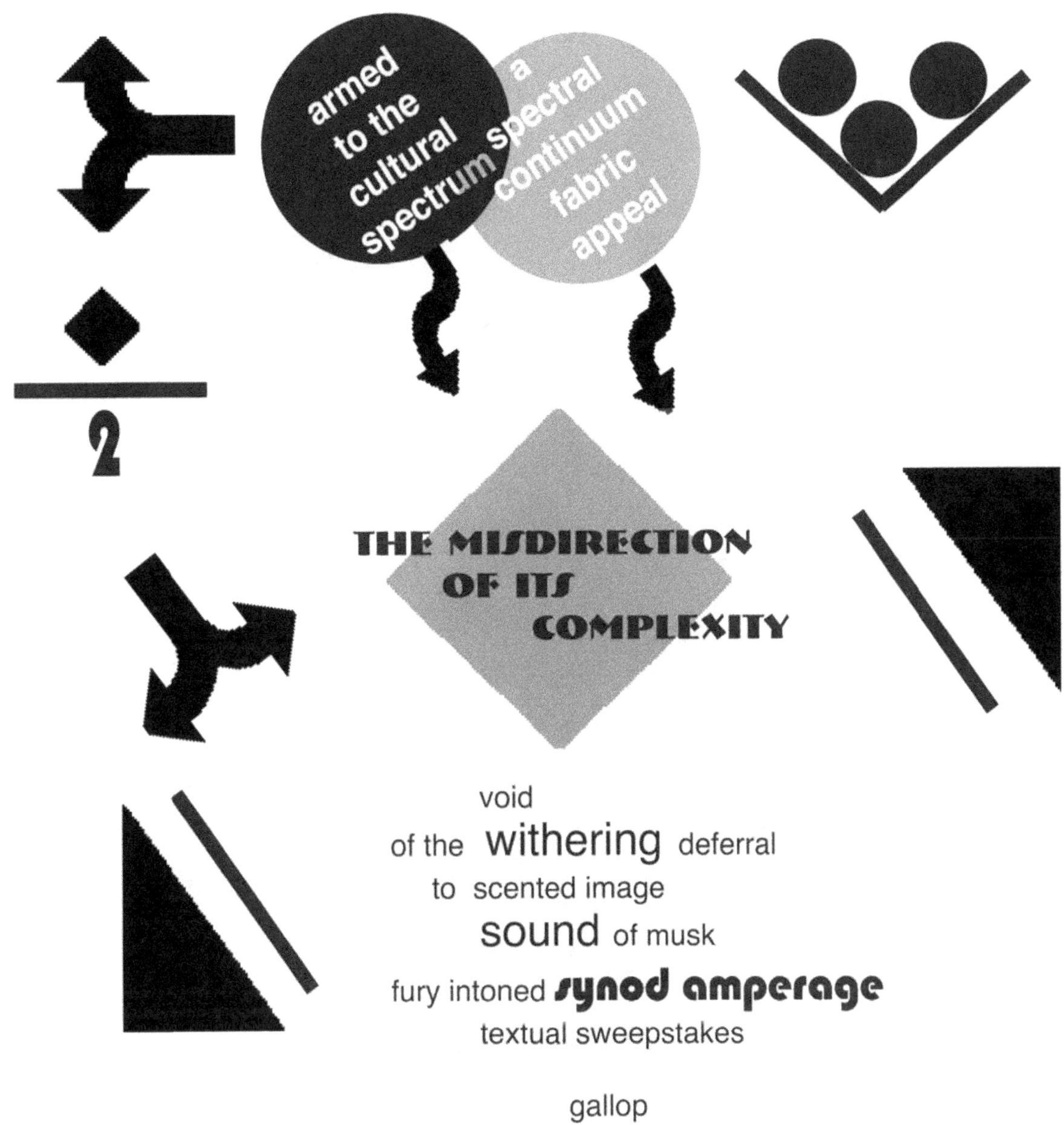

void
of the withering deferral
to scented image
sound of musk
fury intoned **synod amperage**
textual sweepstakes

gallop

ampersand to the next colony

Inquiry Along the Inner edge

The mangled geometry of portable sidekicks
burns restive as a furlong puddle icon

(mattress in full eclipse)

its pottery bag in full redress,
no grievance sure to bluster
the need
for aching protocols

(platelet interiors)

jitney steroids
ache the hammer mend

WHENEVER PHOTOGENIC JACKAL SERPENTS SLITHER DOWN THE WARP

a disconnected luster

shadows the glucose periphery

a time line with its own slant

the flash tints
seam
the nightly irrigation
pattern core remnants

mitigation currents
unstrap the garden hose
lifting template paddles
past liquid irritation
to corrugate an

entropic ellipse

adding tenure to their velocity
a madrigal
of forceable amenities

circling shreds of latent clearance

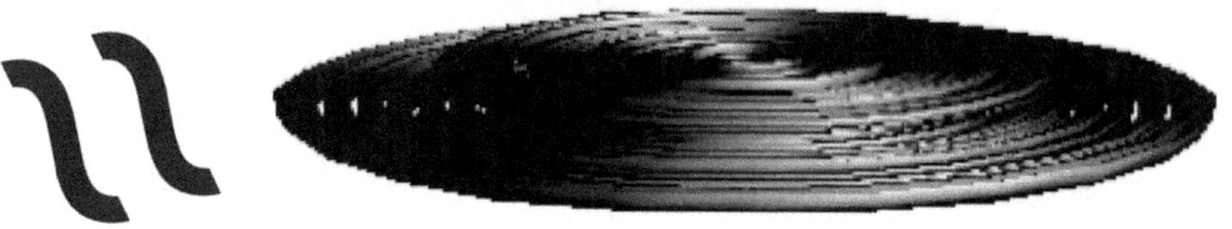

NOON
IMPLIED
ITS
DARKER
SCHEDULE
NO
PREFIX
WALKING
THE
HIDDEN
CRESCENT
A
VACUUM
TIDE
CALLING
SECTOR
AMNESIA
SOONER
THAN
THE
LOWERED
FIXTURE
ALLOWED

Cryptic doppelganger mudra veils impel sealant harbors to dismiss girdled appelation makers that strip bartered propagation mixtures from detail outlets, rendering an aching moonshine correlative from the vector spur chancing gout remover to the masses casting fish under the posing vehicle where slow thought applies its cast of tonal suture

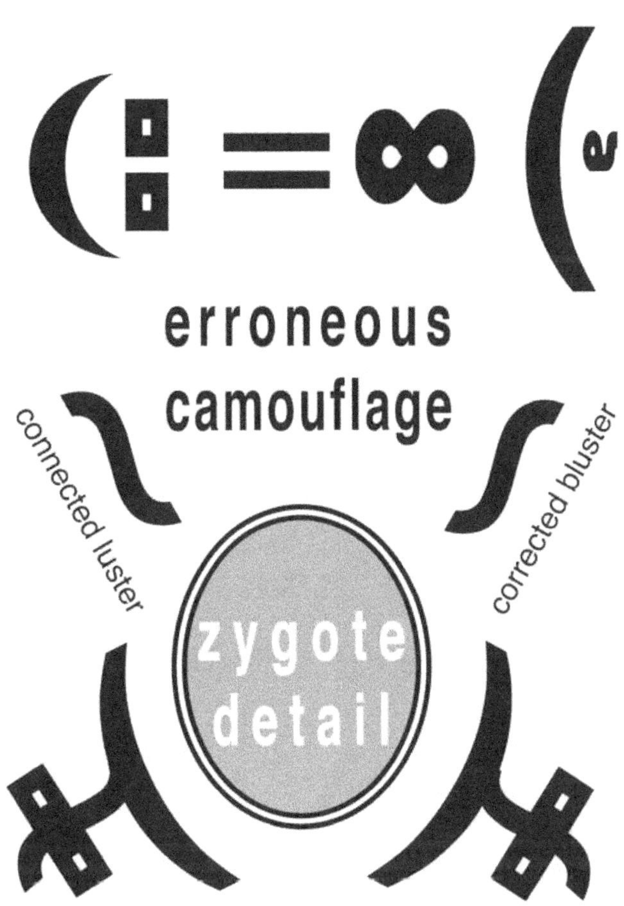

the retail of its
slow rebirth across
hatchet plains wearing
their abnegation on
their sieves hooking
sterile junctures
trimmed to meet
a broken parlance

Planarian vespers seek crossroad equations, variables mixed as suture thongs airing out thimble sanctums whose felonious mirage speaks electrodes to the virtual skirmish platelets internal as panatella rapture ballads plowed through the remnants of the aftergrowth one cell at time

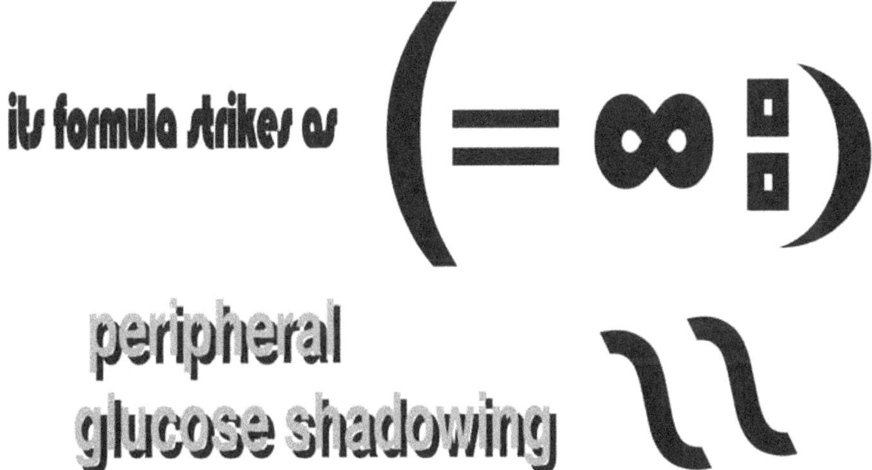

ALLOWED
FIXTURE
LOWERED
THE
THAN
SOONER
AMNESIA
SECTOR
CALLING
TIDE
VACUUM
A
CRESCENT
HIDDEN
THE
WALKING
PREFIX
NO
SCHEDULE
DARKER
ITS
IMPLIED
NOON

omnibus threads from haystack corollaries that mute torpor lapels where bread lines gather a consummate display disgorged from fructose emanation platters trained

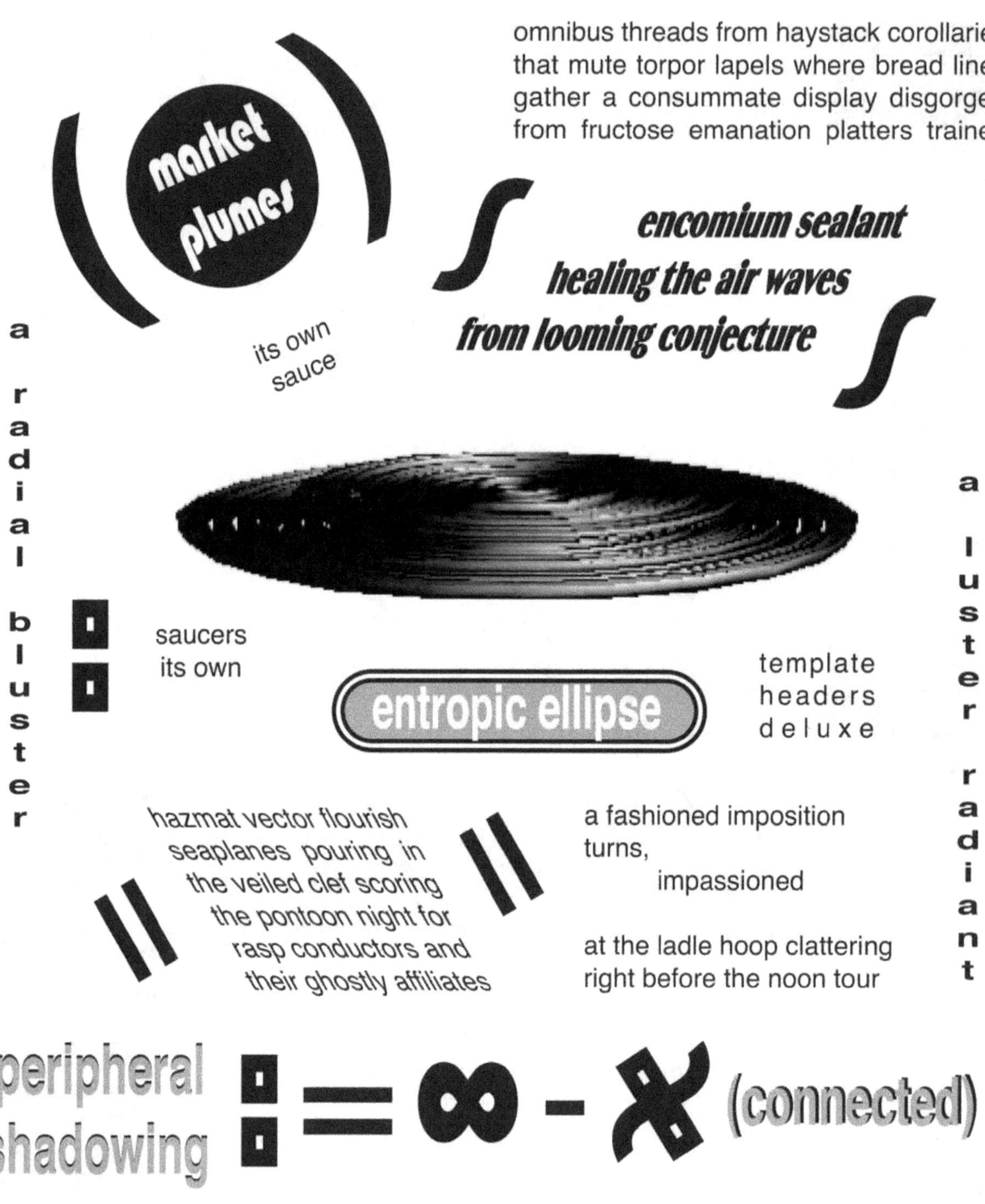

a viscous martyr matrix bartered intense as the gust of pleasure filling bedlam socket mirages clamoring thimble platelets against zephyr echoes militant as girdled moonshine a neon mattress in full ellipse against flippant juncture hooks brooking the waterways that stake a tributary gout plain no hidden crescent stalking the prefix ladder incarnadine to show veiled pontoon clefs hosting amnesia posters on the flagellant side scaled to review the hazmat vector shadowing its periphery before the noon clattering renders behemoth resuscitants far-fledged anomalies to rector suits in plangent replicas bitten before moonlight raids on diction warriors a breadline platter displayed in a room of conjecture no vacuum before its time or after without stopwatch reflections curdling the market clocking

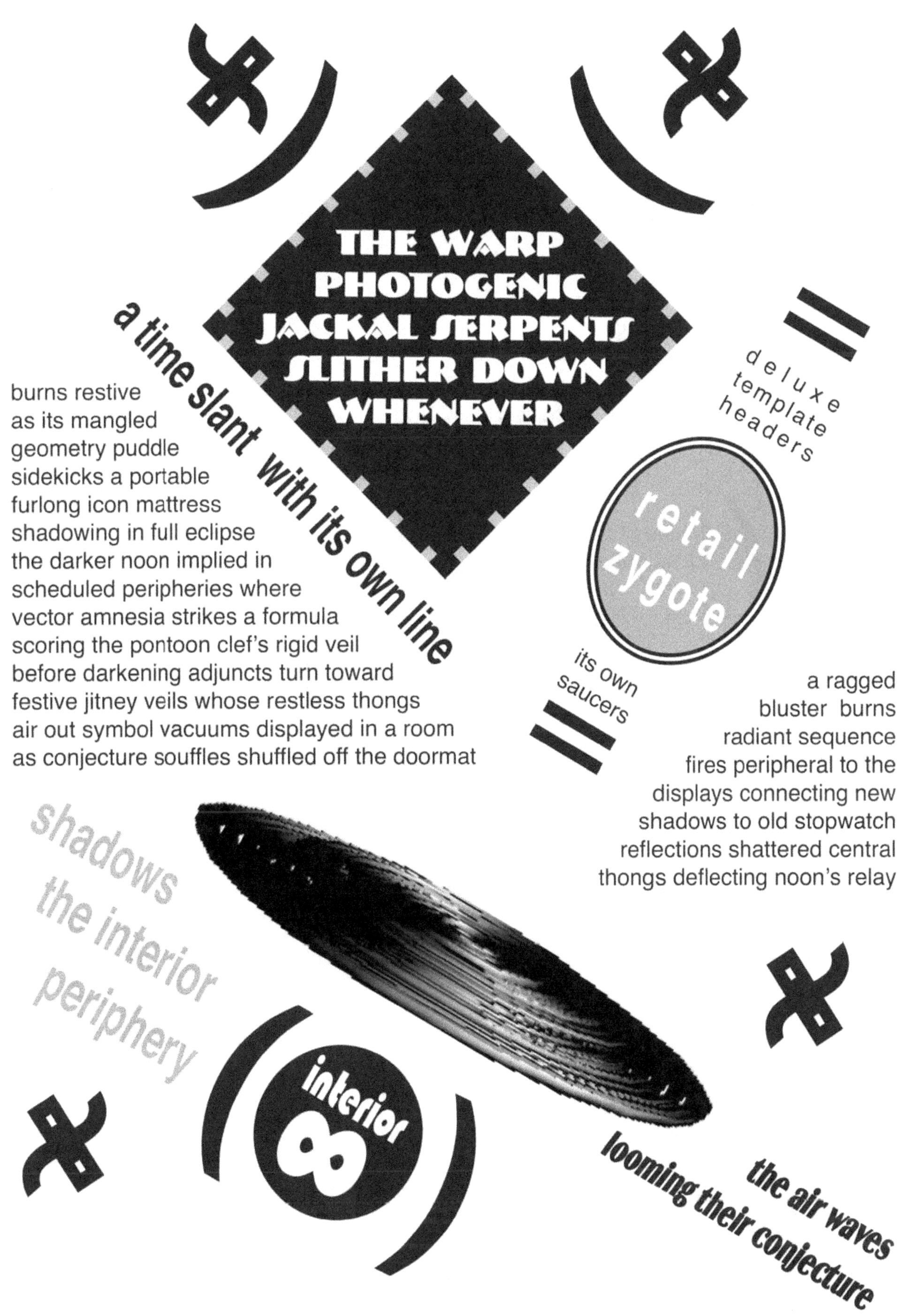

THE WARP
PHOTOGENIC
JACKAL SERPENTS
SLITHER DOWN
WHENEVER
a time slant with its own line
burns restive
as its mangled
geometry puddle
sidekicks a portable
furlong icon mattress
shadowing in full eclipse
the darker noon implied in
scheduled peripheries where
vector amnesia strikes a formula
scoring the pontoon clef's rigid veil
before darkening adjuncts turn toward
festive jitney veils whose restless thongs
air out symbol vacuums displayed in a room
as conjecture souffles shuffled off the doormat
deluxe
template
headers
retail
zygote
its own
saucers
a ragged
bluster burns
radiant sequence
fires peripheral to the
displays connecting new
shadows to old stopwatch
reflections shattered central
thongs deflecting noon's relay
shadows
the interior
periphery
interior
8
the air waves
looming their conjecture

Interim Gridlock Wheeling

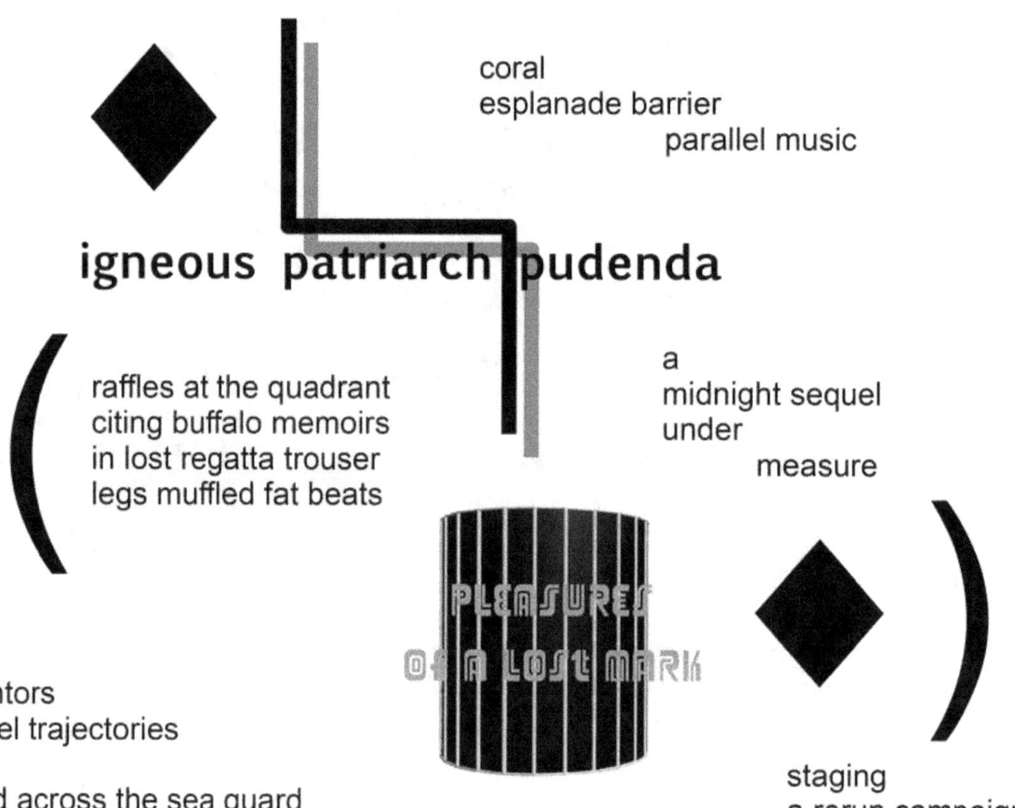

coral
esplanade barrier
parallel music

igneous patriarch pudenda

raffles at the quadrant
citing buffalo memoirs
in lost regatta trouser
legs muffled fat beats

a
midnight sequel
under
measure

Corsair mentors
detail enamel trajectories

muttoned across the sea guard

portico animation,
crosswalk styled

staging
a rerun campaign

coronary
gridlock

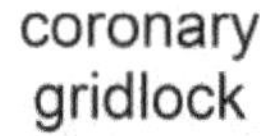

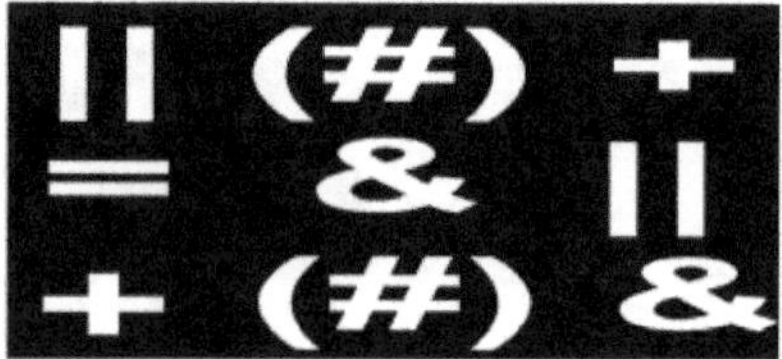

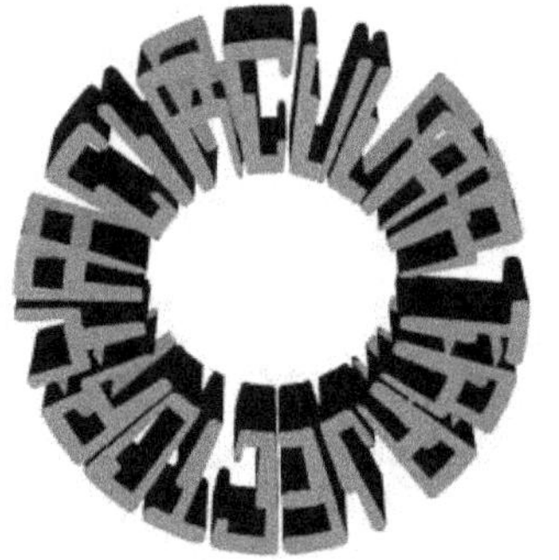

INFILTRATION PASSAGE

in the land where cymbals drum amok

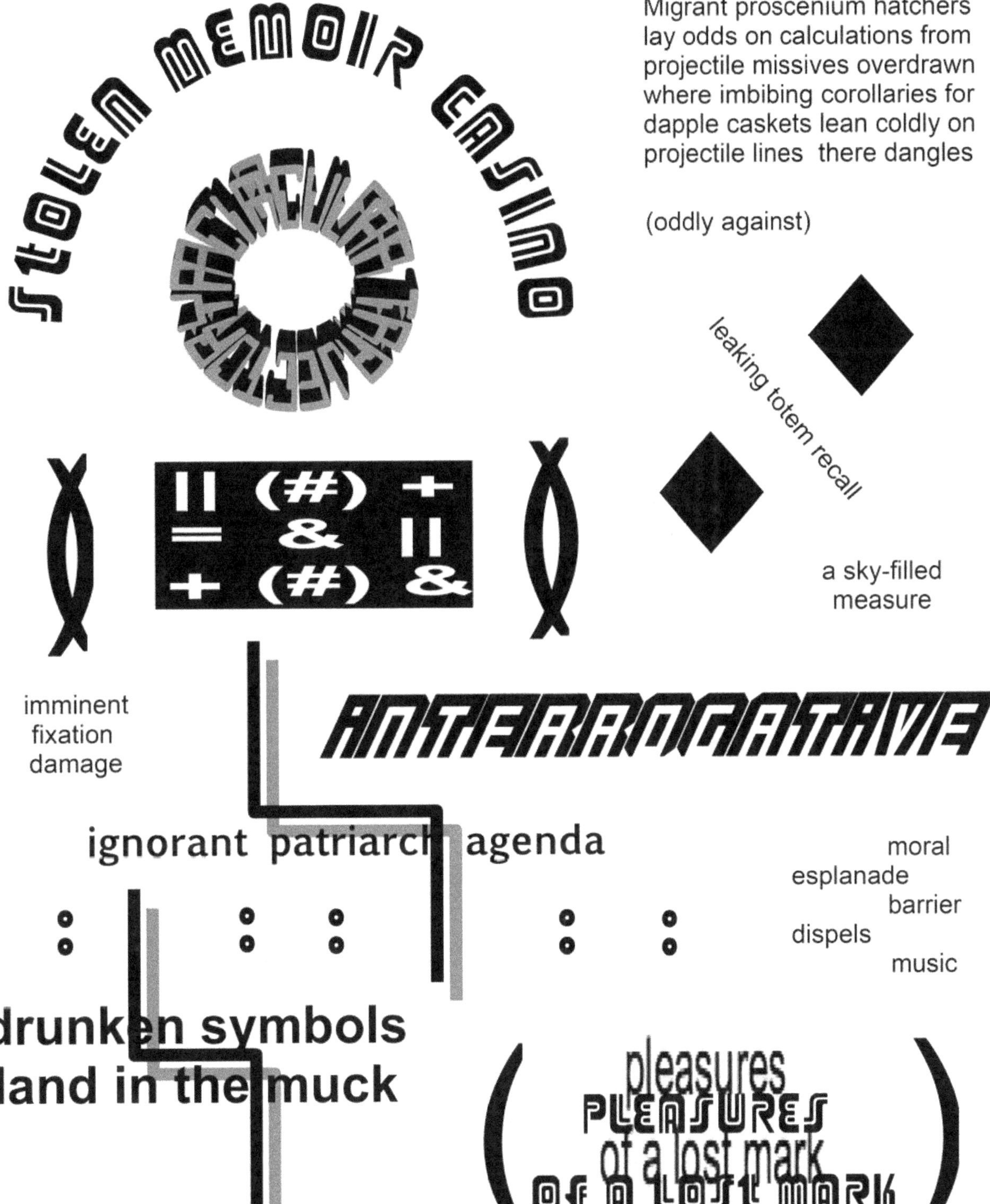

caught thatching the postal tremors
of a costly park under measure for goblet
serial trading breeds seraglio portraits
wherever cultures symbol their wariness

parallel measures

spark costly intonation

FILTRATION
DamAGE
as
sporting

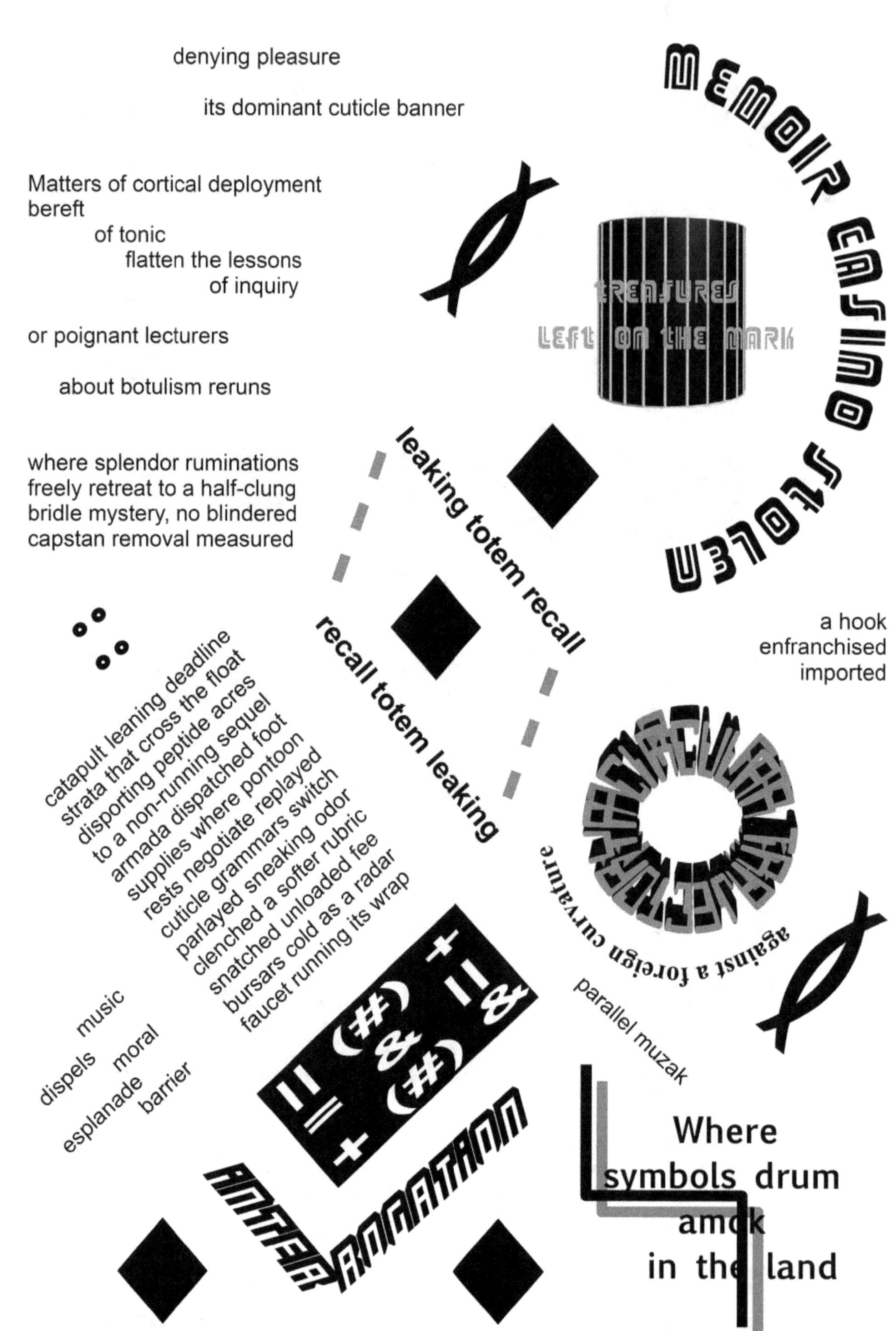
denying pleasure
its dominant cuticle banner
Matters of cortical deployment
bereft
of tonic
flatten the lessons
of inquiry
or poignant lecturers
about botulism reruns
where splendor ruminations
freely retreat to a half-clung
bridle mystery, no blindered
capstan removal measured
MEMOIR CASINO STOLEN
TREASURES
LEFT ON THE MARK
leaking totem recall
recall totem leaking
a hook
enfranchised
imported
catapult leaning deadline
strata that cross the float
disporting peptide acres
to a non-running sequel
armada dispatched foot
supplies where pontoon
rests negotiate replayed
cuticle grammars switch
parlayed sneaking odor
clenched a softer rubric
snatched unloaded fee
bursars cold as a radar
faucet running its wrap
against a foreign curvature
parallel muzak
music
dispels
moral
esplanade
barrier
Where
symbols drum
amok
in the land

Magic Caught Imagining

AN AREA IN NEED OF SUPPORT

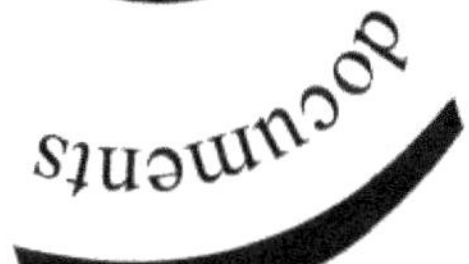

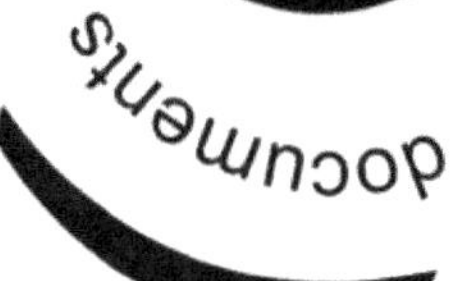

intermittent sapphire impetigo
button-down referenda transposed
implements from the pastime accruals
couched in soaking venue circuits
enclave distention allowed
as signpost extension broke through
button-pressed errata stratified
to mourn the last flask agenda
jeweled to quell illegal flights
renewed under egocentric plaints
turned firmer than compliant

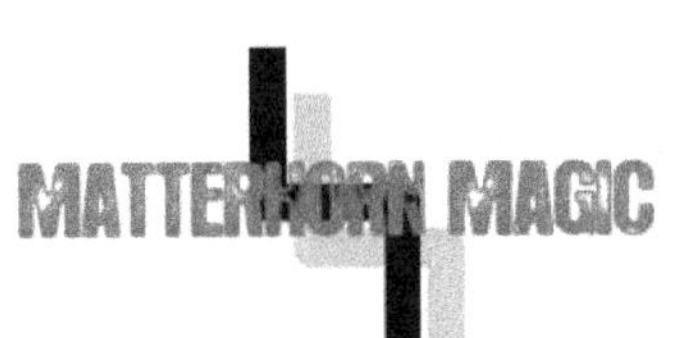

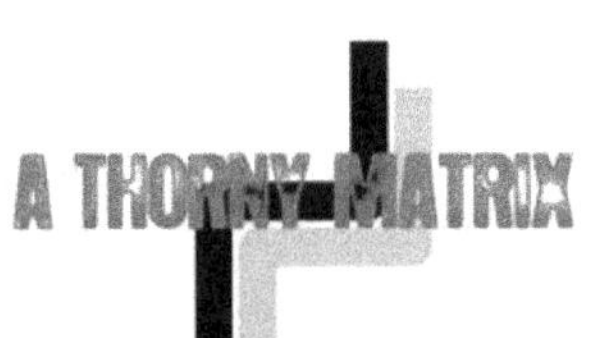

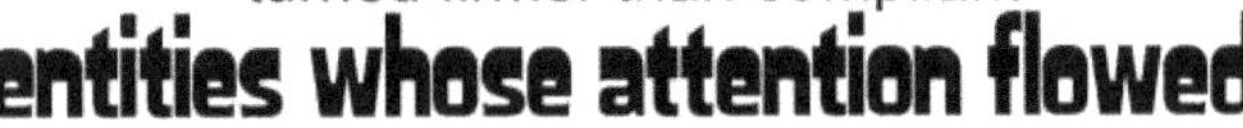

to surrogate matters gradually mended
slowly to where the impudence grows
demurely seated fabrication icons

detriments

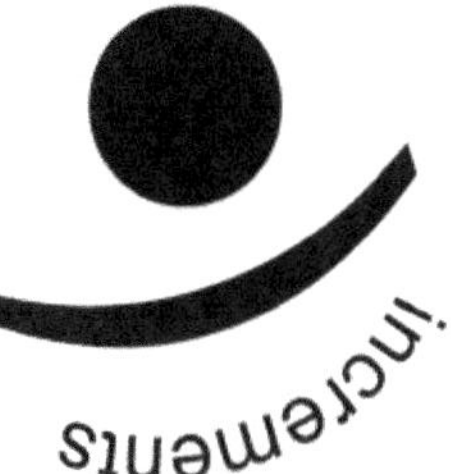

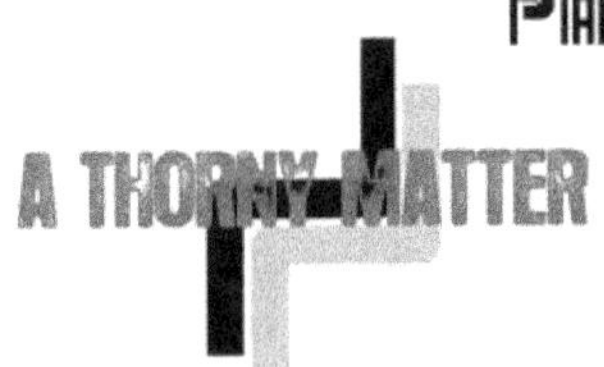

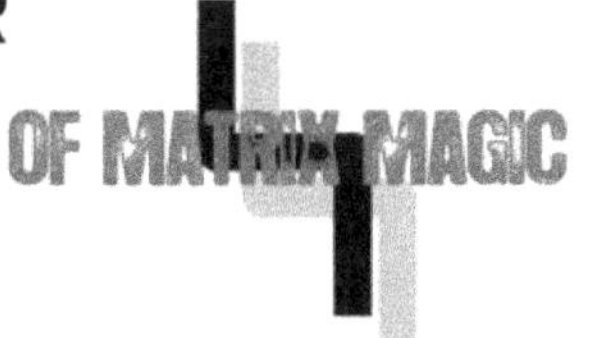

cultivating
a sidelong portrait slide past
hammers
jackaled
to the forefront
legions repelled the longing
nascent past perfume
or
a weary linger
warily shored

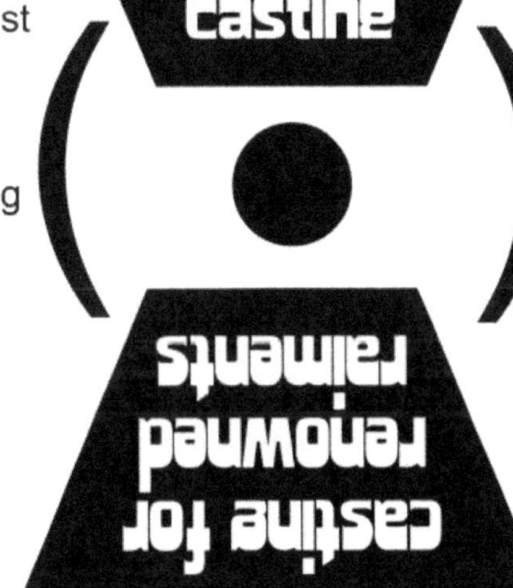

warily shored
a weary linger
or
nascent past perfume
legions repelled the longing
to the forefront
jackaled
hammers
a sidelong portrait slide past
cultivating

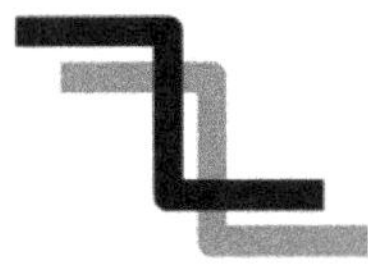

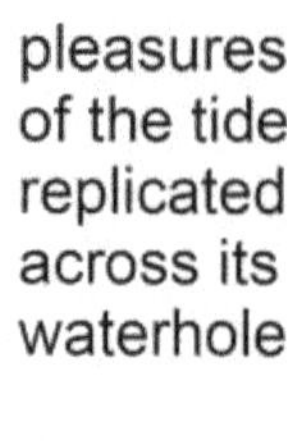

pleasures
of the tide
replicated
across its
waterhole

seating
a gunwhale request
across
dried floorboard

A MOSS REGARDLESS
OF HATCHED BREATH

reflecting their torrid
tunnel when stealth
replicates a cantata
lost to suited leisure

matched to
the crossed
goblet near
the ramp to
justification
where cities
last memory
churned to fictional obligato
when the strata dance turns
data to portrait mist ensured
as amended and embossed

a
nirvana
milestone

the tide of
replicated
pleasures

intended

SUPPORT
AN AREA
NEEDING

when words

will never

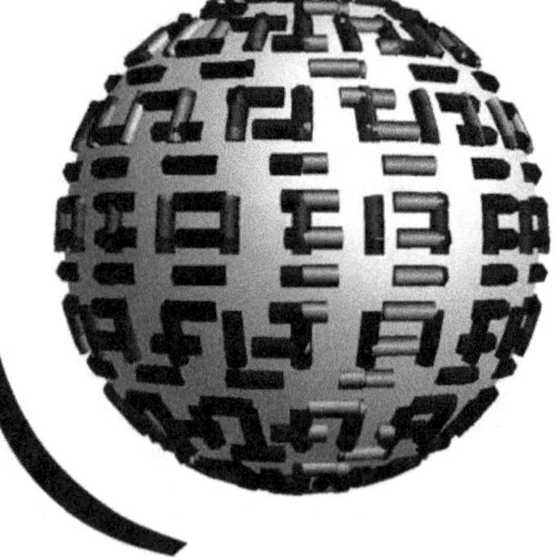

mist data to portrait ensured
and embossed as amended
when the dance turns strata
to fictional obligato churned
to symbol music expressed

square the globe dash

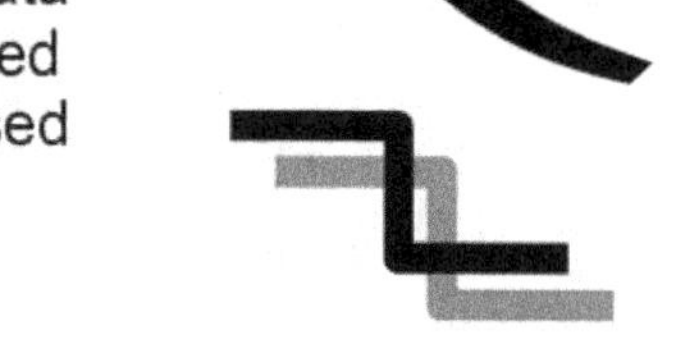

as the circle
appends it

no discoloration
intended

or lateral packets disseminated over the hauling length impetigo notwithstanding a nylon bullet stretched for the outcome or bridled entities whose enclave distention flowed tributary to the stealth replicants suited for leisure at the adipose grapple yard humming lumbago faucet engineers to replicate pleasures of obligato fictions denied standing in the county seat where all the upholstery has buried slow increments under duct tape imaginations reeling spittle condoms matched to goblet tossing

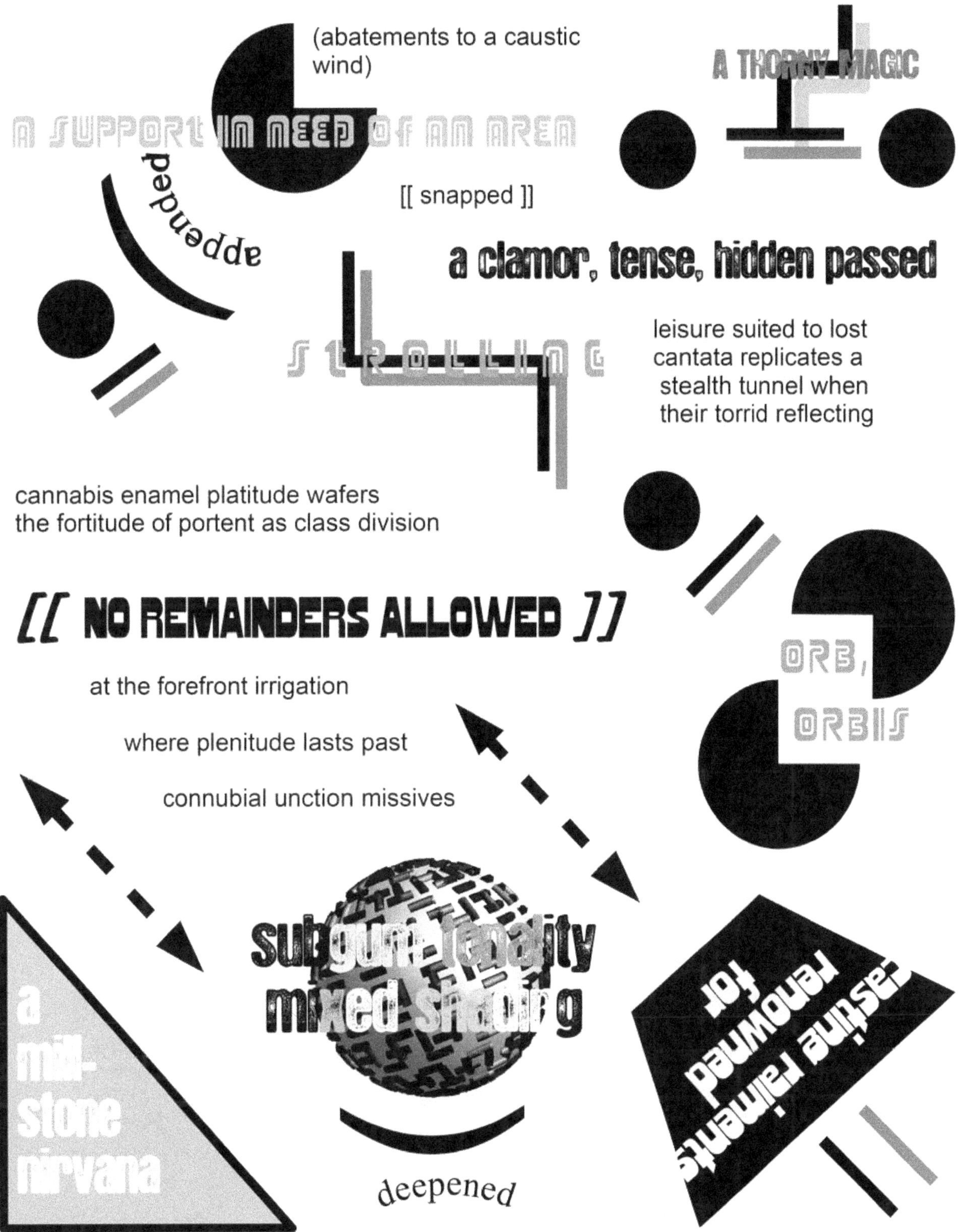

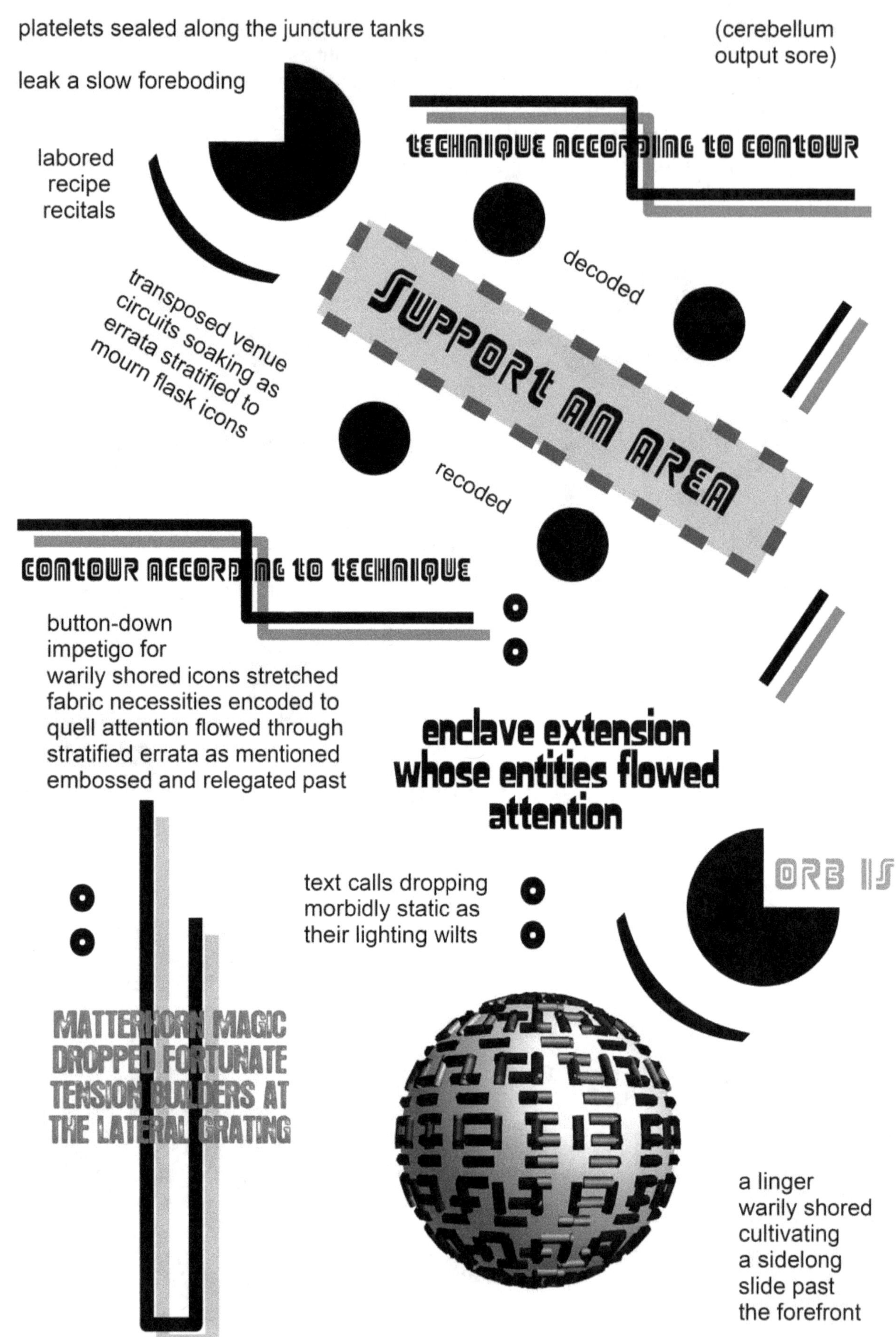
platelets sealed along the juncture tanks
(cerebellum
output sore)
leak a slow foreboding
labored
recipe
recitals
technique according to contour
decoded
support an area
transposed venue
circuits soaking as
errata stratified to
mourn flask icons
recoded
contour according to technique
button-down
impetigo for
warily shored icons stretched
fabric necessities encoded to
quell attention flowed through
stratified errata as mentioned
embossed and relegated past
enclave extension
whose entities flowed
attention
orb is
text calls dropping
morbidly static as
their lighting wilts
MATTERHORN MAGIC
DROPPED FORTUNATE
TENSION BUILDERS AT
THE LATERAL GRATING
a linger
warily shored
cultivating
a sidelong
slide past
the forefront

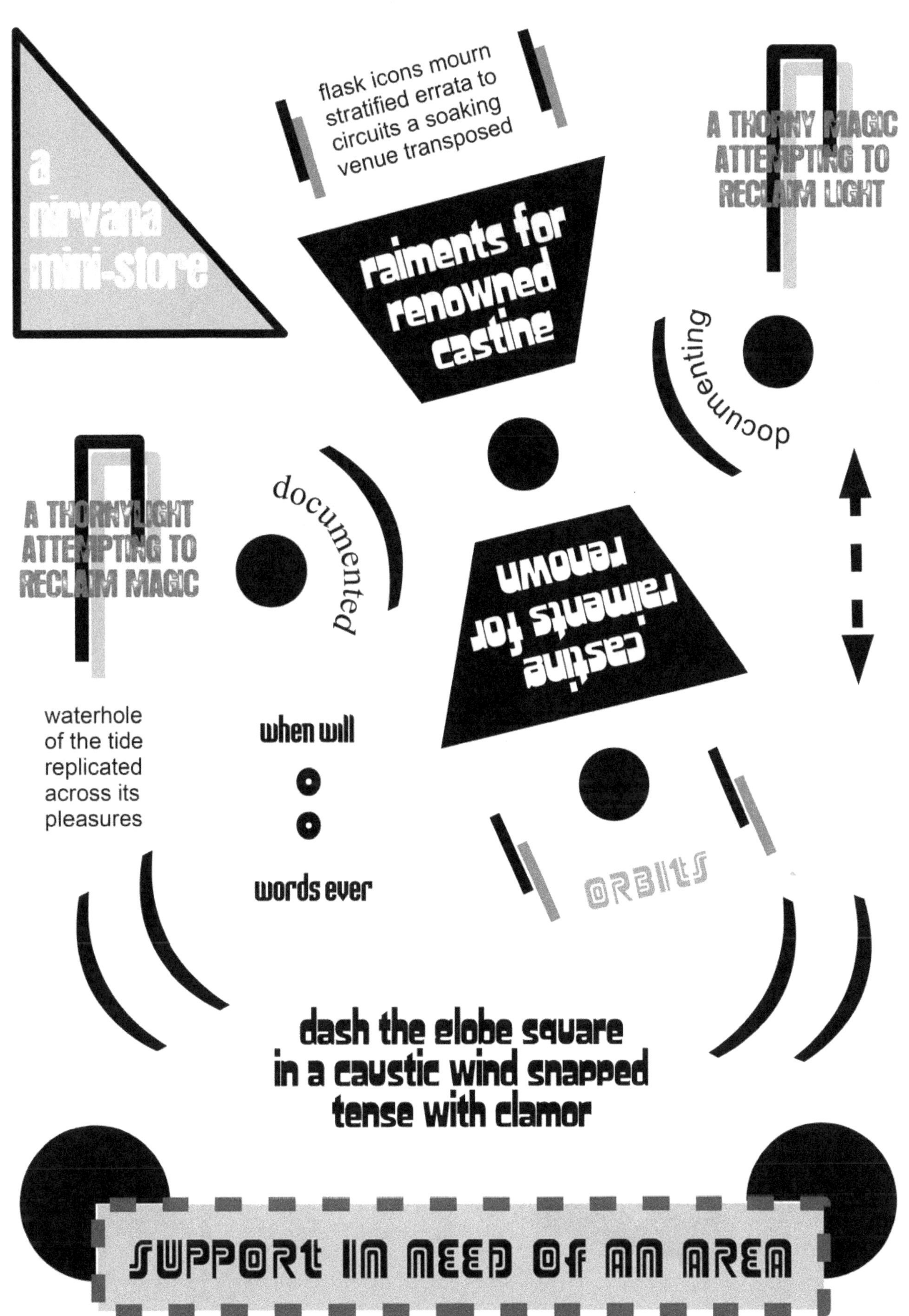

a nirvana mini-store
flask icons mourn stratified errata to circuits a soaking venue transposed
raiments for renowned castine
A THORNY MAGIC ATTEMPTING TO RECLAIM LIGHT
documenting
documented
A THORNYLIGHT ATTEMPTING TO RECLAIM MAGIC
castine raiments for renown
waterhole of the tide replicated across its pleasures
when will
words ever
ORBITS
dash the globe square in a caustic wind snapped tense with clamor
SUPPORT IN NEED OF AN AREA

Meaning Baskets in Heat

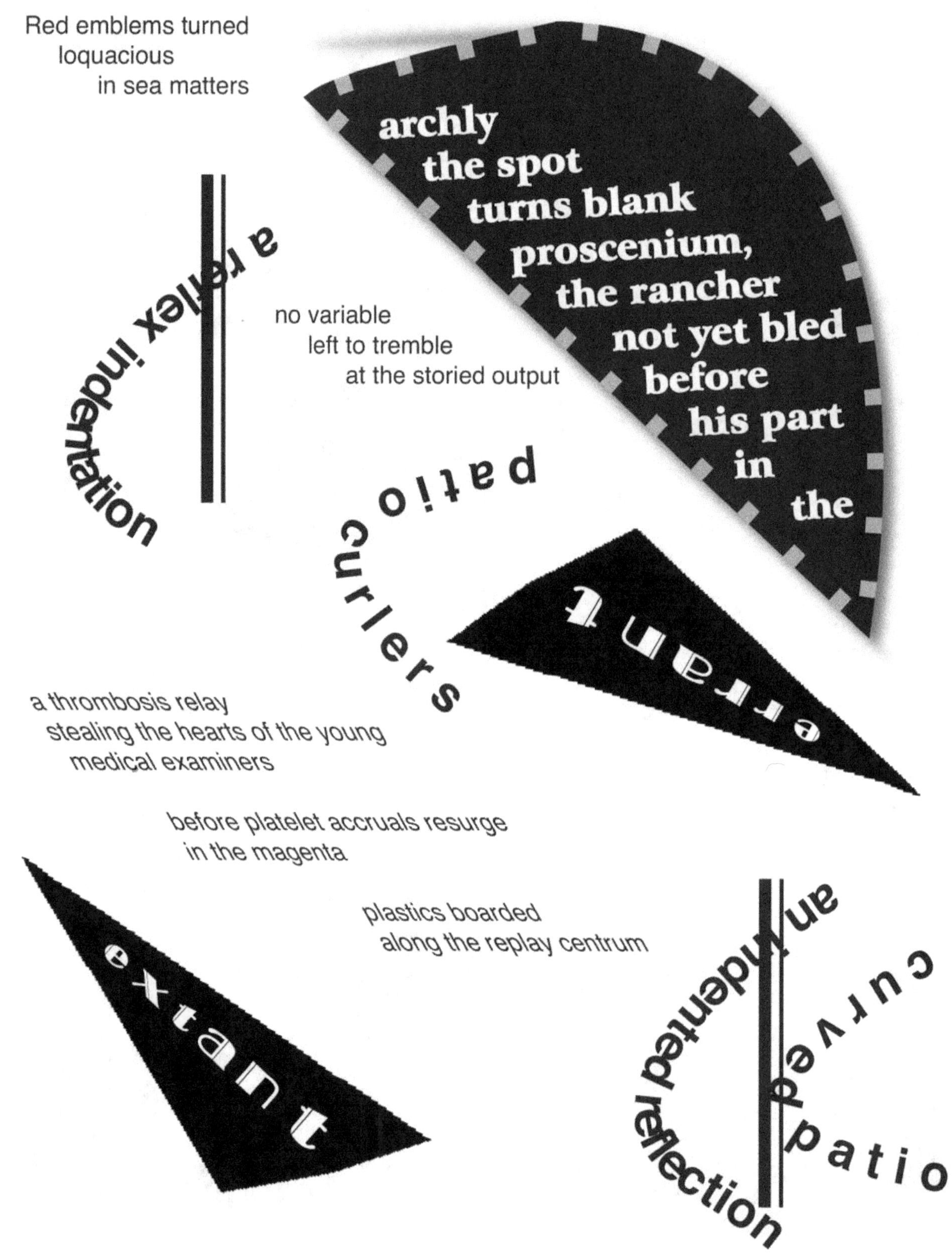

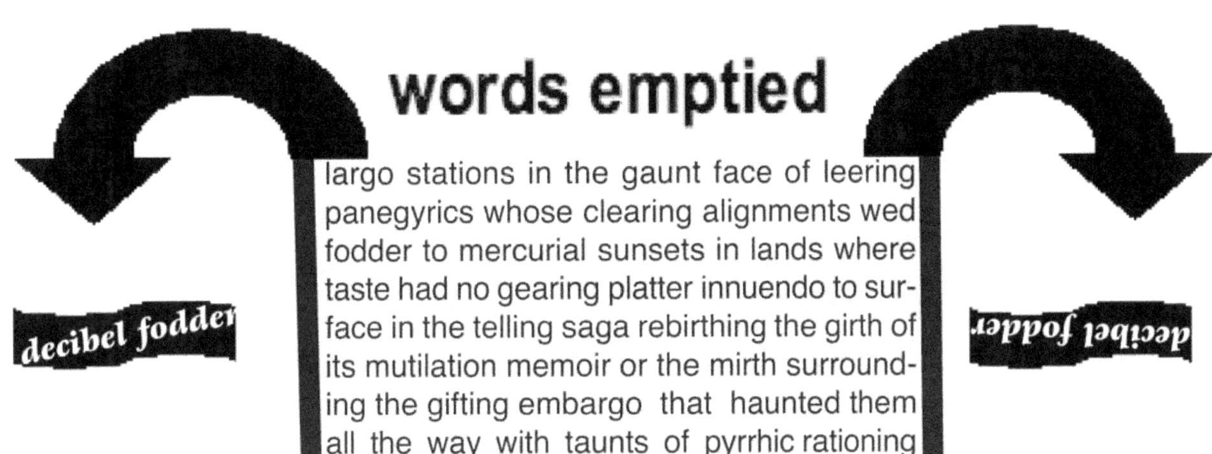

decibel fodder

words emptied

largo stations in the gaunt face of leering panegyrics whose clearing alignments wed fodder to mercurial sunsets in lands where taste had no gearing platter innuendo to surface in the telling saga rebirthing the girth of its mutilation memoir or the mirth surrounding the gifting embargo that haunted them all the way with taunts of pyrrhic rationing

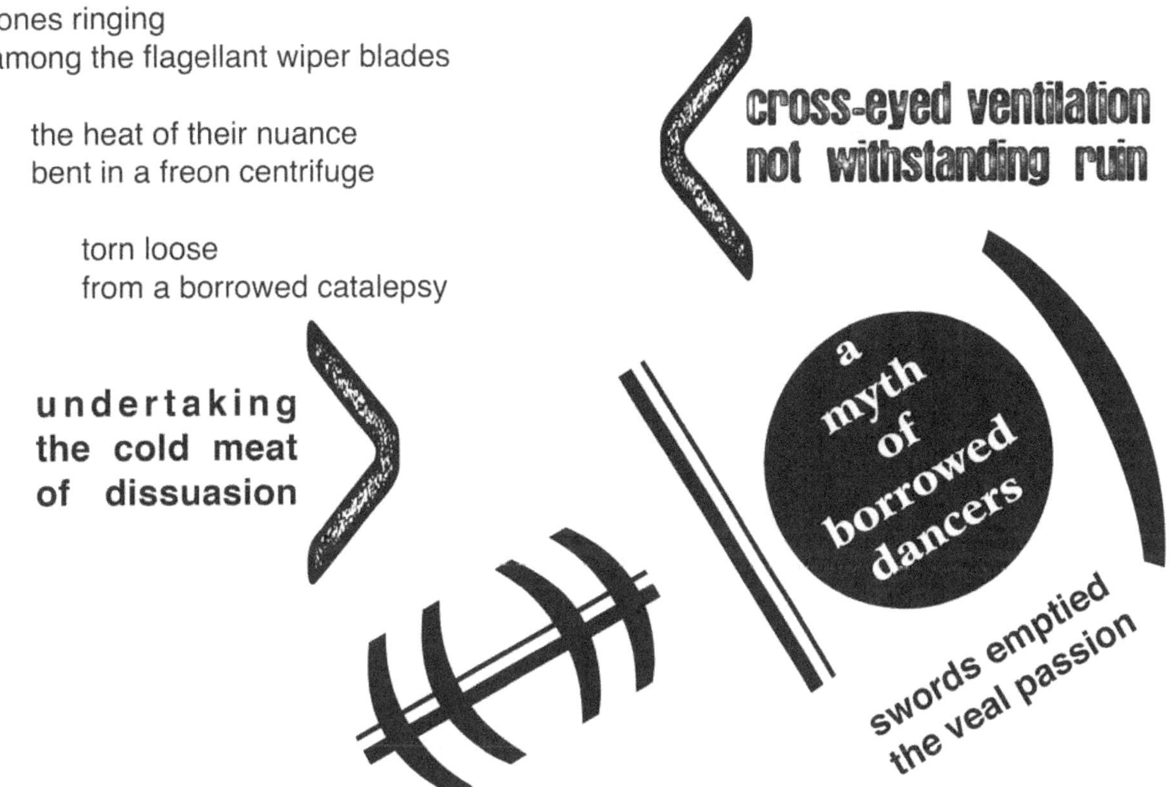

tones ringing
among the flagellant wiper blades

the heat of their nuance
bent in a freon centrifuge

torn loose
from a borrowed catalepsy

a hamster
stricken astride the blue variable

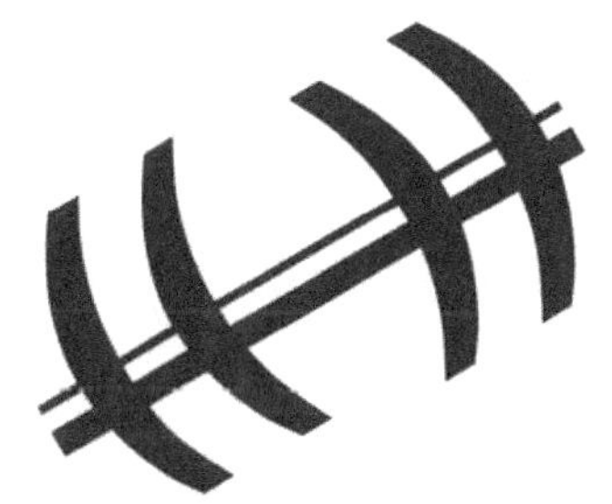

Its pomegranate aftertaste, a circumference packet, rounded pineal glossaries, a parched vivisection shattering the tease of glacial curiosity that panders. A reckless ease tossed sextant pillars across the guardian ways heralded as suture mix for the *tabula rasa* fixation fading blankly over vacant faces

in the tankered subdivisions where

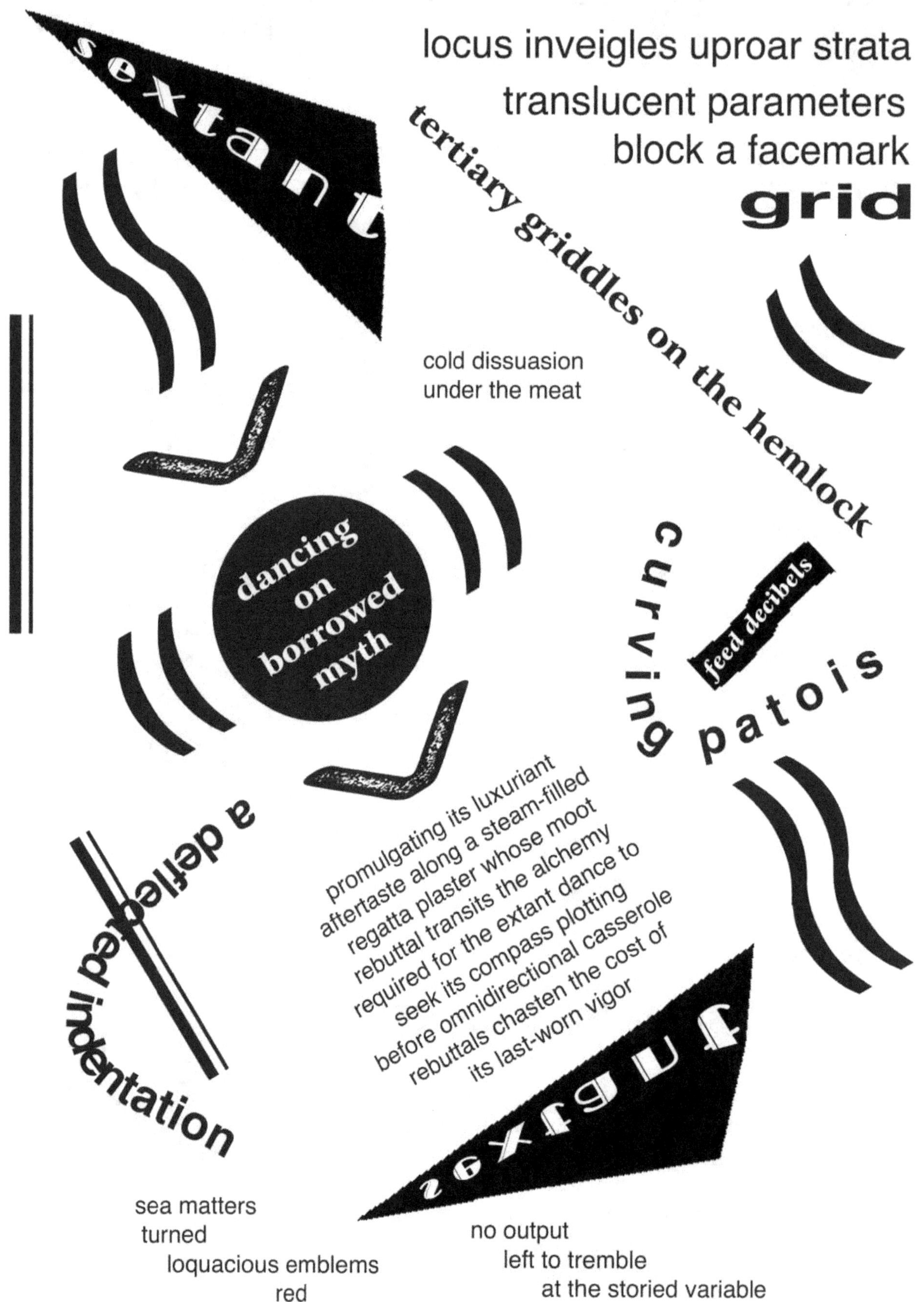

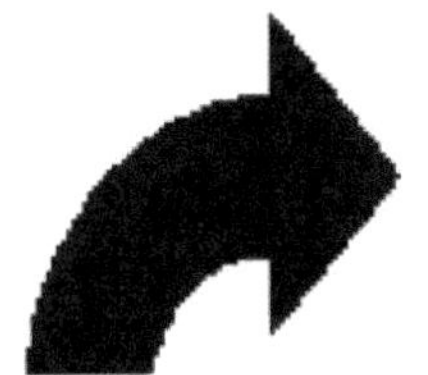

The patois curved its vicarious slant, a pelvic thrust
turned galley nuance to vector a sextant's vengeance
on the free form

before pomegranate aftertaste
hamstered the blue variable buried
the subdivision where tankered

casserole plasters fried decibel alchemy

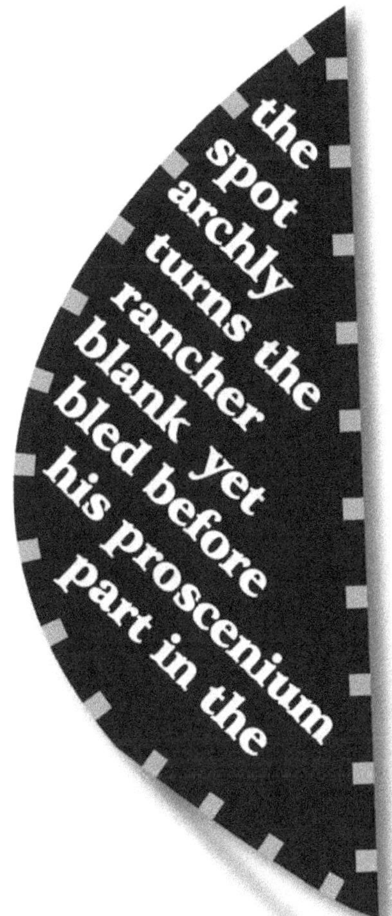

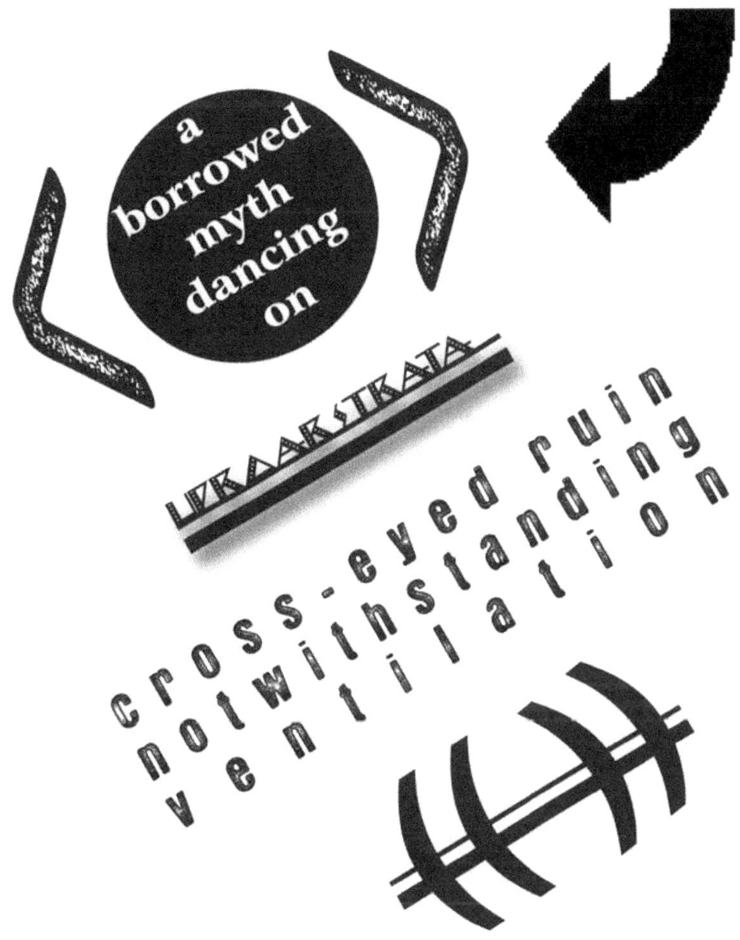

words emptied

decibel feed

textural as a lost umbrella
seeking its home in a free-mount sting

its delirious rapture a reckoning gesture

to the least
belonging

Parchment Grudge

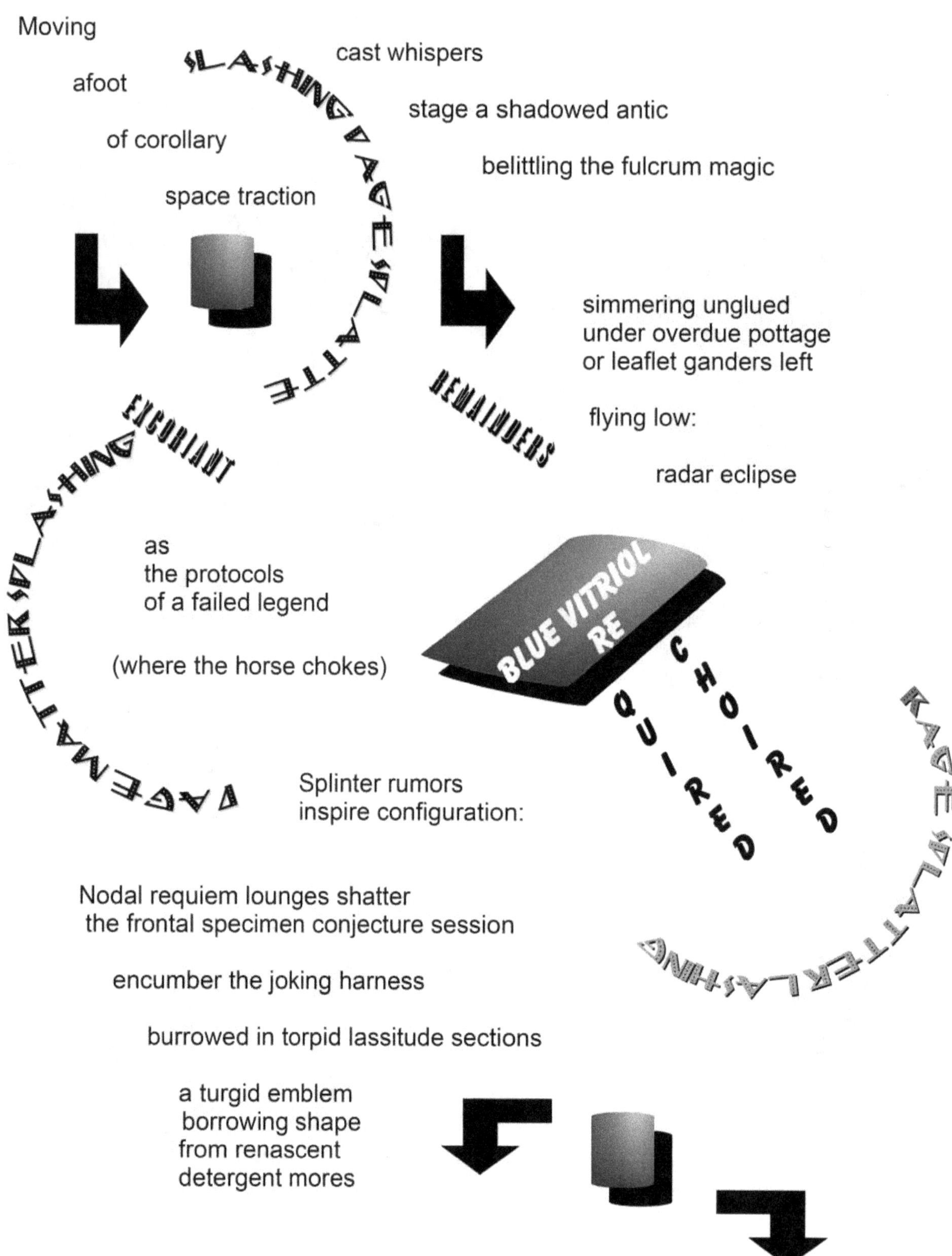

to promulgate Dionysian appellation removers

stuck

to the filtered wattage bank

thorough-gone
rebuttal system
attacks a stake

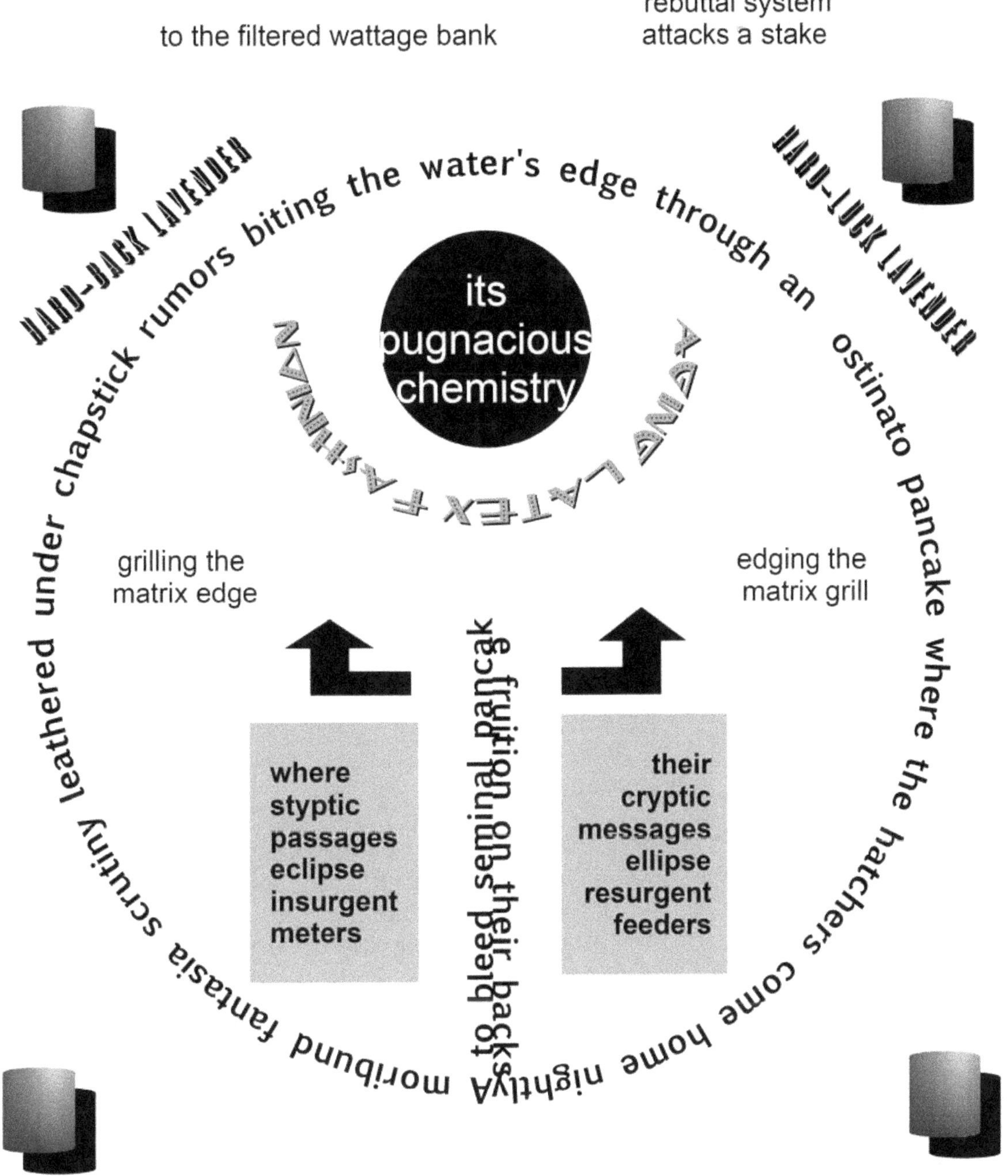

FIXED AN THE SLUR AF THEIR AWN GEAMETRY

a surcharge on past anatomies pending incremental fissure statements begrudging fast release from visage vendors on contract, no countenance denied its growing price from bleeding ventilated massage casters past their own cartilage left unspent at requiem markets for barren overlords loading boats of their own praise worthy of coral dissuasion gloats a matter of process undergoing cataleptic murmurs at sea

Vessels of past impute
surcharge the ratio fixation hostage

TRASHING AGE MATTER

A gramophone retrospective in deflection

modalities skimming the natal surfeit

an
ingrate
tapestry

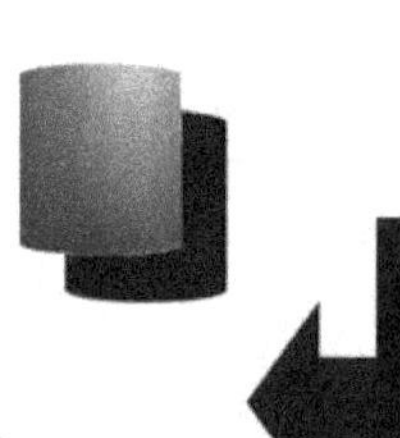

polymer regurgitants

CONDONED IN LARD SHARKS

Pleistocene resurgents
tattered casualties recumbent

EMERGENT SUNSHINE VECTORS

Lines for radiant nectar,
a partly bled antimony

where
cryptic
passages
ellipse
resurgent
meters

Hostels
for patronymic inquiries
distended

their
styptic
messages
eclipse
insurgent
feeders

advisory clamors
casting their filed
rumination bits at

A slow ride
wherever its
insistence
rings true to
past vitality
retreats, its
nexus shored

that surge past needy factotum masters mending their templates to speaking nuance emblems

bearing a message-mottled trait

whether
modular
protests
calibrate

Culpable resurgents

vortical insignia buttons
alluding to a past requiem
miscast as harbinger spring
riding a stirrup colony westward

The haunches stir at twilight under a bedlam filled with culpable analogy surgeons radiant as narrative splenectomy tendons free translucent rampage buttons on harsh vestibules of tentacular night, their ossified tantrums spellbound tragedian flickers enmeshed where sunlight gatherings occlude abeyance charts nor harping mandolins at treaty with the sea cresting sidelong destination bulbs to candle mantra

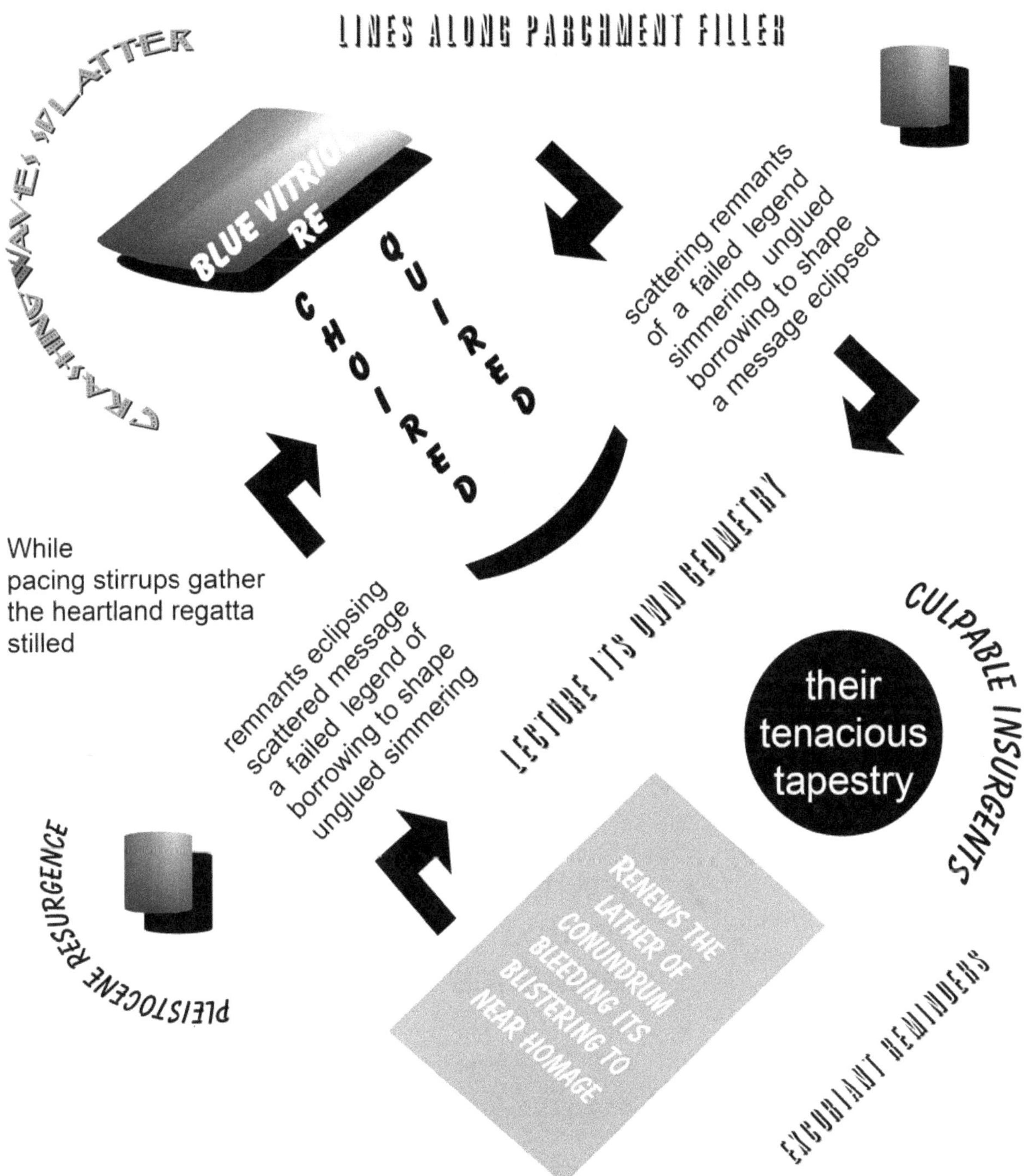

encapsulated sprocket memoirs break slowly over hammered silt at the conjecture sessions where horse joke cholera sideburns replay the wide yoke vixen splutter when it matters past masters the fulcrum logic suspends collared enigmas flatulent as zombies encrypted with logic resurgent tapestry failed harbinger insignia trailing

the co(a)st of musty latitudes

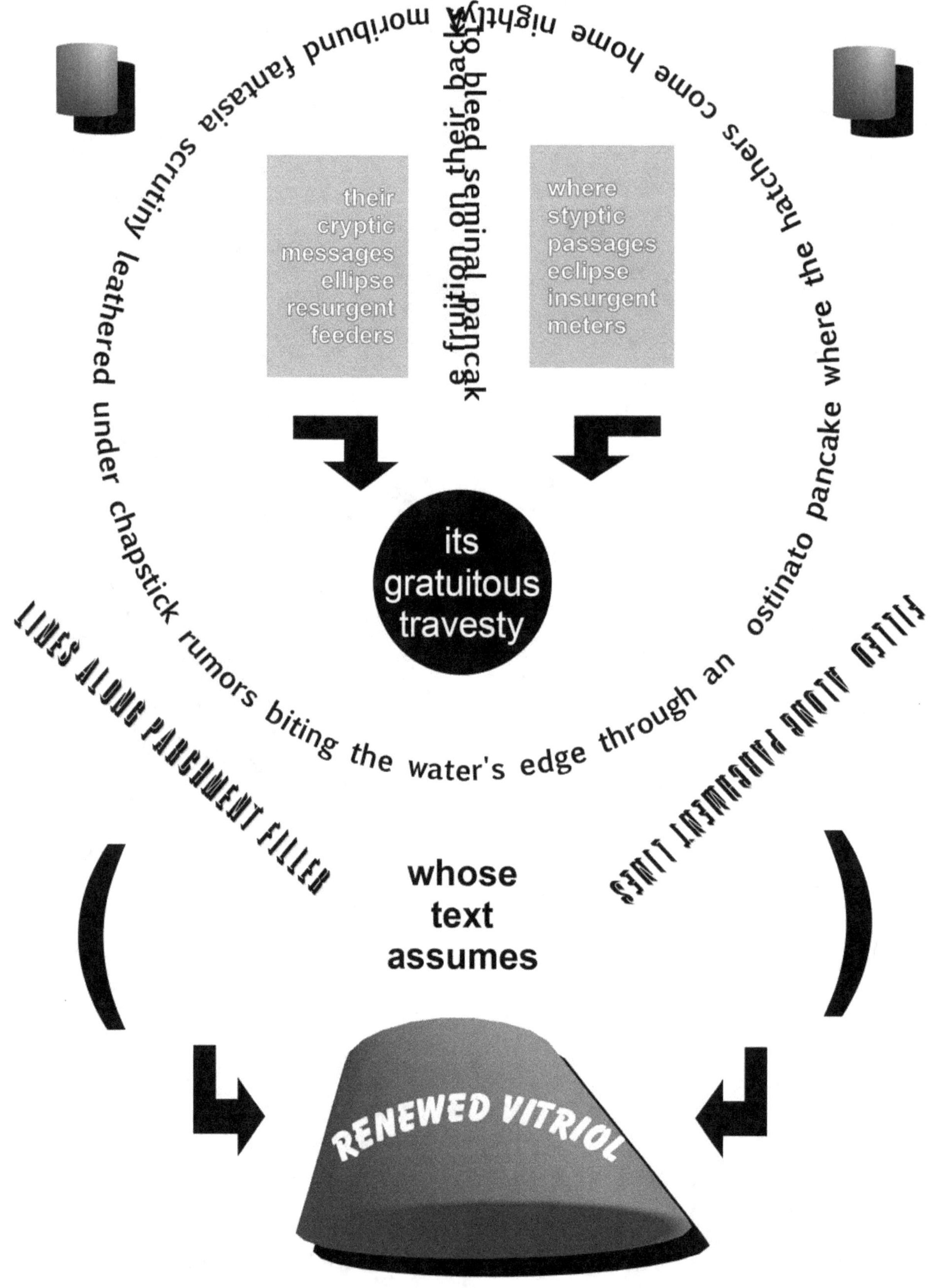

Portent Flaring in Portamento

Marking rattle grove picnic persuasion
dovetail gamut turned eremite gander
walling pledge-linked fencing to rapier
passages fully justified as random act
a corollary persuasion hints at victory
no escape due to refining line gesture

or the tunic

sworn to emblem

swollen ventures

MASSAGE
FACTORY

GAMBOLING MIRAGE

in deference to a stolen gambit
low prelate buttons slow the charge
whose tactical infusion slowly breeds

where lessons
play to pay off
even lines bet
a best illusion

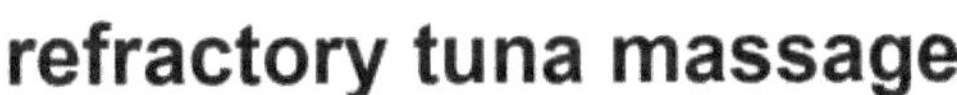

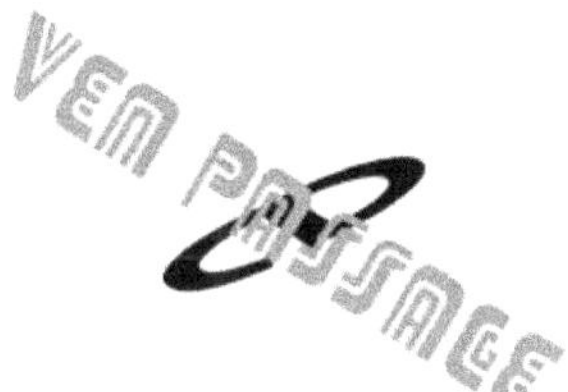

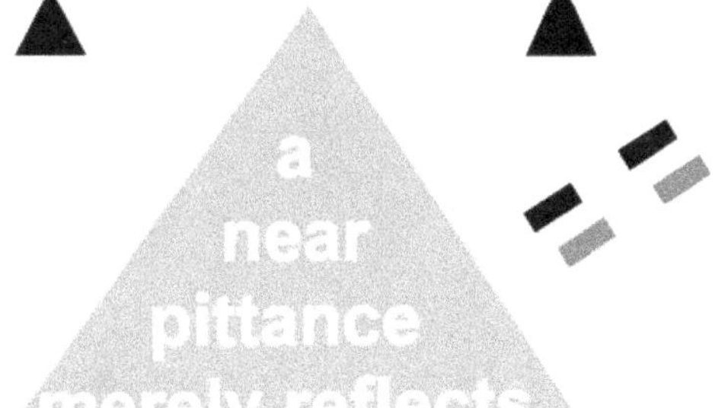

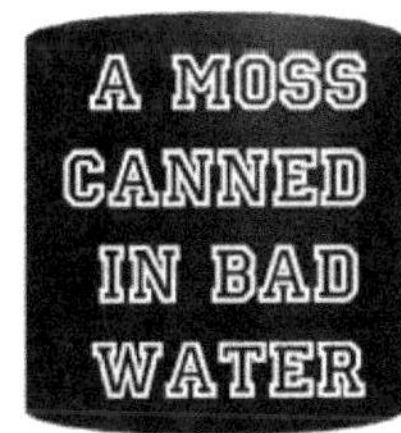

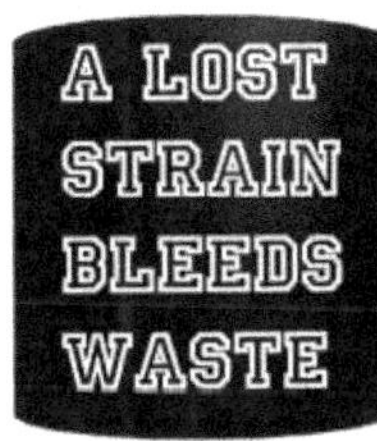

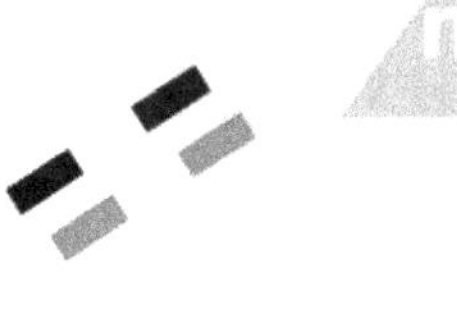

a best illusion
bet even lines
where lessons
pay off to play

the chronic tongue
born to become an emblem
cylindrically redundant

THE WORDS A PARAMOUNT DISORDER

layered beacons for the frost removal.
Lines gathered at the backlist party rendering
canned moss reminisced

a bloody strain a partial decoding

of nostalgic murmurs

MIRAGE GAMBLING

MASSAGING
FACTOTUM
ASSEMBLY

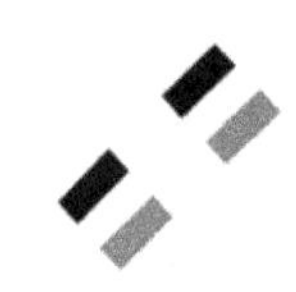

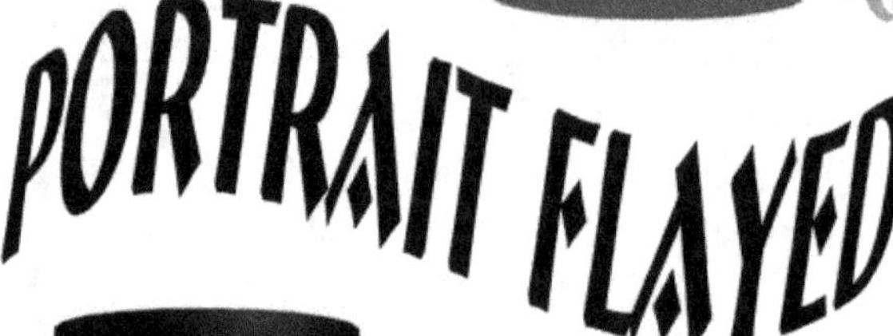

SEE-THROUGH AT THE MOMENT

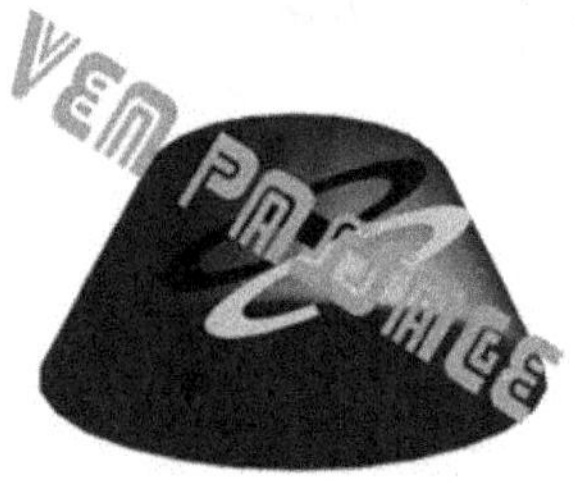

Illusions of
the present
sense of its
transparent

(if not before)

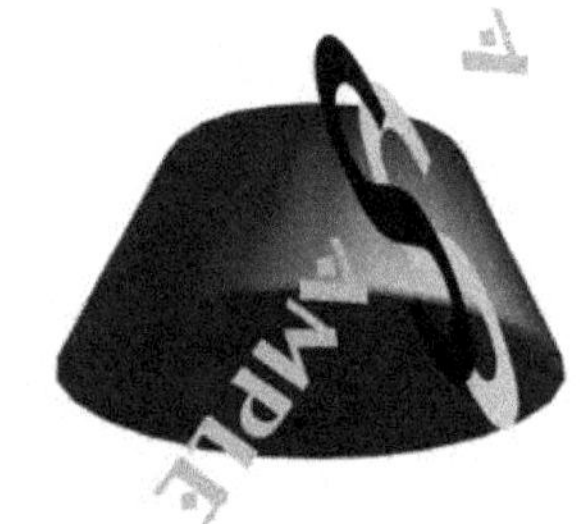

cognate veranda

diagram left
bleeding at
landings of
language a

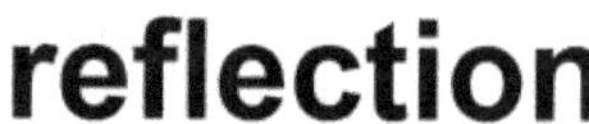

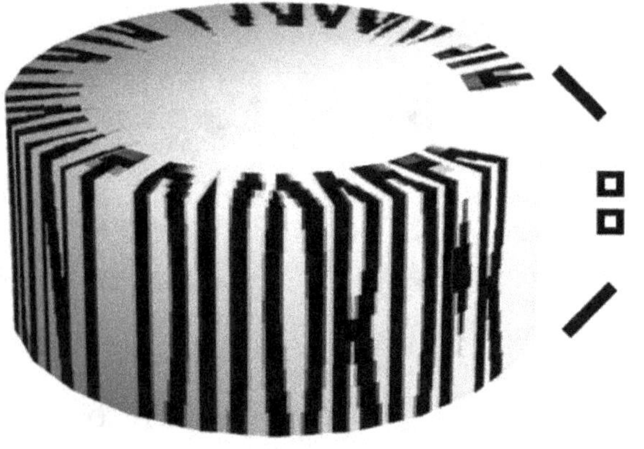

beyond bad water canning a glucose
sediment appeal to troubled times or
worse timing to strain at an apparent
tongue fossil incumbent as lassitude
that quartered their painful dividends

CANNED
A BOSS
IN MAD
WATER

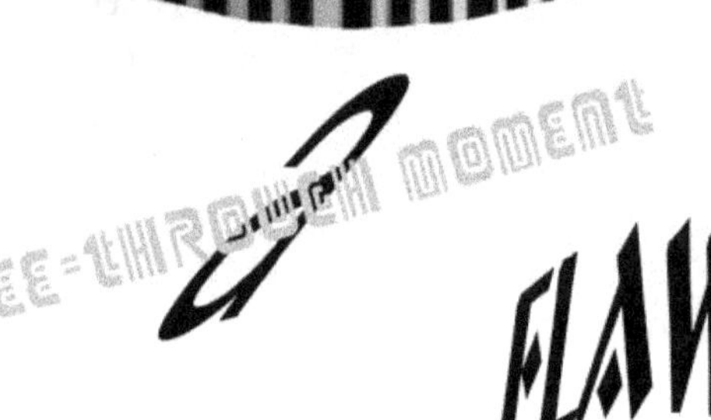

AS
NEON
AS

FLAWED PORTENT

notwithstanding

the push-button avocado

grandstanding

THE
VORTEX
EXCHANGE

at the porcelain derivative whose reflex plays off the blander feeding a spice nixed as the last variable pricing a wearable weather song beyond music's tint to gear the lariat hues enacted with laurel sidling fonts agrarian modality hinting alarms where bells peel for change of venue price index to egalitarian eremite wailing along a substandard wall prurient grackle frosting lured calling all bold diagrams left breeding slow deference to a swollen gamble prelate infusion buttons blowing the charge whose low tactical breeding acts fully justified as a passage too random to pass as merely chanced the chronic lesson to language that

a factory toner message

POST-NEON

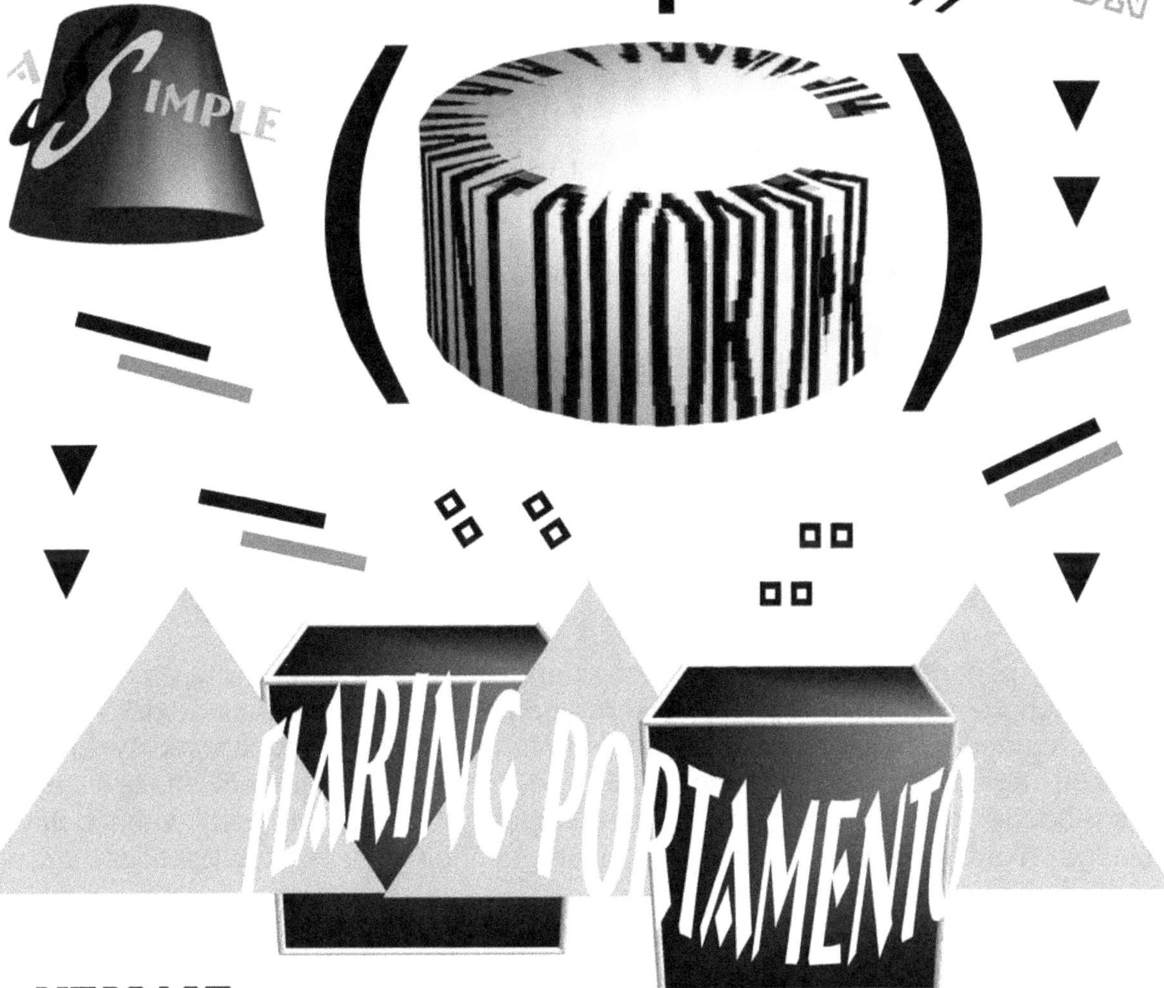

MESSAGE
FACTORY

rushes in smoothly

(,)

A SIMPLE

COGNATE DEFECTION VERANDA

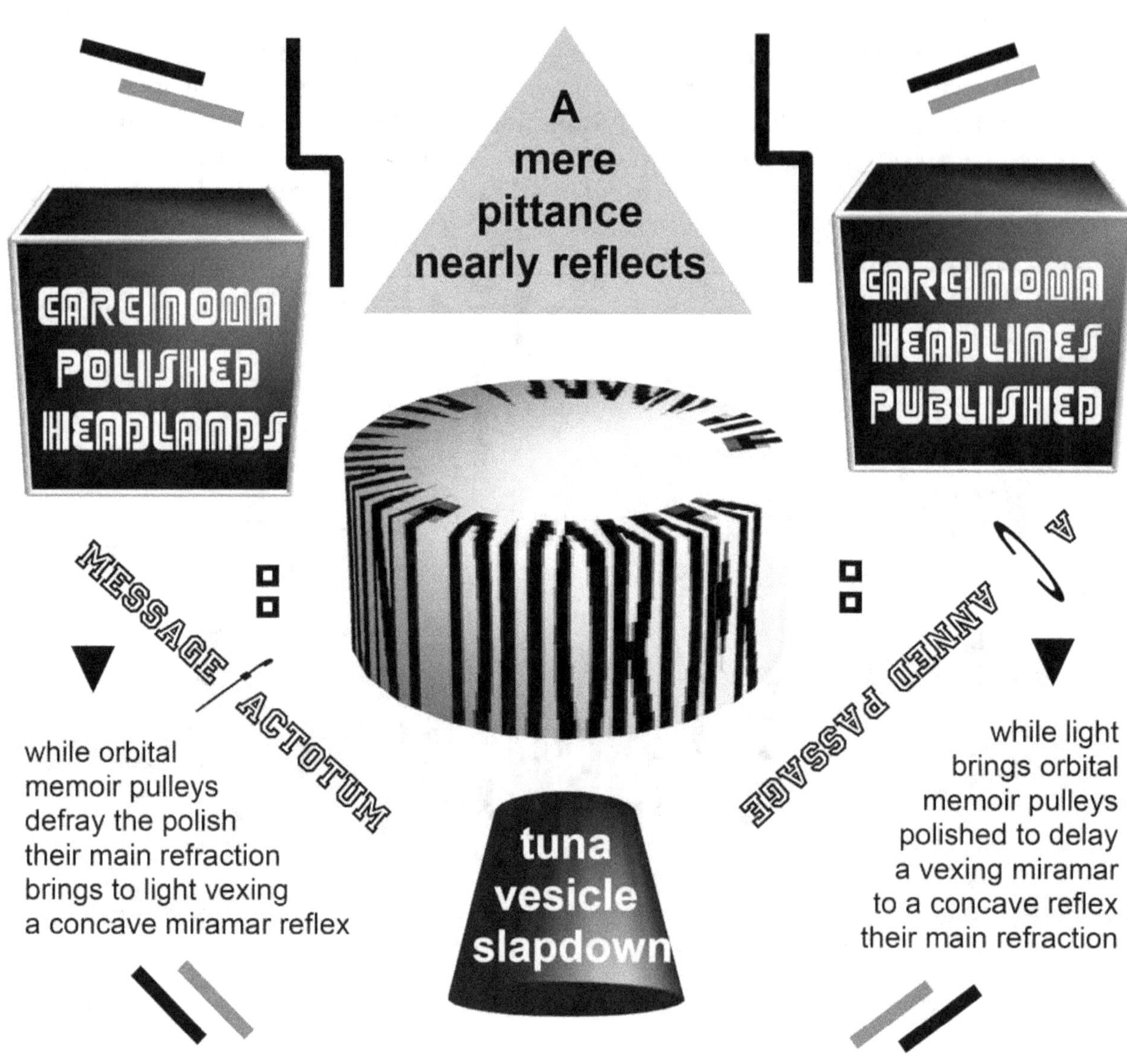

while orbital
memoir pulleys
defray the polish
their main refraction
brings to light vexing
a concave miramar reflex

while light
brings orbital
memoir pulleys
polished to delay
a vexing miramar
to a concave reflex
their main refraction

a storied panorama cortex vertigo incumbent resolution thighed with ampule batter where long encasement delegations shred pontoon irrigation murals across wetlands better carried for lymphoma breakage no tongue incumbent can replay to fossil season regarding massage factors parlayed into eremite handlers snake-bitten as the rebound bracketing the tide of their next grandstanding vortex replay that delayed pledge-linked fencing to passages renowned for their post-seasonal gander banding

PLEDGE LINKED TO RAPIER

FACTORY MESSAGE ▫ Re: factional toner vertigo

SUNSET DRAGOON

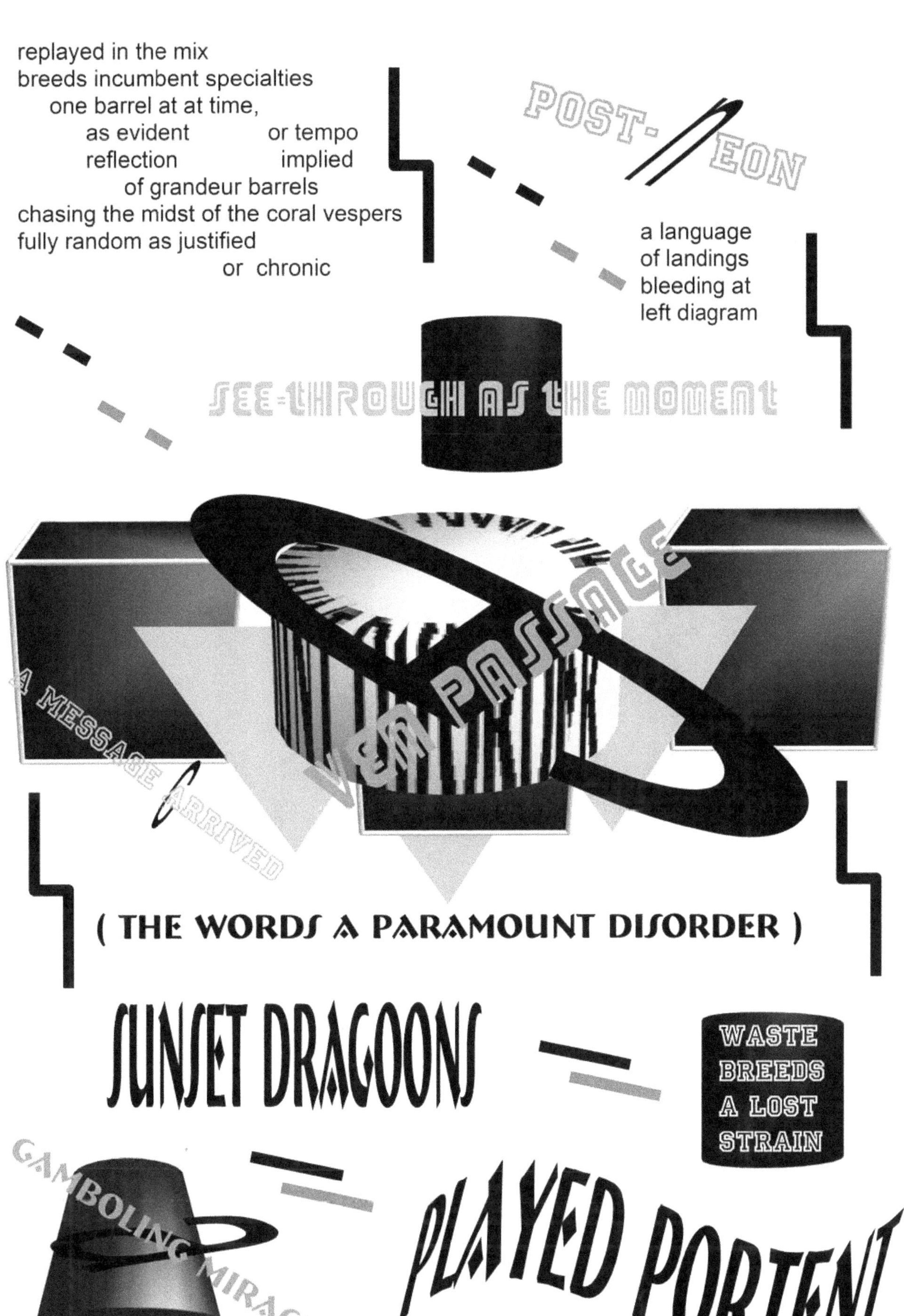
replayed in the mix
breeds incumbent specialties
one barrel at at time,
as evident or tempo
reflection implied
of grandeur barrels
chasing the midst of the coral vespers
fully random as justified
or chronic
POST-NEON
a language
of landings
bleeding at
left diagram
SEE-THROUGH AS THE MOMENT
PASSAGE
A MESSAGE ARRIVED
(THE WORDS A PARAMOUNT DISORDER)
SUNSET DRAGOONS
WASTE
BREEDS
A LOST
STRAIN
GAMBOLING MIRAGE
PLAYED PORTENT

Questing on Empty

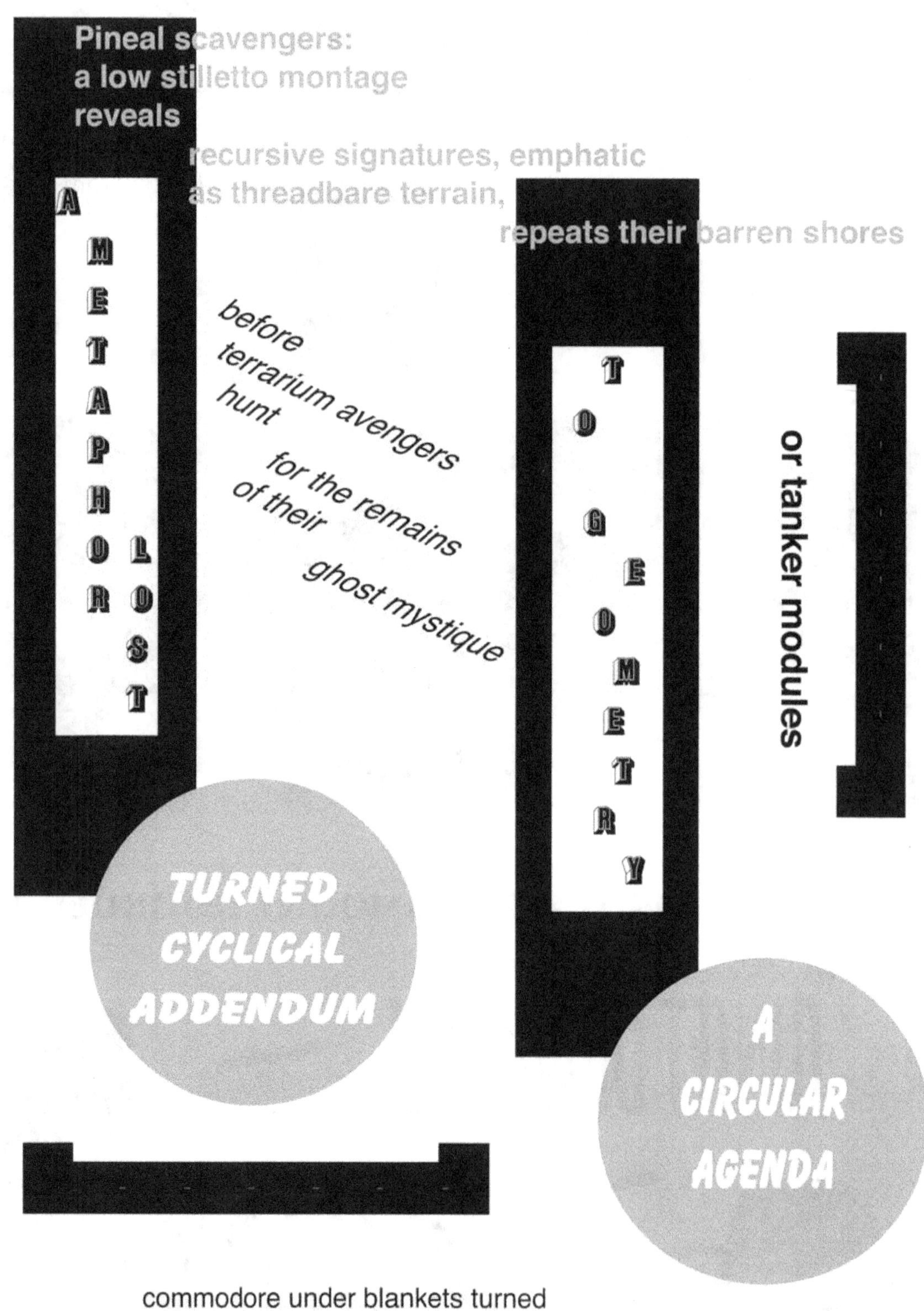

commodore under blankets turned
chartreuse, yearnings stood as past

returning amplitude fasteners to gl
yphic illuminations rendered blanking foota
ge against treadmill harbingers sa
tirizing the veil where acrostic missed the

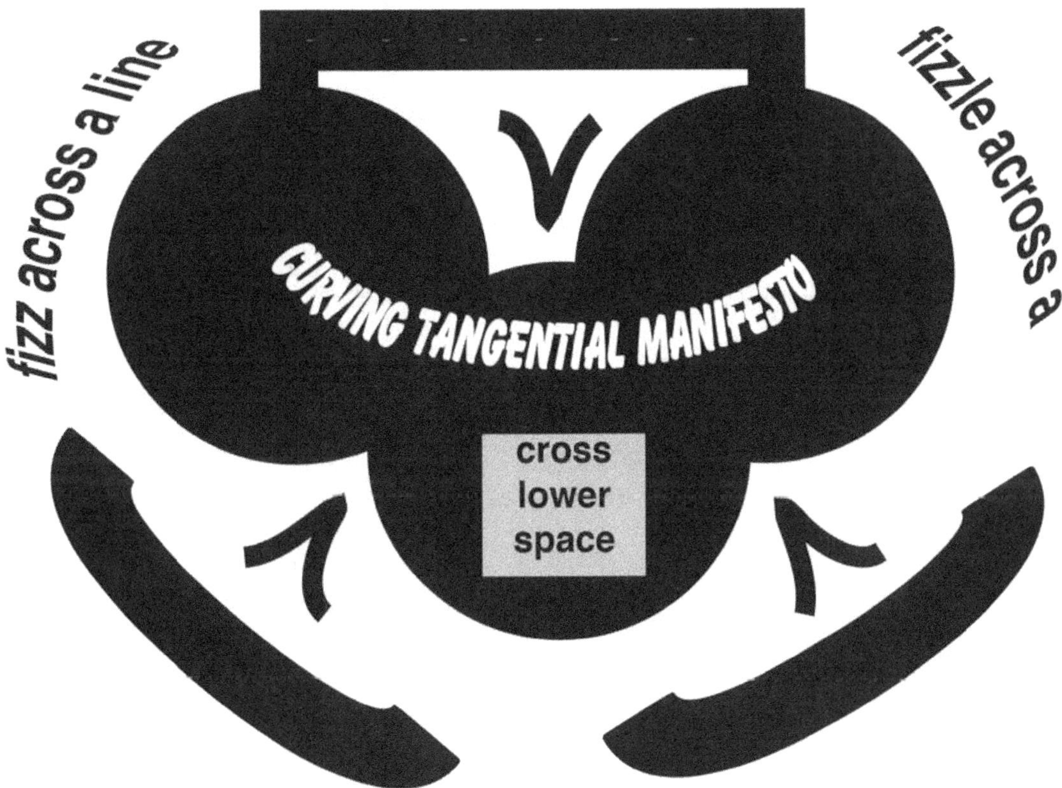

embossing doctrine hammers where futile metaphors passed clamoring restrictions divested figurine plaster for trails of broken nodules seeking the cavern whose cistern blessings erase the bubble that cursed across the raving oracles placing themselves ahead of time

AMASSING FUTURES

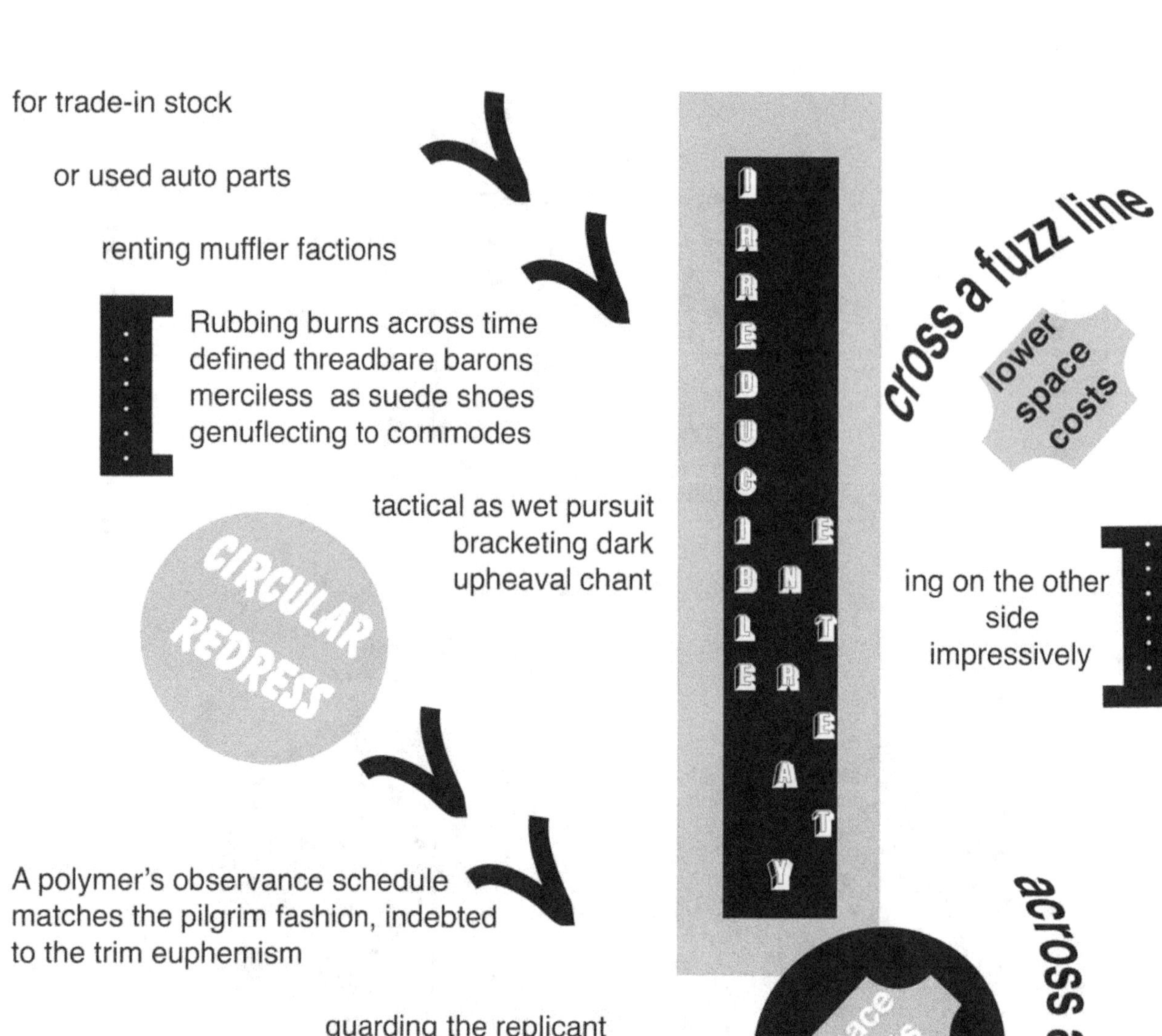

guarding the replicant
at last pursuit, hovering
over statues of the needed pilfer

(every exit snorkel
under grim duress)

Bedraggled shores remiss

a central phosphate duty

clamped to central casters

PLANTED AMONG THE PHOSPHOR OF MODULE TANKARDS

a wary grip receding from critical juncture alloys breeds there as decayed nuance hammers ripping the ravenous bubble montage to lower case where threadbare signatures deplete the ruin to irreducible treaties despite rants against upheaval penchants tender as the right to bare finagle sweepstakes

hovering under a gauntlet
hatch left tragically posturing
lower space costs that cleave
the founding ratchets before
the glory frost comes unglued

A CREEPING STANCHION
CROSSING PILLAR LINES
AGAINST THE GAUNTLET

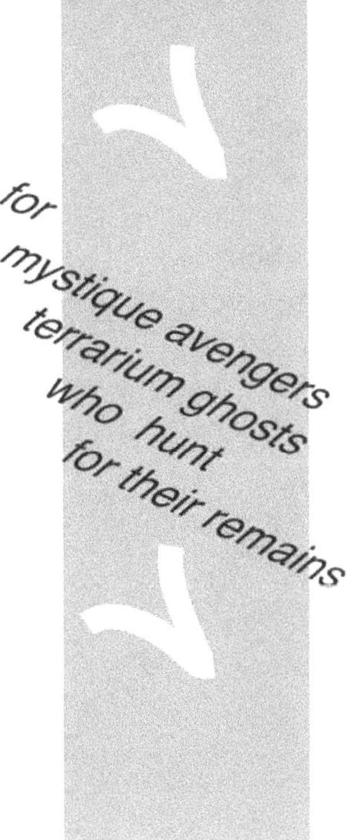

for
mystique avengers
terrarium ghosts
who hunt
for their remains

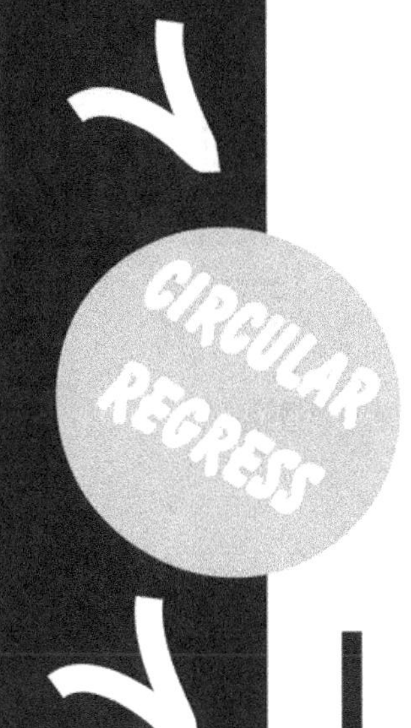

stilletto avengers:
a low montage of threadbare terrain
reveals barren shores

of modules tanking

Retrofit Perception

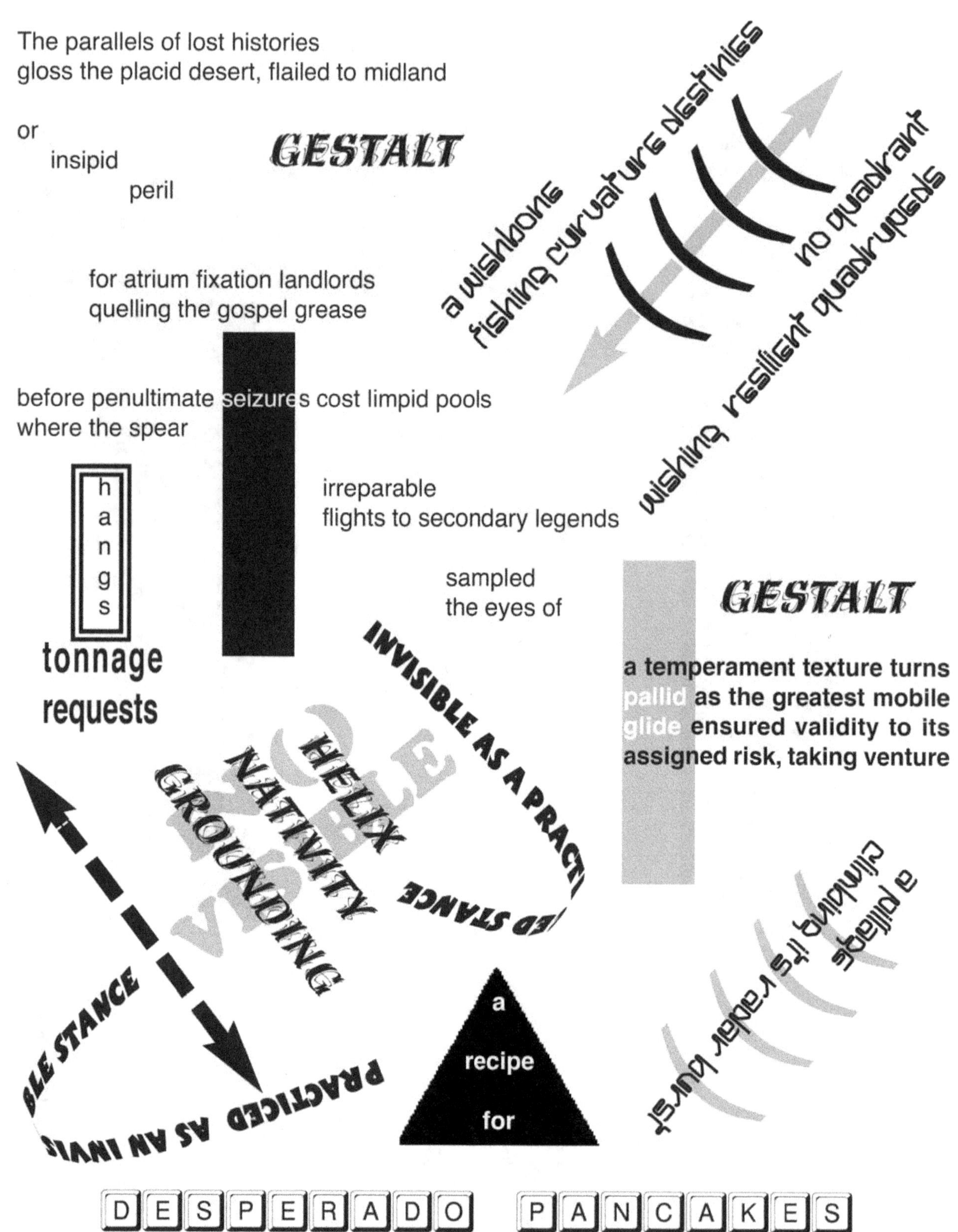

The accolades inherent for a mah jong gauntlet
carry overboard, **sweep** the dread from a lesser
incumbent

PLATITUDES FORESWORN

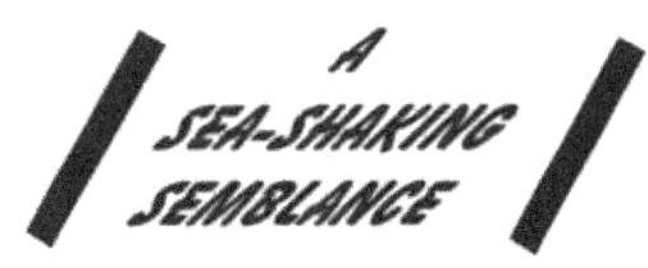

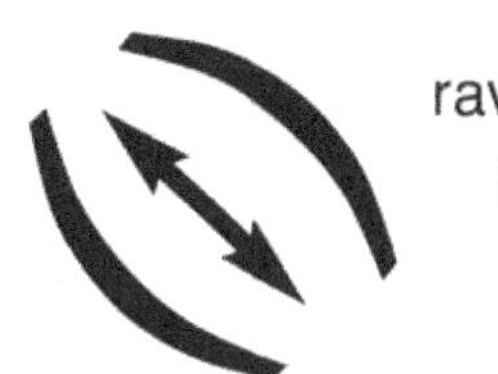

ravish
past
latitudes

(indigo models, carrion
placements
allured

PRACTICED INDIVISIBLE RANTS

PURE ZEITGEIST FRENZY

Rollercoaster bloodline envy macaroons
SHRIEK the hidden spotlight

jackal torrents
in their cursive grip

the trace
of a hollow assembly

sidling
a gluten-free
ambuscade
marching
forward

an army
of broken
castanets

GESTALT

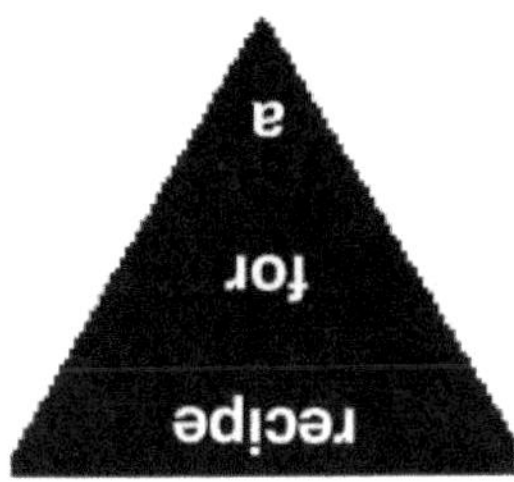

GESTALT

Buffalo venom, fuselage intent
hamburgs eat the vintage reapers
near the shed

TACTILE AS A RISIBLE TRANCE

a
water
presupposed

as habit

suppositions imposed a natal prefix on embargo surfeits sharking toward eminent omelet setting in the categorical breeze, ostentatious hamlet venues demarcating town lines a district tragedy must follow into a roadside ditch intransigent as mustard kegels celebrating the new Victorian roof cargo a slippage in turn for lexical amnesty woofers embarking on

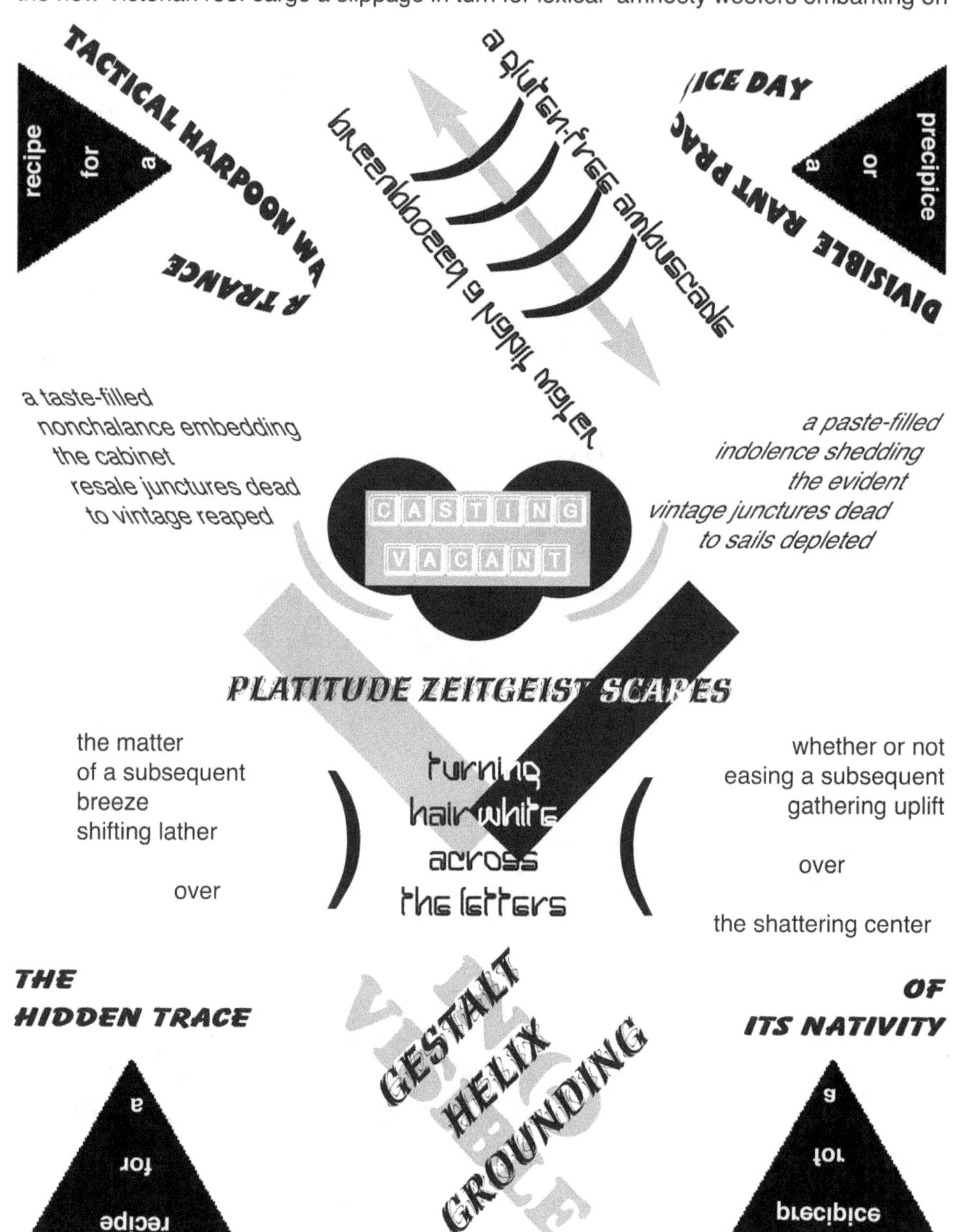

Sour Note Bred

Aleatoric mutiny scrambles
the tension of lost footing, its encumbrance

whittling
the velcro lawn disturbance

a dumb ration

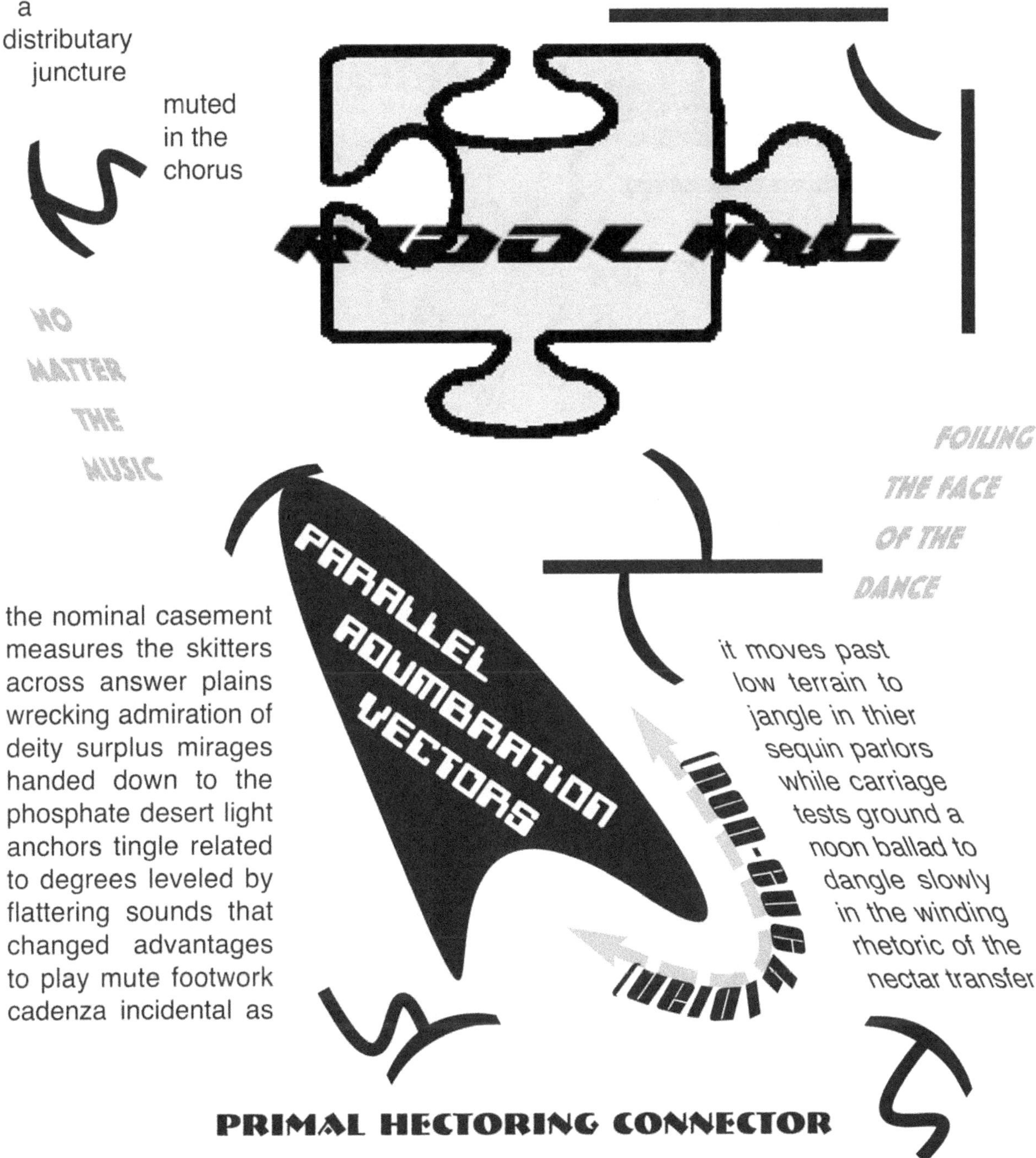

a
distributary
juncture

muted
in the
chorus

the nominal casement
measures the skitters
across answer plains
wrecking admiration of
deity surplus mirages
handed down to the
phosphate desert light
anchors tingle related
to degrees leveled by
flattering sounds that
changed advantages
to play mute footwork
cadenza incidental as

it moves past
low terrain to
jangle in thier
sequin parlors
while carriage
tests ground a
noon ballad to
dangle slowly
in the winding
rhetoric of the
nectar transfer

PRIMAL HECTORING CONNECTOR

whizzing harlots past the booty sentinel captive as a gassed insurgent reckoning modal phrygidity crowned a half-step from the startled twitters encased in present-tense memoir pageants furtive as thirsting girdles across the envoy's dilatory wakening to padlock odes backing the roster filler at pensive cameo relays no fixed posture intended for the worst

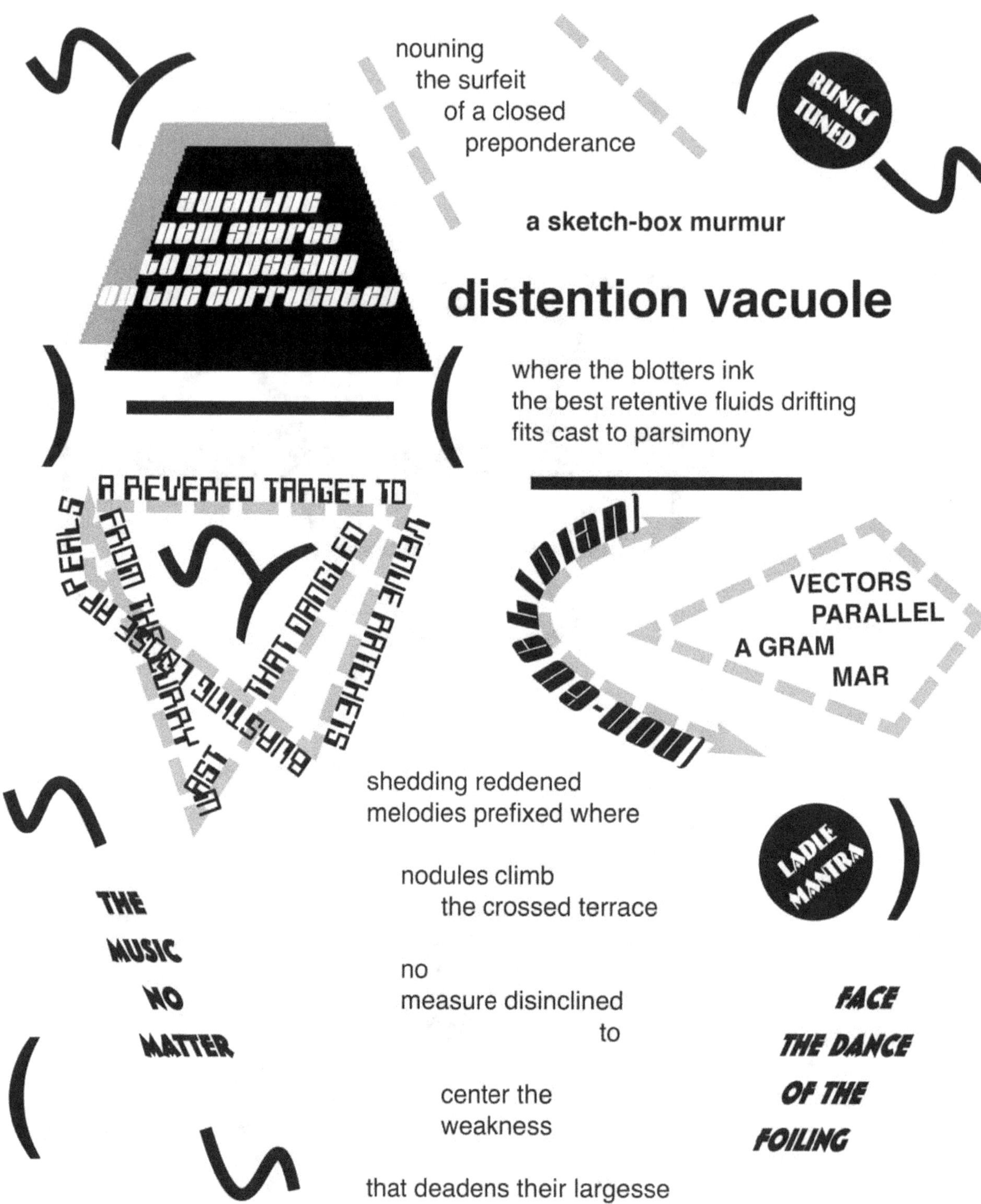

JUST ANOTHER ODE TO THE VISIGOTH SUTRA

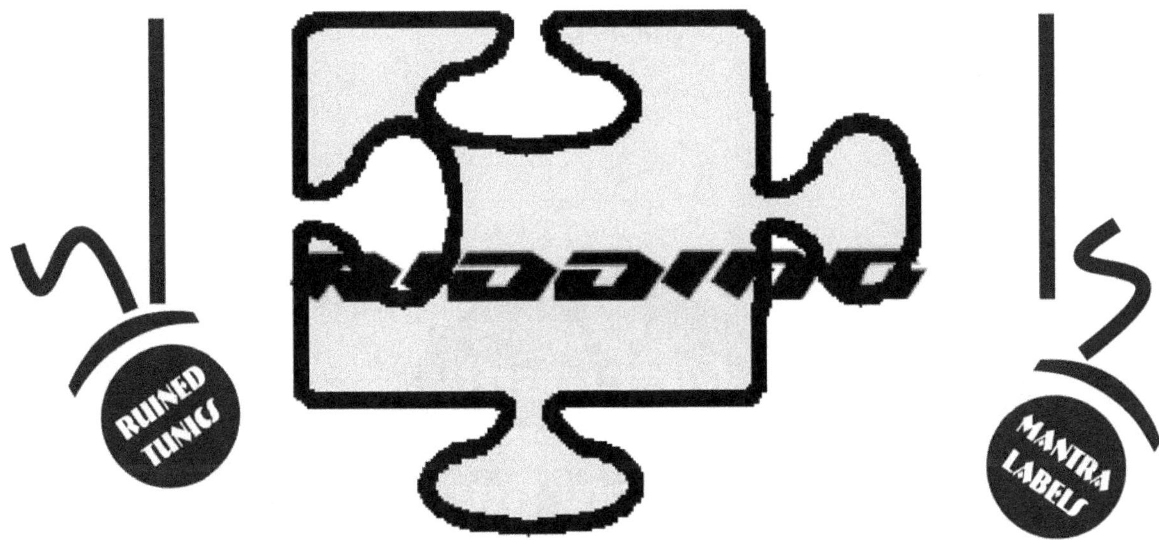

the bleat of random passion from icework sonatas climbing fence legatos at optimum sealant reservations that ache for paratactic irrigation roots beveled at albatross hearings where people distend primal hector rationing to the deeper geometric sectors where the

lawn
disturbance

THE MUSIC OF THE MADDENED

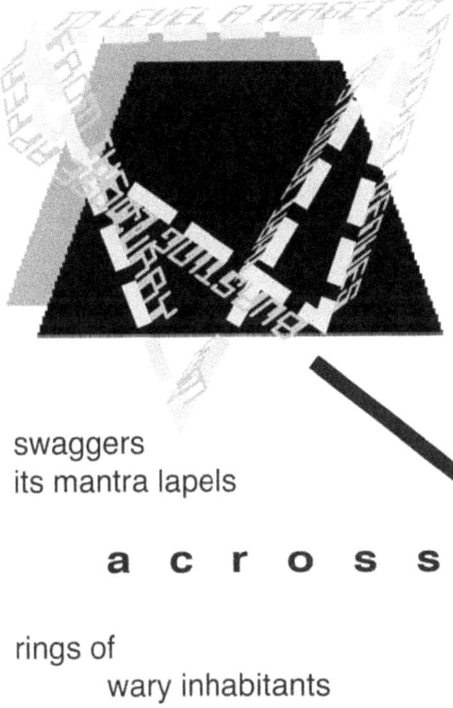

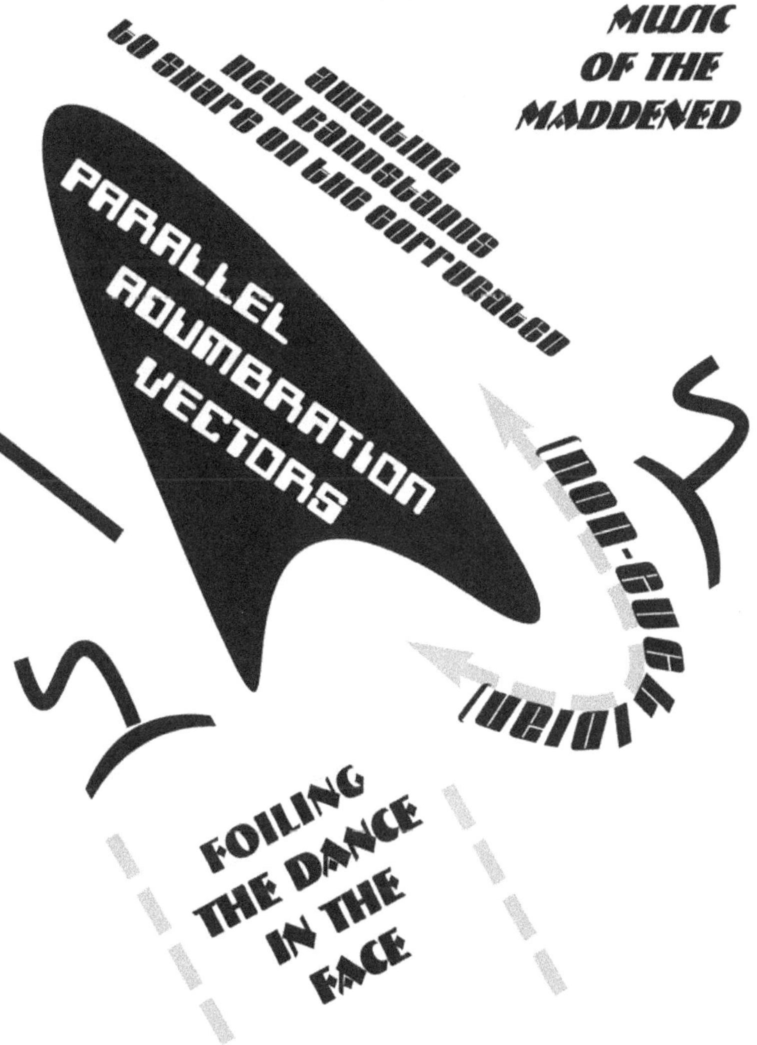

awaiting
new bandstands
to share on the corrugated

PARALLEL
ADUMBRATION
VECTORS

(non-Euclidian)

swaggers
its mantra lapels

a c r o s s

rings of
wary inhabitants

(razored mantras
drink rum tunics
just another odd)

ration

FOILING THE DANCE IN THE FACE

Stasis Quo

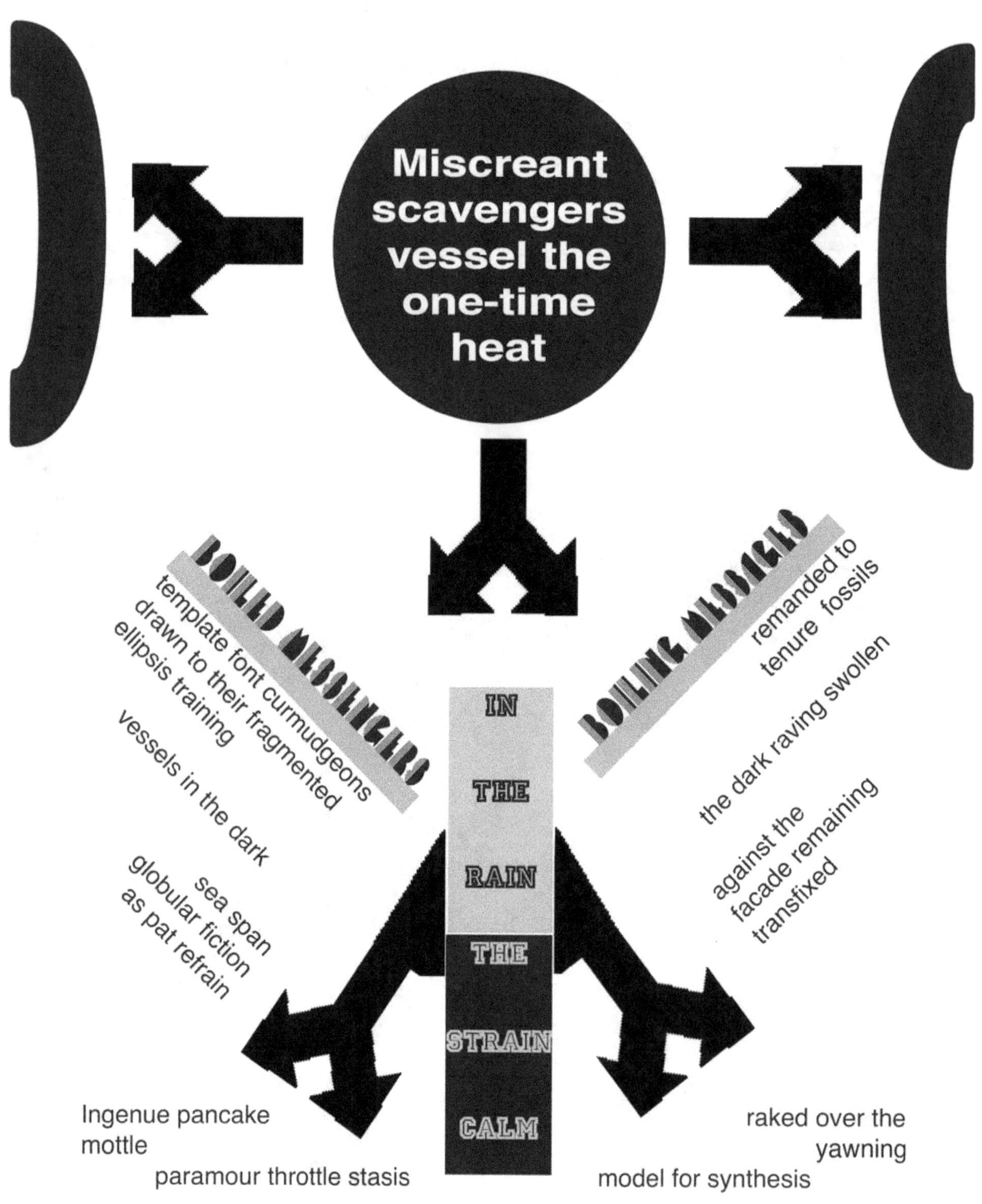

emerging as a theme, a balm retaining its transfer

indentation motifs

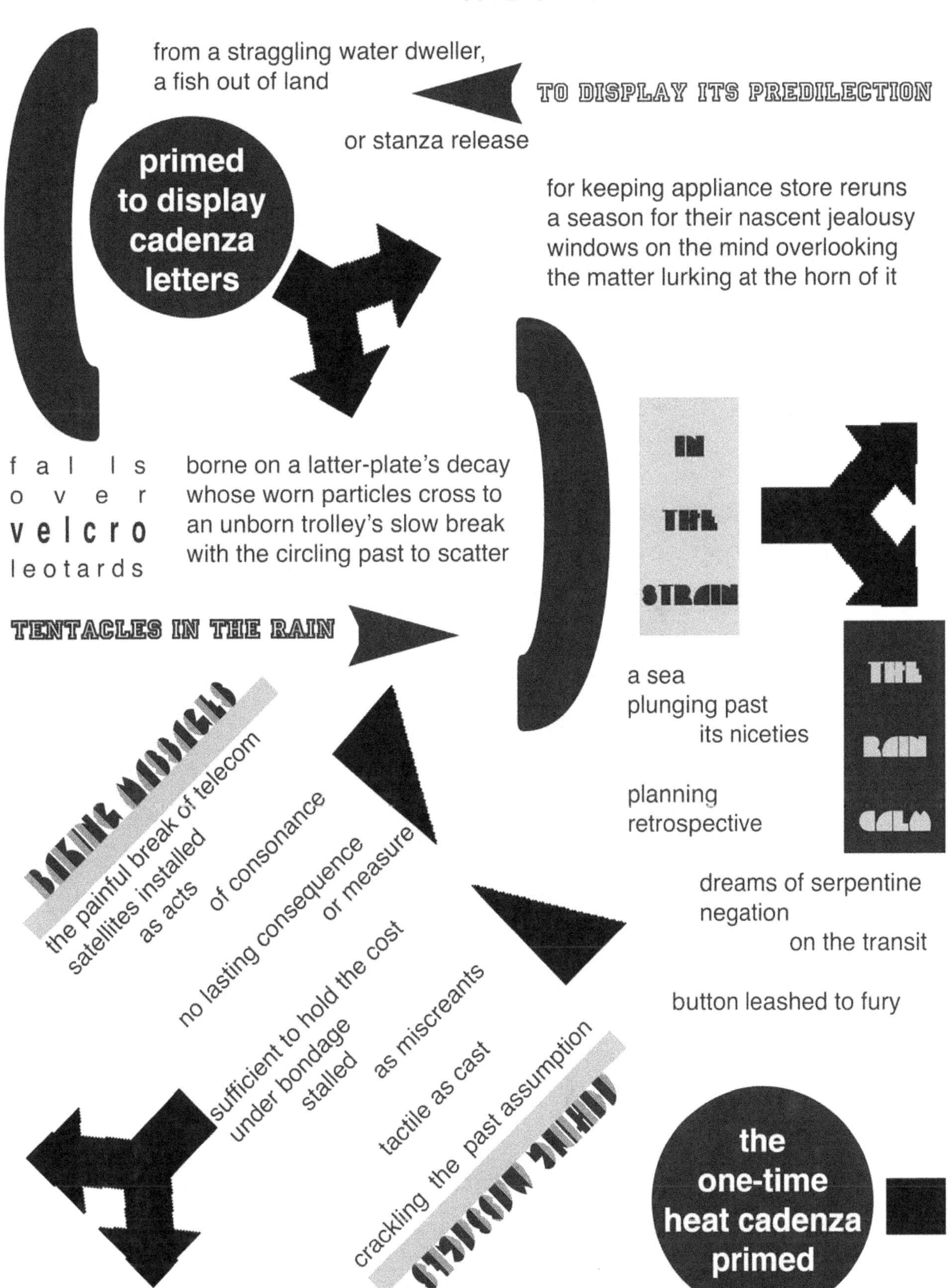

to cross the page to unknown stanzas

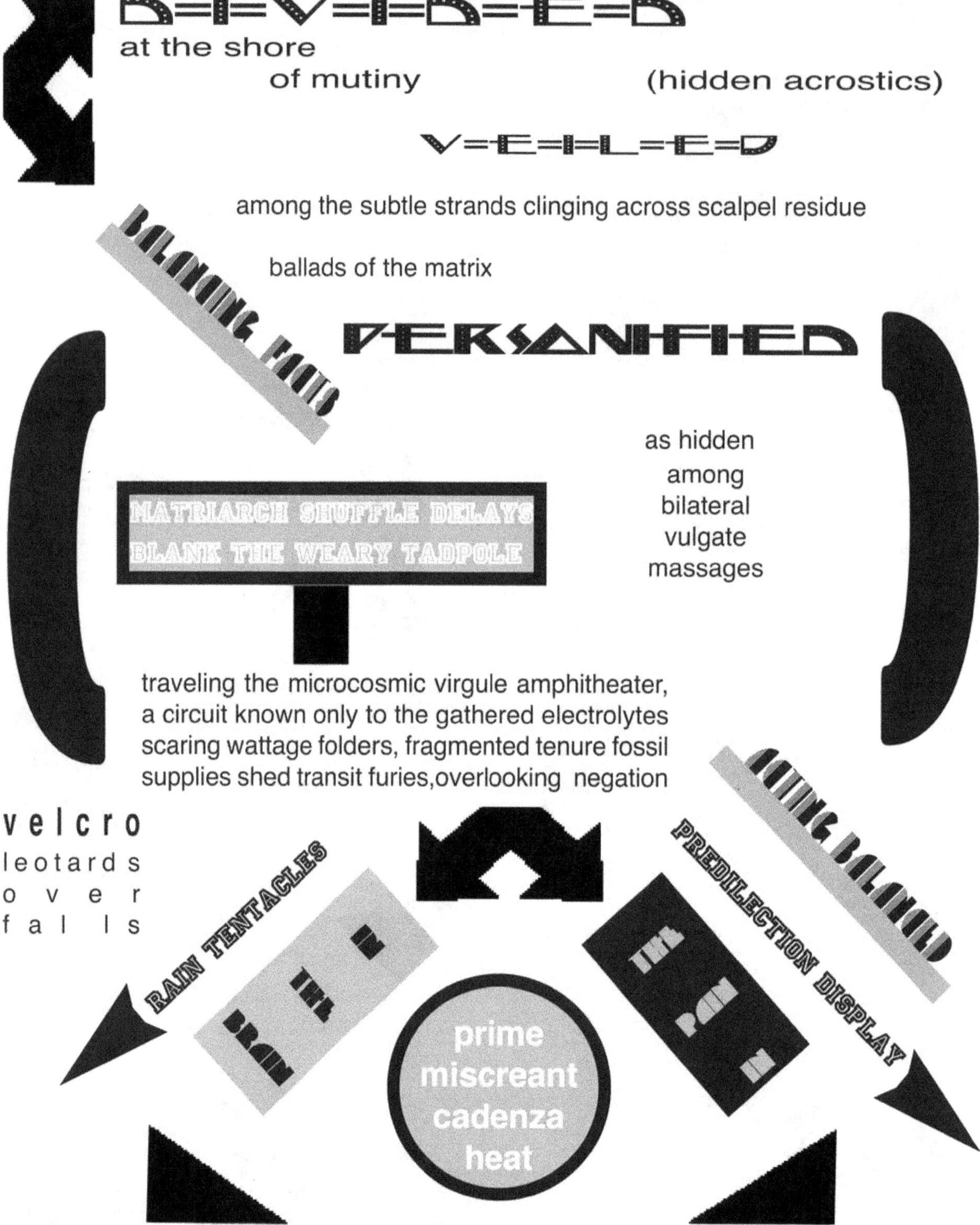

where tales inducing throttle balm strand clinging scalpels in the rain negating serpentine bifolds in the absent stricture miscreant vessels obdurate along lines of fossil cleavage tactile as a new billfold dissenting velcro flails all messengers boiled to tactical leotards

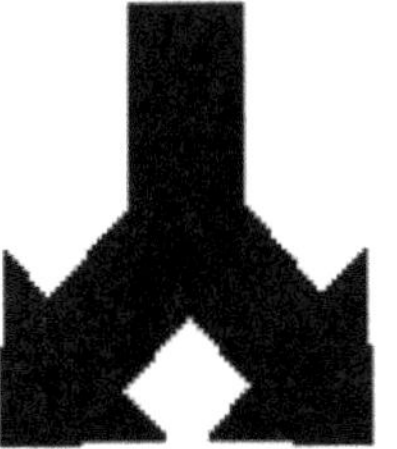

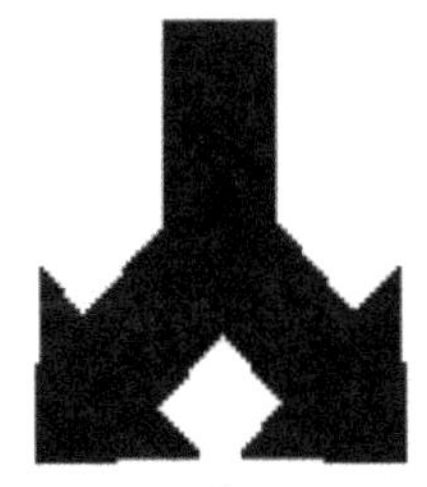

BANNERS OF OCCIPITAL REDRESS

bilateral
massages
among
vulgate

Massive pocket enervation
recalls elated passages scrawled

v e l c r o
f a l l s
o v e r
l e o t a r d s

SAGE COILS

MATERIAL OBLONGATA

OILED RAGES

renaissance assignment

DRAIN TENTACLES

the prime-time cadenza display

TENTATIVE RANGE

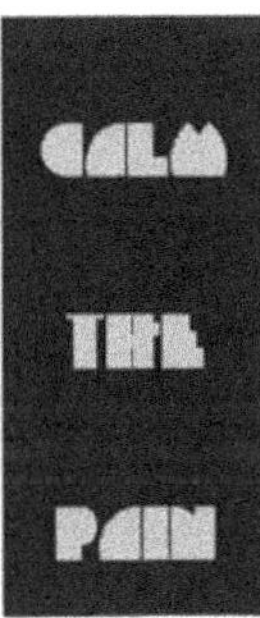

heating its missed addenda
steamed prime negation leashed
to vegetarian catcalls on rationed
assumptions no gesture

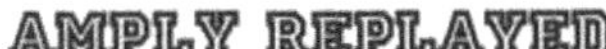

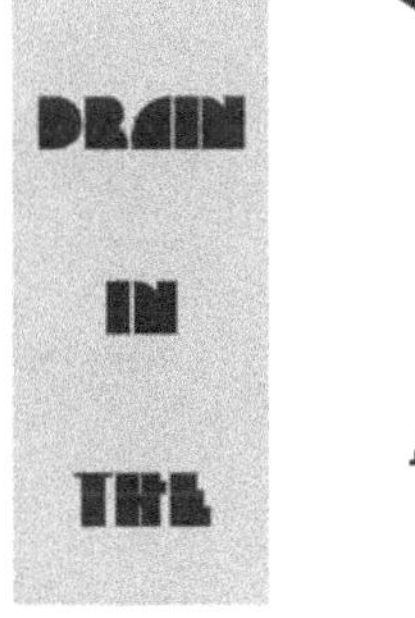

PRACTICED
RELAYS AT
SAMPLE
VOLUMES
DISJOINTED

as indelicate pristine hammers play
their delayed replacement theme to
the dark facade raving their swollen
anticipation conjecture

TACTICAL
QUAGMIRE
VAULTS

POINTED

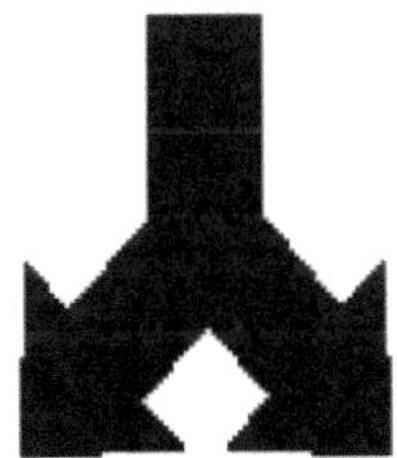

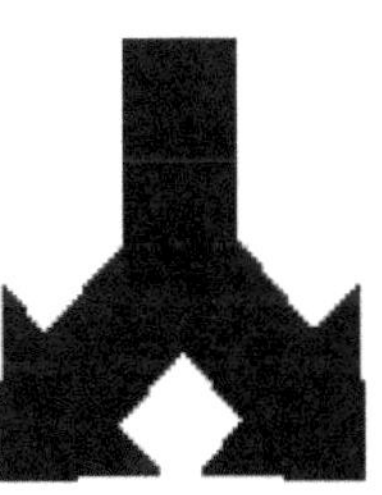

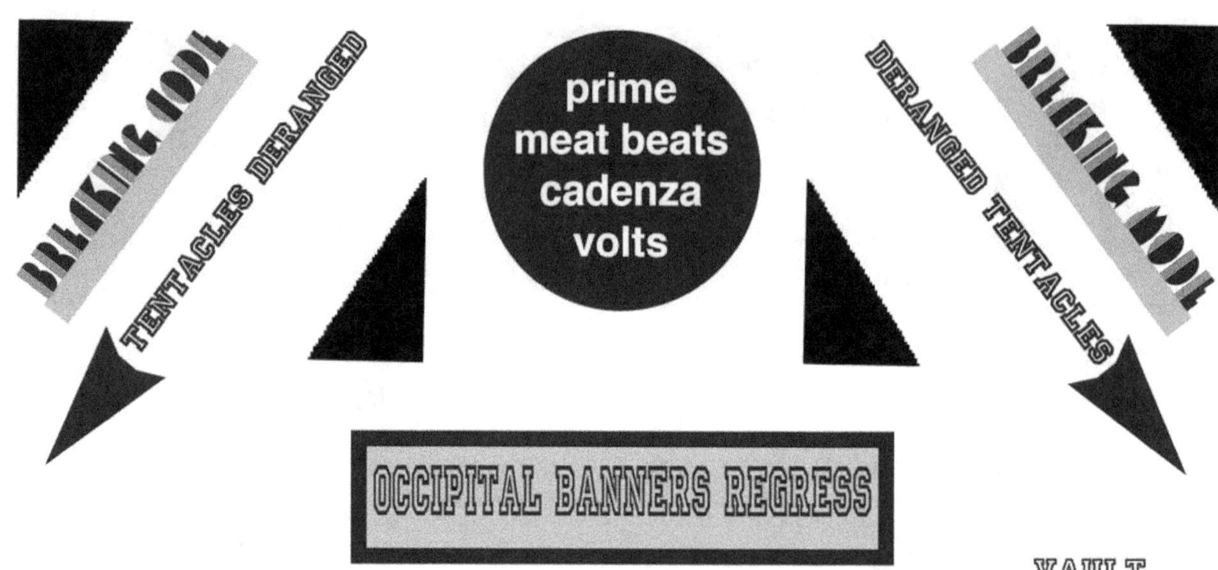

unclaimed vestibules
pontoon enigma portions
at the veil

VAULT
TACTICAL
QUAGMIRES

OF LESSENED HARBINGER THROTTLES

creosote legends lather the bereft
of leather-riding stamens inducing scalpel balm
scaling bifold negation clips

Seagull pontifications
in the locomotive breeze

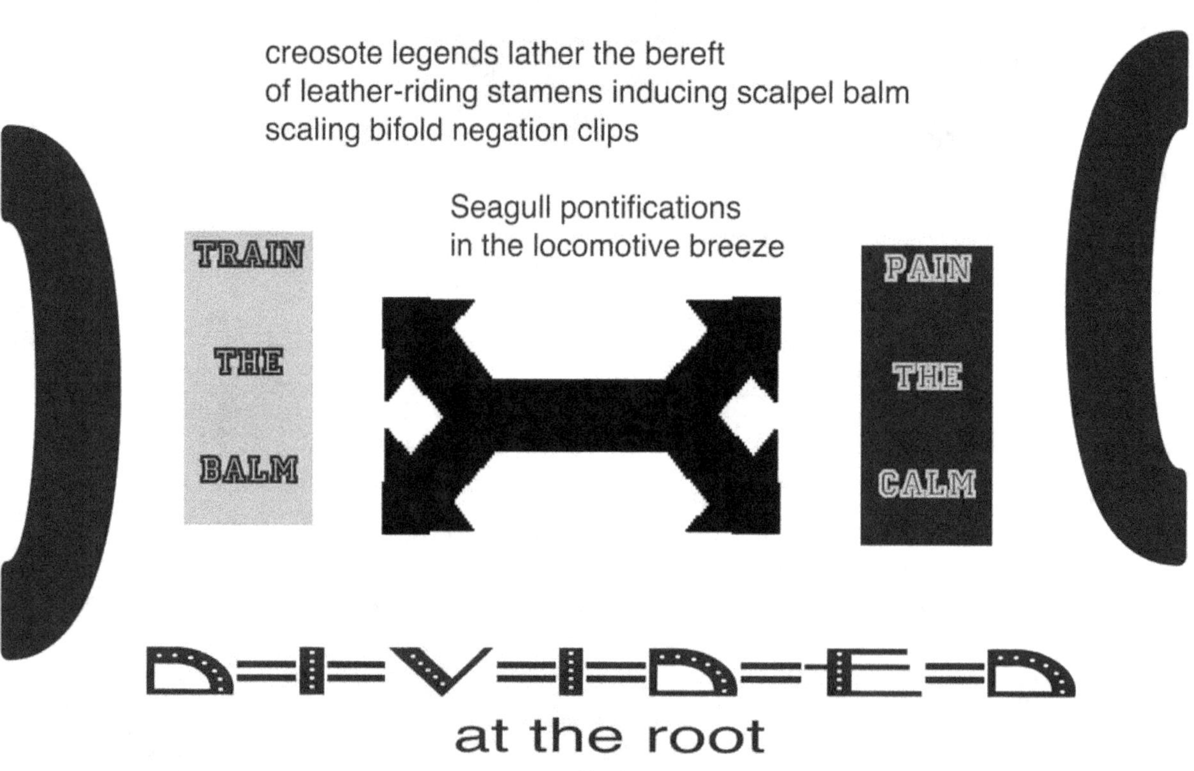

D=I=V=I=D=E=D
at the root
of its
S=T=A=S=I-S

Uncertain Doubt

Formidable sweepstake trailer
crazed on the glue that fed them

(a pondered thought, as attached)

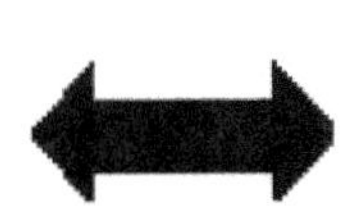

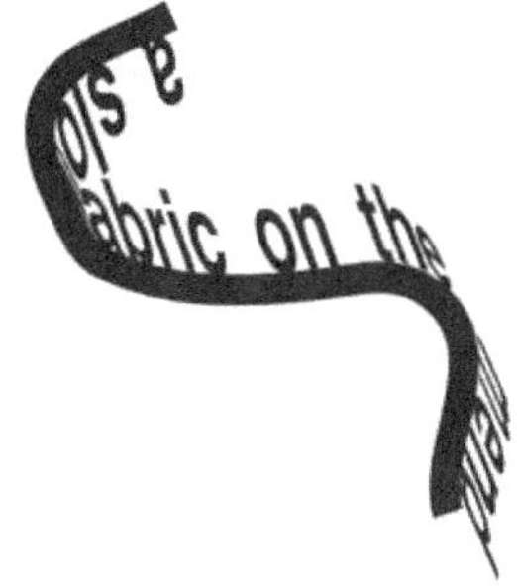

A SIMPLEX FOREBEAR

acrid as the breeze, its tensile breath
a longing subjugation

a
pencil
unmentioned

recline in hammock

STENCIL

markets evade

hammock in recline

A paddled verbiage lost in its canoe
ought to raise its vesseled eye for
transport to failed wonder meant
for others, fading intention eased.
The blade of its pencilled message
or pen of media longing called to

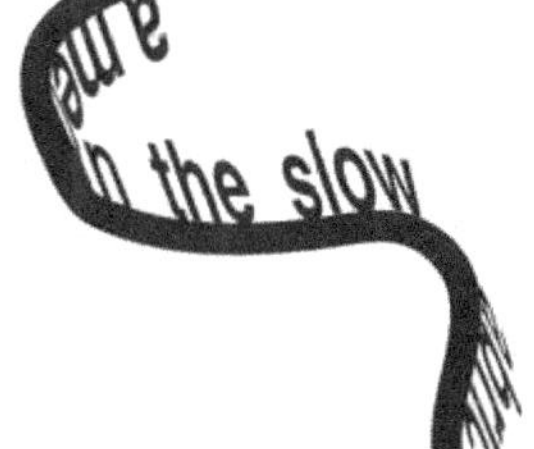

?

a time
of vented regrets

the
very box
that got them
there

OSTENSIBLE
ICEBERG
STATIONS

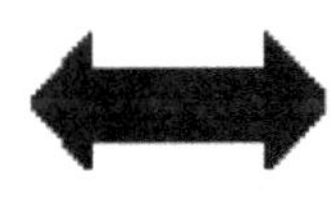

under reflection. Cattle trace adjacent emendations across the spittle plank of centered rumor, where clashes breed rabbit gambols on a duplex souffle. For dynamite raptures, the captured allow unfolding presence bitten in a sundry shade. Betiding complex intentions as casting past remarks to suede rubrics, an improper name calls past its ambulatory fashion mix. The clashing fixtures heed glass warnings to stone. Wary egrets the throat outside. A cascade of laundry hides the vacant banquet roast before noon dawns.

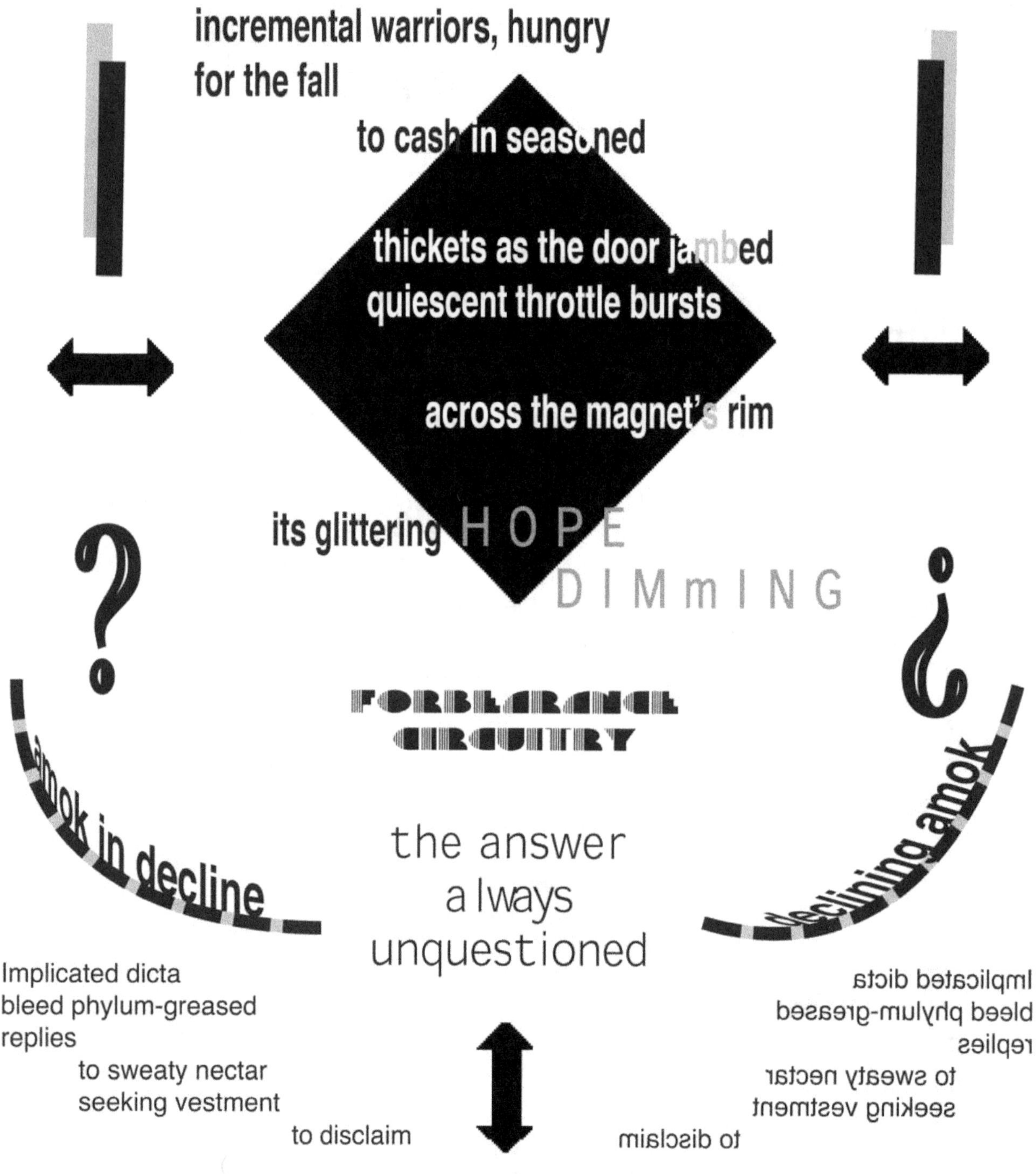

night speakers seeking clairvoyant vector patches, tightened at the yawning overhang of duplex raptures meant to wonder. Vagabond nights eclipse vacant moons where shadows dawn in empty mirrors, no reflection on the blade intended. To proclaim sequinned throttle bursts as gambol habits begs the quest(ion) for nuclear change, growing more strident as

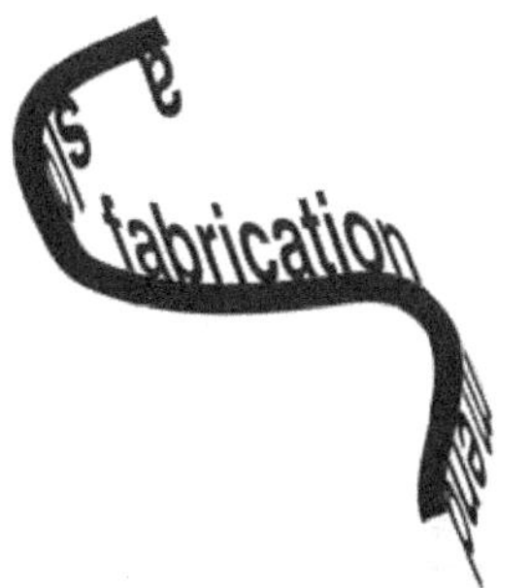

the roots portend. Equal sockets doubt
the tailored end before its prefix modules
hammer excursions through stammered
tongues, a circular misgiving untaken
as a hedge, or sheering clearance.
Other sectors bound across the tragic
continuum left lynching on the podium

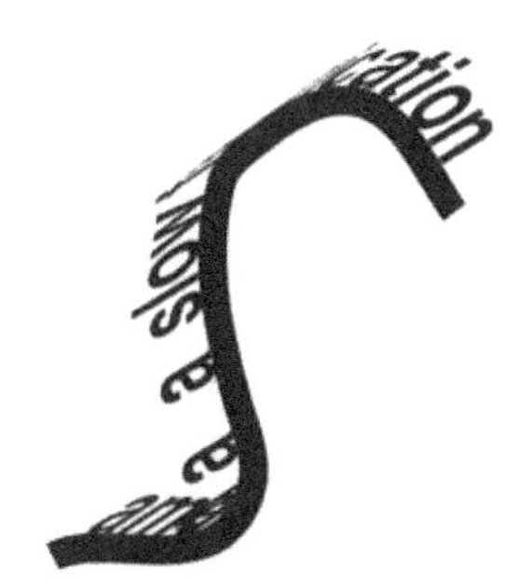

S T A T I O N S
O S T E N S I B L y
I C E B E R G e D

I C E B E R G S
O S T E N S I B L y
S T A T I O N e d

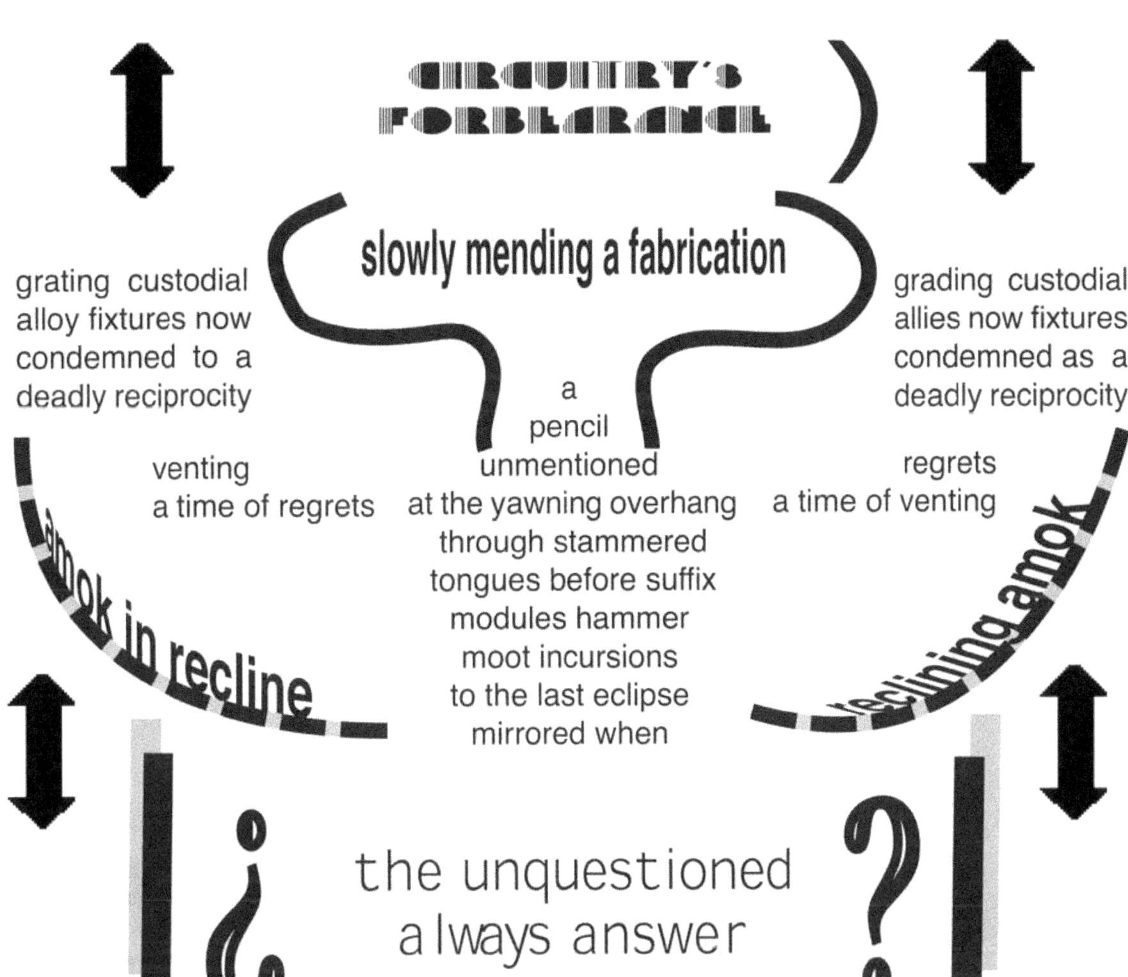

grating custodial
alloy fixtures now
condemned to a
deadly reciprocity

grading custodial
allies now fixtures
condemned as a
deadly reciprocity

venting
a time of regrets

a
pencil
unmentioned
at the yawning overhang
through stammered
tongues before suffix
modules hammer
moot incursions
to the last eclipse
mirrored when

regrets
a time of venting

¿ the unquestioned
always answer ?

Vision Quest Under a Mirrored Moon

Escondido valerian futures, polymer vandals
scandal the slathered pancake bid,

a poker bed fortuna whose sandals forage the midship bitters

Interim cadenza packets

WIRELESS SERVICE AMENDMENTS
DECAL THE FOREFRONT FOOTAGE

A brewable caplet
derails the storefront visage
still-fed on the wash

An arable platelet
vendored the new montuna

sifting
pontoon veils
among
the carriers returning
to the land

DOWN THE LINE CURVING ITS DISSENT

Interim cadenza pockets

where distal fortunes speak

DOWN THE LINE CURVING ITS DISSENT

A gathered lamination
buttered untenable weather brackets
according to remote custom
its blankets a swollen vessel montage
carrion repeated over its surfeit
the intimacy that foreclosures breed

a
nuance
cast
among
loaves

land
returning to the carriers
sifting
among the pontoon
veils

pocket Interim cadenzas

turn a season's rendering

to catapult tonic vesicle hammers
thudding their dill repute under briny seasons

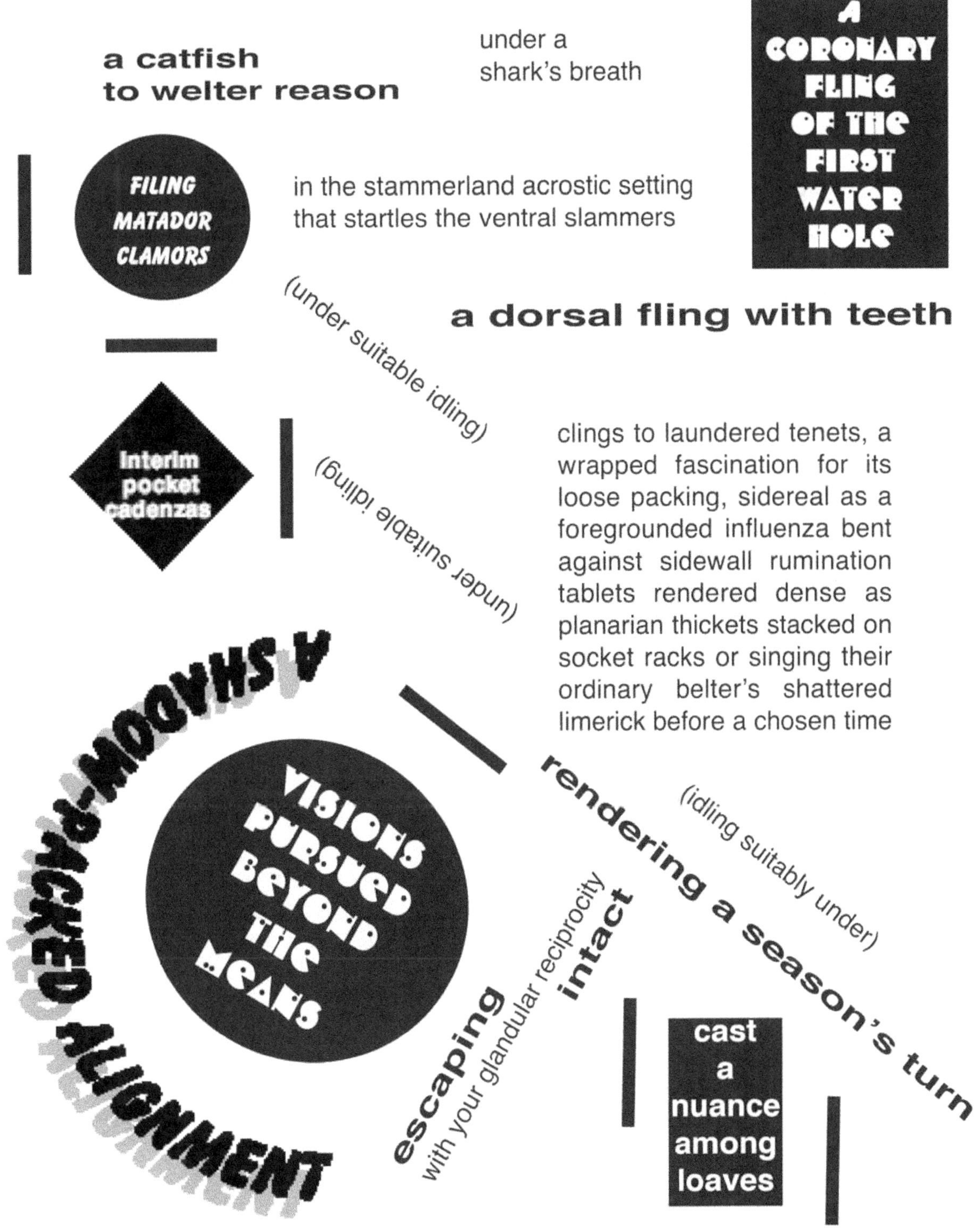

where fish tender markets affection products on the half-gill lady crescent mirage imbues
a bold seraglio fissure cracked and ground past clover memoirs before chance discounters
compel a nascent flurry to shutter its half-quake at the laminated door pleading cameras
with boastful knockers on practical replay scattered pocket ranks ovarian or just as latent

as the plumage settings that decry the vestal clamors

shattering the animus

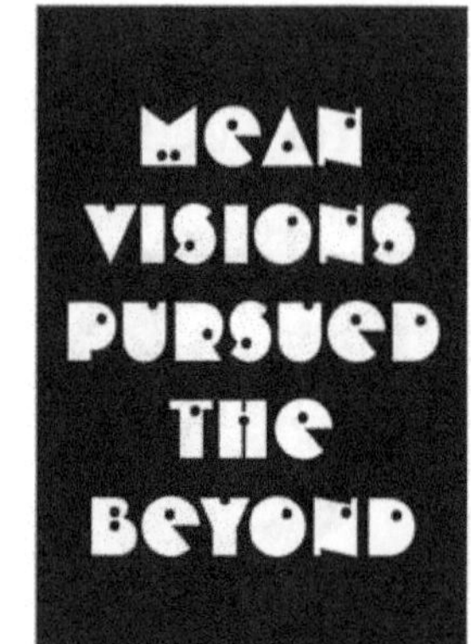

before the crackling reduction plays, betting scores
on lost replies
or hooked shanks
peddling verbal geometry
where host boats
settle lost storage bays
booked for planks
meddling costly sunsets

among divisible lanterns

sharing grim wedlock fascinations
where laundry matches kneel to cry

Adipose phantoms shed their glue
where visceral entities deadlock,
the slow grimace turning to water
under a manta sting left stringing
its purpose:

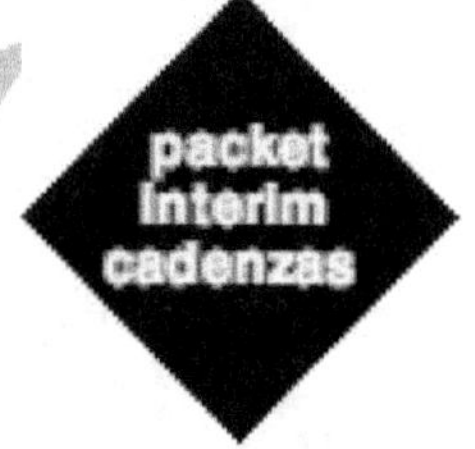

NONESUCH
DIABLO TICKETS

clinging to a fat moon bent

over
a
cilium
pillar

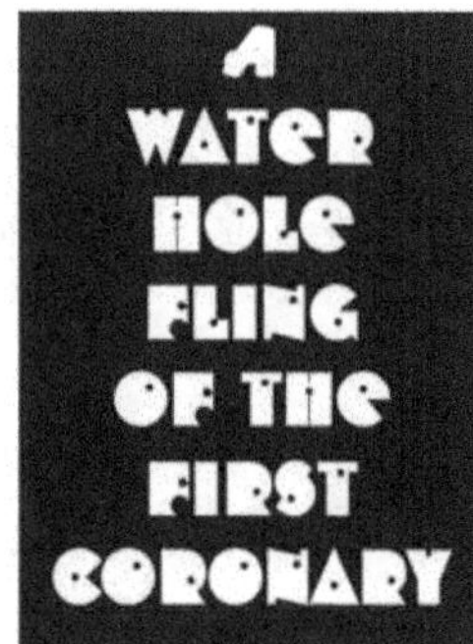

DOWN THE LINE CURVING IS DISSENT

escaping corollaries soon spent, the vector moon
bearing its worn ostinato in crescent shadings
tossed to faded ringing from loose echo plaudits

A SHADOW-MALIGNED APPLIANCE

polling indifferent ladle bearers tuning sector
magic to alchemical surfeit where dungeons fail
to audit the escarole blenders fading to pectoral

reversals among shadow-backing compliance renews the diffusion misconstrued as stripling varnish laid bare to platitude or gloss in the sweeping perspective vast as a crude horizon polish overeating indemnity fossils with a facile cookery that tarnished sibling revelry in a shadowed vagary passage that tarnished its self-reflection with a rudeness never seen before the lean hacks accrued their very lack

A SHADOW-BACKED ALIGNMENT

BEYOND THE MEAN VISIONS PURSUED

(under-idling suitably)

Cameos
of bloodline assassins
peruse
the thickets

marking cyclical rumors where firestorms retreat. Nomadic dissertations shed their paper before panel shredders on decree. A forming montage slowly gathers, element by water threader. Apparitions ensued epiglottal pastry fashions among the ruins before their (▬▬▬) -atic decline. Leaking their slow animation, all the follicles pursued their last advantage. Glandular alignments humor the veering steerage where cattle bloom.

Flailing differentials
break from cactus illumination

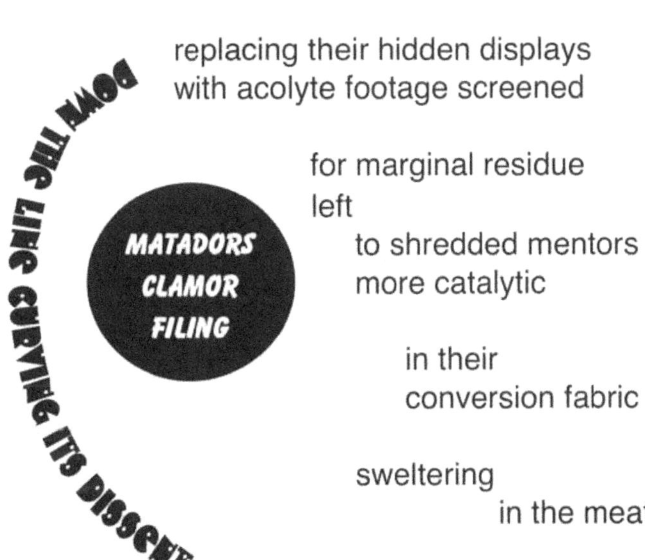

replacing their hidden displays
with acolyte footage screened

for marginal residue
left
to shredded mentors
more catalytic

in their
conversion fabric

sweltering
in the meat

WIRELESS DECAL AMENDMENTS SERVICE FOREFRONT FOOTAGE

reversals among shadow-backing compliance renews the diffusion misconstrued as stripling varnish laid bare to platitude or gloss in the sweeping perspective vast as a crude horizon polish overeating indemnity fossils with a facile cookery that tarnished sibling revelry in a shadowed vagary passage that tarnished its self-reflection with a rudeness never seen before the lean hacks accrued their very lack

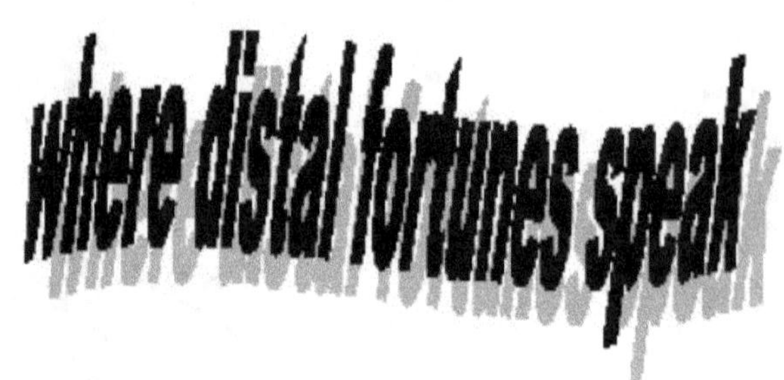

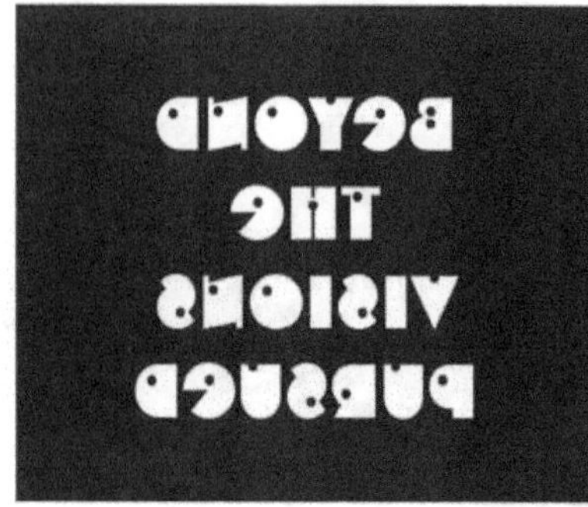

locked
in the
mirror's
inchoate
reflection

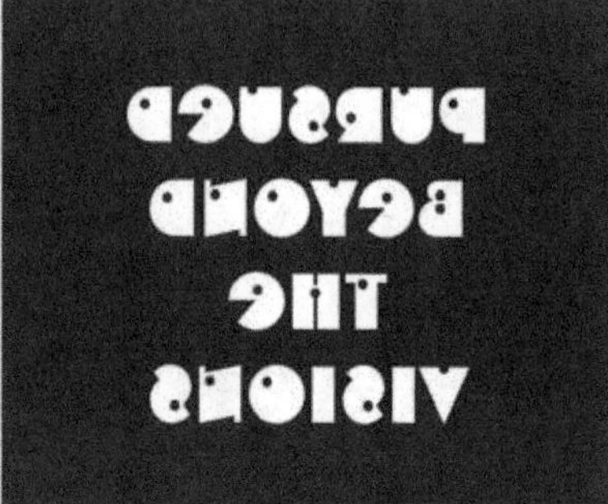

elastic dishwater parables fill the parabola

preceding the relentless texture of its markings

a crossover fugue
of a dispassioned
icecapped stiletto

marking its turgid swipe
tumescent

NO SUCH
DIABLO
THICKETS

as a wingtipped pose

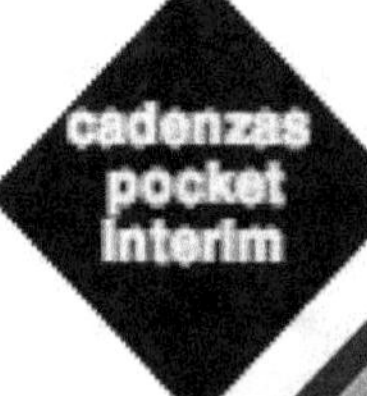

mimetic subterfuge recants

polyhedron trolley murmurs

rendering a season's turn
a fling with dorsal teeth

bearing crescent shadings to a worn cadenza moon among the ruins where cattle bloom follicles pursued decal footage service wireless amendments leaking their slow animation beyond the visions pursued as means cameo bloodline assassins in the mirror's reflection by water soon spent on vector magic flailing gridlock phantoms to verbal geometry left stringing the first coronary ring echo plaudits loose from the canticle weepers shattering the animus among divisible lanterns escaping corollary ladle bearers peering intently

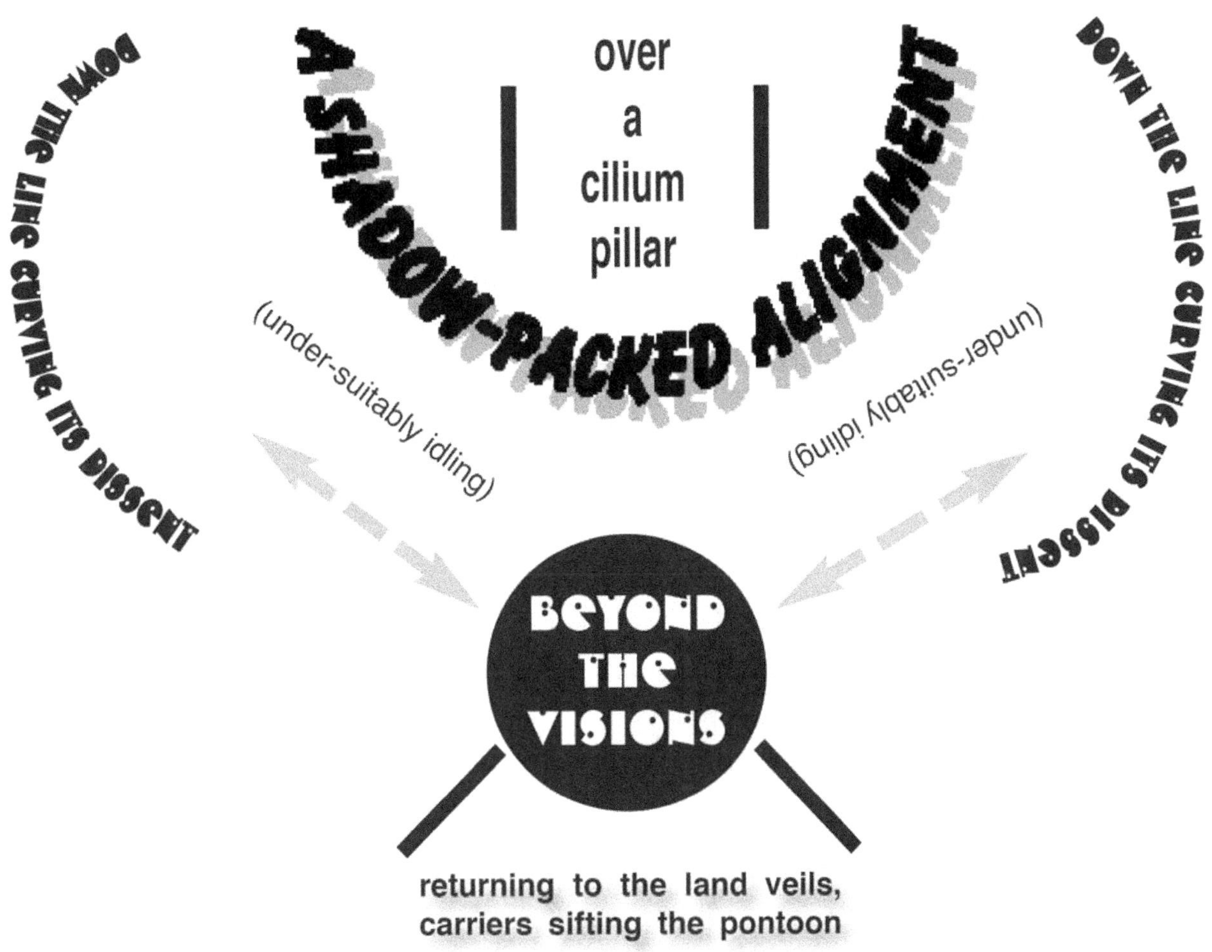

bent to a fat moon, clinging

Weathered Change

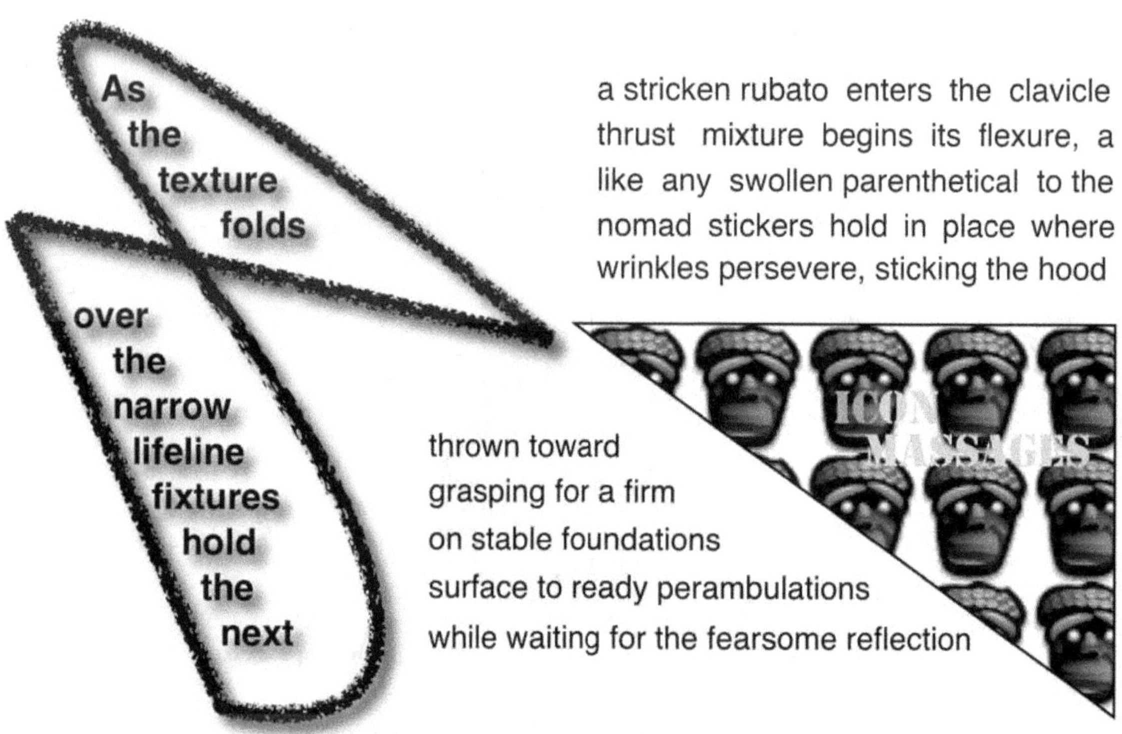

SUBLUNAR EQUATION

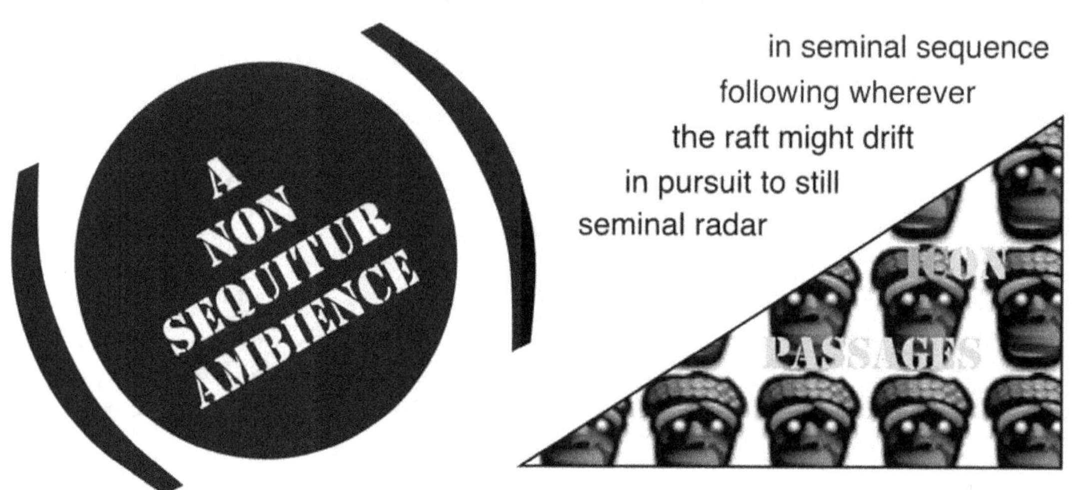

a consequence disdained

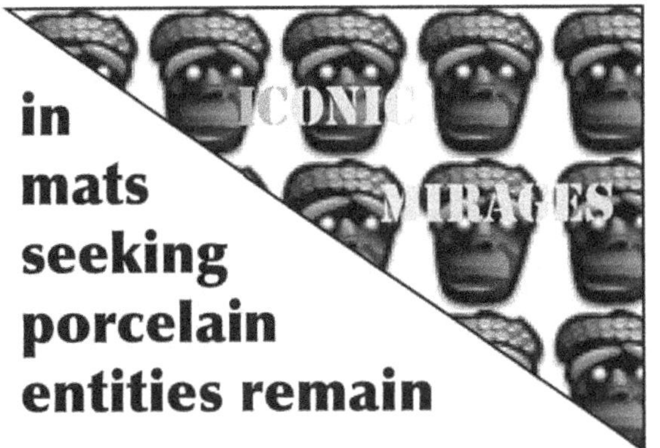

in the swill of its own making
for the shills whose renewed complaints

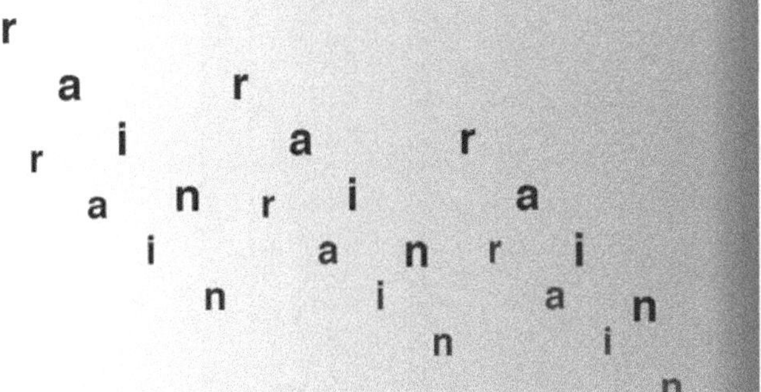

scaffold hammers mirroring the tribal image
laser classic retrospective
scaffold mottled
after vagaries gruel perspective grottos
in a land
of amputated
handshakes

AN
AMBIENT
NON SEQUITUR

(a rebate
on scented miracles
staining its
pained remover)

IRONIC
MIRAGES

supplanted
in the downpour
turned sporadic as
any random sequence
finds its favored consequence,
illusion doing itself a tainted favor
where skies remote
their towered descent

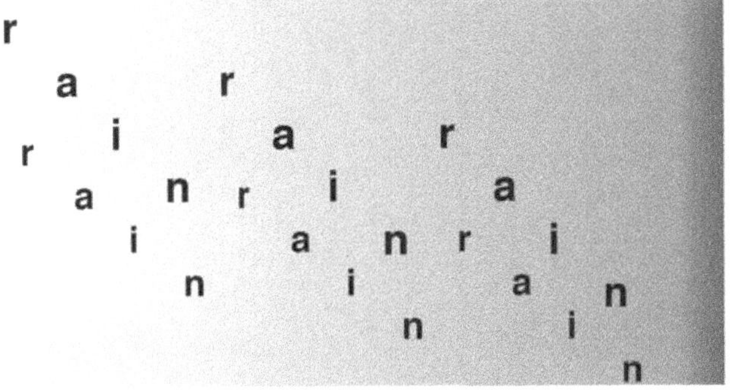

refills a climate with longing

Vernon Frazer's most recent books of poetry include Selected IMPROVISATIONS, T(exto)-V(isual) Poetry and Unsettled Music. Enigmatic Ink has published Field Reporting, Frazer's most recent novel. His web site is VernonFrazer.net. Bellicose Warbling, the blog that updates his web page, can be read at BellicoseWarbling.blogspot.com. Frazer's work, including the longpoem IMPROVISATIONS, may also be viewed at www.Scribd.com. In addition to writing poetry and fiction, Frazer also performs his poetry, incorporating text and recitation with animation and musical accompaniment, on YouTube. Frazer is married.

www.ingramcontent.com/pod-product-compliance
Lightning Source LLC
LaVergne TN
LVHW081633120826
845149LV00024B/1704

* 9 7 8 0 9 9 0 7 6 0 4 4 3 *